Andrea Vance is a senior journalist at Stuff. Born in Northern Ireland, she worked in the Press Gallery at the New Zealand Parliament for nearly a decade, first with Stuff and then TVNZ. She spent seven years as an investigative journalist with the *News of the World* and was night news editor at *The Scotsman*. She is a Press Fellow of Wolfson College, University of Cambridge.

BLUE BLOOD

ANDREA VANCE

HarperCollinsPublishers

HarperCollins*Publishers*
Australia • Brazil • Canada • France • Germany • Holland • India
Italy • Japan • Mexico • New Zealand • Poland • Spain • Sweden
Switzerland • United Kingdom • United States of America

First published in 2022
by HarperCollins*Publishers* (New Zealand) Limited
Unit D1, 63 Apollo Drive, Rosedale, Auckland 0632, New Zealand
harpercollins.co.nz

Copyright © Andrea Vance 2022

Andrea Vance asserts the moral right to be identified as the author of this work. This work is
copyright. All rights reserved. No part of this publication may be reproduced, copied, scanned,
stored in a retrieval system, recorded, or transmitted, in any form or by any means, without the
prior written permission of the publisher.

A catalogue record for this book is available from the National Library of New Zealand

ISBN 978 1 7755 4215 5 (pbk)
ISBN 978 1 7754 9246 7 (ebook)

Cover design by Darren Holt, HarperCollins Design Studio
Cover images: John Key by Bradley Kanaris/ Getty Images; Simon Bridges by Hagen Hopkins/
Getty Images; Judith Collins by Hagen Hopkins/ Getty Images; Christopher Luxon by Radio
New Zealand/Angus Dreaver
Typeset in Adobe Garamond Pro by Kirby Jones
Printed and bound in Australia by McPherson's Printing Group

MIX
Paper from
responsible sources
FSC
www.fsc.org   FSC® C001695

For Sam and Dubh

CONTENTS

1

LOST KEY

JOHN KEY WAS EXHAUSTED. He'd escaped Auckland, retreating to the family's holiday home in Hawaii for the summer break. As the sun dipped below the Pacific Ocean horizon, Key turned to wife Bronagh and said: 'I'm certain it's my last year.'

The year 2015 had been bruising for the prime minister. It opened with sustained attacks on the government over public funding for SkyCity's multi-million-dollar convention centre. Before the casino operator was finally dissuaded from its $100-million demands for a top-up of taxpayer cash for the controversial development, there were days of damaging headlines.

Ever since, Key's National Party was dogged by the sense it was becoming 'out of touch'. Key upset a waitress at his local café by repeatedly yanking her hair, creating a storm that would become known as 'ponytail-gate'. Steven Joyce, one of his most trusted ministers, was beset by details of extravagant spending on hair-straighteners, sun decks and enormous televisions at the business and employment super-ministry MBIE, one of his pet projects.

By mid-year, protests objecting to the Trans-Pacific Partnership (TPP) trade deal had reached fever pitch. Over the winter, thousands rallied in the streets to oppose the international pact, anxious it gave too much power to large, foreign corporations.

A row about the deportation of New Zealand-born criminals from Australia also drove much of the political agenda. Although the Beehive was powerless to influence the hard-line and domestically popular Canberra policy, Key found himself having to answer for the desperate plight of New Zealanders stuck in detention centres. In a testy Parliamentary debate he made a rare misstep, admonishing Labour for its stance on the issue by saying the party supported rapists, child molesters and murderers. The clumsy remark sparked a walkout by 12 female Opposition MPs and made headlines around the world.

Even the prime minister's bold mission to change the New Zealand flag was unravelling. After public disappointment at the official choice of four designs, he had to bow to a social media campaign to include the 'Red Peak' flag in the shortlist.

There were other disappointments that would have lasting impacts too. March saw National's candidate Mark Osborne humiliated by Winston Peters in a by-election in Northland. Peters, once National's favourite son, was now its *bête noir*.

Northland was a messy campaign. Only weeks after the 2014 general election, it emerged second-term National MP Mike Sabin was the subject of a police investigation regarding an alleged assault. Sabin, a former police officer who was on the verge of being appointed a minister, was forced to step down in late January, and the party was under considerable pressure to reveal what it knew about the assault allegations, and when.

Aware that National was in trouble and that incumbent governments are often defeated in by-elections, Key dispatched four young, ambitious MPs to bolster the campaign. They were on hand to support Osborne, a virtual unknown, with local meetings and media opportunities. A promise to upgrade 10 one-way bridges became a central focus of the campaign. Over a few weeks, Mark Mitchell, Alfred Ngaro, Chris Bishop and Todd Muller bonded over the loss of a seat National had held for close to two decades. Later, they would become known as the 'Four Amigos', an alliance that would dramatically shape the fortunes of the party.

Winning Northland gave Peters's New Zealand First party an extra MP, and at the same time weakened National's ability to push policies through Parliament. A long-promised package to reform the *Resource Management Act*, the country's critical planning and environment legislation, was consequently much weakened when revealed in November.

Even Key family holidays were not exempt from controversy. The prime minister's 20-year-old son, Max, created a minor fuss by posting an envy-inducing YouTube holiday video while staying at the family's 322-square-metre Hawaii townhouse. Quartered in a luxury gated community, with its cherry-wood cabinetry, private lift and golf-course views, it was an untimely reminder of how far removed Key's life was from his constituents'. The prime minister found himself having to defend his family from accusations of indulging in a lavish lifestyle at a time when the national debate was beginning to shift to unaffordable housing, an issue that would persist through the next two elections.

At times it felt as though the government was being attacked on all sides. A lift in the refugee quota to welcome 750 Syrians, as Europe was besieged by desperate migrants, was dismissed as 'too token'. Senior minister Paula Bennett was taking fire over plans to sell off tens of thousands of state houses, the biggest shake-up of the system in 80 years. Finance Minister Bill English risked appearing mean-spirited when he applied a rarely used financial veto to torpedo Labour's bill to increase paid parental leave.

Even so, Key had plenty of reasons to smile as he relaxed into his Maui holiday. Media pundits and the Opposition were bent on suggesting National was showing the early signs of third-term-itis, an affliction caused by a mixture of arrogance and a public itch for change. But this was wishful thinking: those sentiments were not yet resonating with voters. The first public poll of 2015 showed National with 49.8 per cent support, and Labour languishing on 29. The year closed with National retaining that commanding lead: the final Roy Morgan poll put National on 49 per cent, while combined support for the Labour/Green vote could only reach 41.5 per cent.

But a conversation with US President Barack Obama was playing on Key's mind. The pair were elected to lead their countries within four days of each other in November 2008 and had developed a warm friendship after first meeting at a lunch hosted in New York the following year by UN Secretary-General Ban Ki-moon.

During Key's previous summer break, at the end of 2014, he and Max had met Obama for a round of golf at a military base near the US president's rented holiday home on the island of Oahu. As Key was contemplating his future in politics, Obama was beginning his last full year in the job. Key had long believed that most prime ministers stayed on one election too many, and thought the US system, which limited presidents to two terms, had merit.

He had a long talk with Obama and asked him what he would do if he had the opportunity to run for another term — would he take it? Both men concluded they wouldn't. 'There was something nice about that: that you throw everything at it, but there's a finality about it,' Key thought. Only months earlier another world leader, British Prime Minister David Cameron, had clearly been grappling with the same conundrum. Announcing in 2015 that he would not seek a third term as prime minister if his Conservative Party remained in government, he told the BBC: 'Terms are like Shredded Wheat — two are wonderful, but three might just be too many.'

As Key weighed up his own options in early 2016, he was keenly aware that this year would be an important one for setting the party up for the 2017 general election. He reflected on the experience of former Australian Prime Minister John Howard, who was toppled in 2007 from the seat he'd held for 33 years: if the most successful Australasian prime minister in a lifetime could lose an unlosable seat, then there was a reason. Key thought he might suffer the same fate if he stayed one election too many, admitting to himself that 'everything they [voters] like about you for a long period of time, at some point they don't like'.

From the moment Key entered the political fray, during the tumultuous 2002 election campaign and through eight years in government, Bronagh was loyal to his ambitions. While she was a member of the National Party, she was not an activist. Key says, 'She's the most understated person, so she is happy having a life out of the limelight. She doesn't feel the need for me to be there for status. But the job [as MP and PM] is pretty 24/7. You are away one hell of a lot, and when you are home you are busy.'

Much has been made about Bronagh's influence on Key's decision to quit politics, with speculation she issued an ultimatum. There was a final demand — but not the one journalists would later assume. As that evening on Maui in 2016 cooled and they relaxed over drinks, she told him: 'Look, you've been in this for 15 years and you've been busy for 35. So, if you want to do one more and have four terms I'm 100 per cent with you. But, if you do go, please tell me you won't go back [again after that].'

When Key returned to New Zealand from holiday, it was to one of the most tempestuous years since the economic and societal changes of the 1930s. It would see political earthquakes like the election of Donald Trump, Brexit, Islamic terror attacks across Europe and the strengthening influence of Russia's Vladamir Putin. The 'Shaky Isles' would experience their fair share of ructions too.

There were early warning signs that 2016 would be a difficult year. In February, Steven Joyce copped a flying, flesh-toned dildo to the face as he spoke to journalists ahead of Waitangi Day celebrations. The sex toy was thrown by Josie Butler, a Christchurch nurse who claimed to be protesting against the TPP, shouting: 'That's for raping our sovereignty'. Sizeable demonstrations against the pact continued, with thousands blocking streets and motorway on-ramps as Pacific rim trade ministers inked the deal at Auckland's SkyCity.

Although National was still polling well, the public mood was unmistakably scratchy. In March, Kiwis rejected Key's bid to change the national flag, opting to retain the traditional Union Jack design. He would later say the referendum failure was his biggest regret. Third-term blues also saw Key spending more time in front of microphones, soothing the voter. Cracks were beginning to show in key public services, which National had made a virtue of making 'more efficient'. The themes that would dominate the 2017 election began to emerge: housing inequality, water quality and inadequate health services.

Key was also feeling the pressure of what seemed like a relentless barrage of issues that distracted from the main work at hand. A good example was the year-long wrangle over the infamous 'Saudi sheep deal'. The $11.5 million agreement to set up a farm in the desert using taxpayer funds had created a political storm. Murray McCully drew much of the flak, and Key came under considerable pressure to sack his foreign minister. The project was an effort to placate businessman Sheikh Hamood Al-Ali Al-Khalaf. The Saudi exporter had earlier bought farms to breed Awassi sheep to be slaughtered in Saudi Arabia, only to be thwarted by New Zealand's ban on live sheep exports. His subsequent threats to sue were souring chances of a free trade agreement, or FTA, with the Gulf States, which stalled after 12 years of negotiations. McCully was hoping that establishing a joint agri-hub in Saudi Arabia would sort matters out and put trade relations back on track. The demonstration farm, which would be owned by Al-Khalaf, was a form of compensation, which also doubled as a way of showcasing New Zealand's agricultural technologies.

The irregular arrangement only came to light in April 2015 after Key held talks in Riyadh to try to get the trade deal back on track. Key knew the proposal was controversial, and Cabinet had discussed the problem at least four times, looking for a creative solution that would be in any way acceptable. The government claimed legal advice was that the exporter had a legitimate lawsuit. Given the FTA was in jeopardy, Key thought it was worth it. But it came at a high price.

Opposition parties called it a bribe, and over the following months the government was variously accused of breaking rules of political process and being secretive, deceitful and incompetent. Much of 2016 was spent defending the decision to send 900 ewes to Damman, and it squandered valuable political capital. While ultimately Auditor-General Lyn Provost found no evidence of corruption, this did little to dilute the impression that National was willing to bend the rules for the wealthy.

By September, Key was in New York for a week-long meeting of the UN General Assembly, the world's most important diplomatic convocation. It was the culmination of New Zealand's two years of presidency on the Security Council, a major diplomatic accomplishment. He was to chair a high-level meeting on the unfolding Syrian crisis. It was also a crucial moment to lobby for former Prime Minister Helen Clark, who was competing for the UN Secretary-General role. The trip was gruelling, with Key's flight to Houston diverted to Tahiti for a medical emergency. On their delayed arrival, the PM's entourage was greeted with news of a bombing just blocks from the UN headquarters, which injured 29 and put the leaders' security teams on edge.

The 19 September attack on a UN aid convoy close to Aleppo in Syria further set the scene for a tense meeting, with Britain and the United States blaming Russia. There was scant progress: New Zealand's presidency would lapse in October with no resolutions in place.

On the long flight back to Auckland, Key finally turned his attention to his exit, telling Bronagh he had made up his mind: he would retire by the end of the year.

At two minutes past midnight on 14 November, a magnitude 7.8 earthquake jolted the northeastern coast of the South Island. Two people died, and the shake caused widespread damage to the road and rail routes leading to the tourist town of Kaikōura and closed State Highway 1. Buildings in Wellington were later condemned and insurance claims eventually topped $1.8 billion.

The natural disaster delayed Key's intended retirement announcement by some weeks. Earlier in the year he had confided his intentions to some of his closest colleagues, who believed they'd talked him out of stepping down. As one former minister in the Key Cabinet confided: 'I thought he'd got past the point — only just — but past the point where he was going to pull the pin.'

Nothing was further from the truth. The fractious nature of 2016 had only hardened Key's resolve. It wasn't a matter of not feeling physically up to the challenge; more a sense of dispiritedness. A realisation that even though he was working as hard as he possibly could, he was left dealing with a seemingly endless stream of contentious issues and conflicts.

Initially, only Bronagh and Key's equanimous chief of staff Wayne Eagleson were in the know. But there would be many more late nights to come in the Beehive, sustained by packets of nuts, tinned baked beans and pinot noir, before the PM would tell the public. Key barely wavered in his decision, being someone who generally sleeps well. But there were other considerations, including that the contracts of his staff ended when he was no longer leader.

He also worried about National's fortunes. Key, with his affable personality and political astuteness, *was* the party. He was not unaware of this, and, given his deep wish for National to 'be the government in every day of the week', he battled with thoughts that resigning would be selfish and not in the best interests of the party. This was no lack of humility; it was a clear-eyed assessment of historical fact.

For the past decade, Key had been National's centre of gravity, and he was about to send it spinning out of control. He was the embodiment of the party's self-help credo: a rags-to-riches story of a state-house child from Christchurch who worked his way into owning a mansion with a swimming pool and tennis court on one of Auckland's wealthiest streets.

Key's ascension through the National Party ranks to the top job may have been swift, but it was not the result of some spurof-the-moment whim. He'd nurtured the ambition to be prime minister from the age of 11. As a 16-year-old, on one of his first dates with high-school sweetheart Bronagh, at the rural A&P show, he had shared how he wanted to be prime minister. So his later political aspirations came as no surprise to her.

They graduated Christchurch's Burnside High School in the late 1970s and married in 1984. And while Key had ambitions for public office, Bronagh's were firmly focused on family. It was her role to keep their family life intact as Key's career as a foreign exchange dealer took them to Singapore, where Max was born when daughter Stephie was still a toddler, and then on to London, Sydney and New York. Hers was a supporting role that enabled his public achievements.

In 2001, aged 40, Key left banking for politics. He had calculated that the average length of time it took to rise from the backbenches of Parliament to prime minister was 18 years. It took him six — the fastest rise to the top in a century of New Zealand politics. However, the National Party he inherited in 2006 had been demoralised and divided, cycling through leaders and recovering from the worst election defeat in its nearly 70-year history.

Key instilled discipline and focus. He ended almost a decade of Labour Party rule, guiding National through three terms in office. His time in power included the global financial crisis (GFC), a series of devastating earthquakes and the Pike River mine disaster. Under New Zealand's proportional representation voting system, he formed a minority government with the support of three minor parties: libertarian ACT, centrist United Future and Te Pāti Māori (the Māori Party). These alliances endured for his entire time in office.

Astonishingly popular, Key also changed the face of political communication in New Zealand. Before Donald Trump, Boris

Johnson or Jacinda Ardern, Key recognised and exploited the personalisation of politics. He was a celebrity, appearing on talk shows, music radio stations and the covers of women's magazines. His appeal was partly down to his ability to appeal to the average voter by conveying his ordinariness. His favourite movie was spy spoof *Johnny English*, and he frequently fan-boyed over All Blacks captain Richie McCaw.

He also possessed extraordinary political intuition, usually in lock-step with what the public would accept. On the rare occasions when he strayed over to the wrong side of the argument, he evinced remarkable dexterity, smoothly changing position rather than compromising his popularity. Under Key, National re-established its reputation as a prudent economic steward against an apparently fiscally irresponsible Labour Party. The narrative would dominate for a decade.

But the position of the National Party when Key arrived at Parliament, as MP for Helensville, in 2002 was anything but dominant. While Key himself was undoubtedly already a success story, being Parliament's richest MP, then worth an estimated $50 million, this stood in stark contrast with his party. At the time National was at its lowest ebb, its caucus reduced to 27 members, and its support at an all-time low of 20.9 per cent.

The crushing electoral defeat signalled a phoenix moment. It was time for a fresh start after a series of missteps, the last of which had seen, the year before the election, a young, laconic Southlander, Bill English, inheriting a divided party from Jenny Shipley. Still smarting from losing to the Labour Party led by Helen Clark, the party was ideologically confused and became paralysed by internal warring. The first change came when former Reserve Bank governor Don Brash replaced English in 2003.

Under Brash, Key rose from 26 in the diminished party ranks to become the finance spokesman and was the star of National's 2005 campaign, easily matching Labour veteran Michael Cullen in debates. Cullen, in a memorable but waspish retort, would later call his opposite mark 'a rich prick'.

In fact, Key was affable, with an easy grin and unnerving self-confidence. Before long the public was charmed, and shortly after the 2005 election he began to appear in the preferred prime minister ratings of opinion polls. But according to one of Key's inner circle, he didn't do a lot of manoeuvring to become the leader. 'He waited for quite some time to let the conditions deliver the leadership change rather than forcing it. He just had a natural understanding of a team environment.'

Brash was lamed by allegations of an extramarital affair, involvement with the Exclusive Brethren evangelical sect, and revelations about the party's election strategies in Nicky Hager's book *The Hollow Men*. When Brash resigned in November 2006, Key seemed to be the obvious contender, with his 'numbers man' Murray McCully counting potential votes. Key wanted Ilam MP Gerry Brownlee to stay on as his number two.

But another MP stepped out of the wings: Bill English saw a second chance. Significantly, doing the numbers for English was Rangitīkei MP Simon Power, now Television New Zealand's chief executive but then seen as the unofficial leader of the 1999 intake of MPs, a substantial voting bloc. While English had taken a lower profile with the education portfolio, he still had leadership ambitions. A fellow MP remembers that English made it clear that he wanted to contest the leadership; that he was frustrated that he'd 'never really got a good shot' in his previous term as leader.

At that point National was outstripping Labour in the polls. It could ill-afford to squander that momentum with another messy public battle. There were doubts about Key within caucus. Some disliked his naked ambition. Second-term MP and Brash loyalist Judith Collins would later write: 'He had come into politics with a very clear agenda of being Prime Minister. It seemed to me from his actions … that John Key was on a course where nothing would get in his way.' Others were unsure of what he stood for and wary of a tendency to equivocate on policy. English was experienced, respected and a more accomplished performer in the House. But, crucially, he trailed behind Key in opinion polls. And he carried the mark of his previous failure, National's worst-ever defeat.

The day after Brash's resignation, Key invited English to his Parnell home. They were joined on that Saturday by McCully and Power. An accommodation was reached: the leader-in-waiting rang Brownlee and confided that he had agreed to make English his deputy, an arrangement he would soon have to make public. It was not a difficult conversation. Brownlee, a staunch party man, offered to hold a press conference in Wellington the next day to announce he was stepping aside. It would be a very deliberate demonstration of unity. The way was cleared for one of the great double-acts of New Zealand politics: John Key and Bill English.

Although John Key was the right person for leader, the only way he would get a good run at it was if the team was tight. With English accepting the deputy role, his supporters were placated and discontent stifled. Effectively, they would get the best of both worlds.

Jonathan Coleman, elected to Auckland's Northcote electorate in 2005, believes the group was simply tired of losing. Although a cycle of destruction, losing and bad polling is a natural part of renewal and comes to every party from time to time, it can lead to desperation. People pull in different directions, and into the mix go egos and jostling for position. 'In the end, they came to the realisation that unless we settled down and fell in line as a team, we were never going to get anywhere,' Coleman says. 'There were senior roles for all of them. They just had to back this guy. There was a strong desire to win.'

From the Parnell machinations, Key built his 'kitchen Cabinet', the political management group that saw him through his entire time in office, with only modest changes. Essential to its success was that it included the key players from both sides of the caucus. For his first term of government, the inner circle would include English, Power, Brownlee and McCully. They would be joined by Eagleson and, when Power stepped down, Paula Bennett.

The electoral decimation of 2002 and near-miss of 2005 had cleaned out a lot of deadwood. When English and Key did the deal, they rallied the remaining troops, established a hierarchy and organised themselves into a very professional machine.

With the power structure settled, Coleman says Key's charisma began to shine through. 'I don't think his personality was really unveiled until he became leader. He was a quiet, relatively serious guy in caucus. This playful, exuberant side had not really been evident to people. I think it was very deliberate. Once he got the leadership, his real personality emerged. And it was strongly optimistic, there was a lot of fun. And he gave people a huge amount of confidence.' Journalists and colleagues soon fell under his spell.

There was one other pivotal figure: Steven Joyce, a wealthy broadcasting entrepreneur and the party's election campaign manager. Joyce had flirted with electioneering, having briefly appeared on the party's draft list in 2002, but was never a confirmed candidate. He had exceptional qualities that would hugely improve the party's chance at a rebuild but would first have to be persuaded to enter Parliament. McCully and Eagleson went to see Key. The suggestion was floated of getting Joyce to stand on the list, with a commitment that he would become a key cabinet minister. The advantages of being a list MP are multiple: there is no need to fight an election head-to-head, as their place is decided by the number of votes the party receives; they are not tied to a geographical electorate and are unencumbered by constituency duties. In the case of Joyce, this had the added advantage for the party that his sole focus could be on bigger-picture campaigning and strategising.

Joyce would guide the party through the 2008 election, with the help of Australian strategist Mark Textor, of the influential consultancy Crosby Textor. Now known as C|T Group, the conservative-aligned firm has been used by Australia's Liberal Party and Britain's Tories, including Boris Johnson's London mayoral campaign. The campaign was built around Key as a political cleanskin with a sunny outlook, and a risk-averse manifesto. It was a decisive victory, sweeping a tired-looking third-term Labour-led government and, at the same time, New Zealand First from the Beehive.

A new dynasty had begun, one that would dominate politics for the next decade. It would only start to crumble on 5 December 2016 when Key resigned, leaving a leadership vacuum and a party that had sacrificed too many principles on the altar of political pragmatism. Within a few short years, the reputation for financial and party discipline lay in ruins, along with the political careers of the four leaders who attempted to fill Key's shoes.

2

THE STAYER AND THE SPRINTER

Bill English cut a sad figure, crushed and humiliated, as he left Parliament's grounds on a cool spring afternoon in October 2003. In the grey marble buildings behind him, the MPs who backed Don Brash in a leadership challenge were rallying around their new boss. As he went, English stopped to thank the 25 staff in the party's research unit, who had also technically lost their jobs. His voice occasionally breaking with emotion, English joked they had shown more loyalty than his MPs.

'Loser!' jeered a rabble of anti-GM protestors gathered on the lawn as he passed by. English, briefcase in one hand, lifted his arm to give a wave before he registered the heckle. Photographer Phil Reid captured the glum spectacle. It would be splashed across page one of the next day's *Dominion Post*.

All recent National Party leaders — Jim McLay, Jim Bolger and Jenny Shipley — had come and gone in the same way. In three short years, Brash, too, would be ousted by a restless caucus, after taking the party to the cusp of victory.

English's exit was a bitter example of the ruthlessness of party politics. He'd lost by one vote; for years English loyalists wrongly assumed it was John Key's. No friend or colleague was there to accompany English on his solitary walk, to find him a car or take him for a quiet drink at the Backbencher pub across the street.

The image lingered in John Key's mind. Thirteen years later he would hand English the chance for redemption. And Key would go out on his own terms: 'The day he got sworn in [as prime minister], I thought that's a great bookend to that picture.'

Over a decade the two men had forged a loyal partnership. Built out of political necessity in 2006, it was cemented when they took office in the midst of a financial crisis. As finance minister, English steered the country through a recession induced by the global credit crunch, which wiped billions from the nation's balance sheet, and the collapse and $1.6 billion bail-out of locally owned South Canterbury Finance.

Inheriting stability, low government debt and a new trading relationship with China from the Helen Clark–Michael Cullen complement of the previous nine years, English was able to spend liberally on reconstruction in the years that followed the Canterbury earthquakes. A housing boom was powered by low interest rates and growing immigration and a surge in dairy exports to China. The Key–English management of the financial system earned the label 'rock-star economy'. It was a term that would haunt National in the 2017 election as wealth inequality grew.

The pair's chemistry was a constant source of fascination for political watchers, who were always searching for any cracks or hidden tensions in the jokes they often made at each other's expense. It certainly wasn't a bromance. Although just months apart in age, the ebullient, rich Auckland banker and dry farmer-turned-Treasury-analyst were very different men. But

Key believed that they were very similar in their core beliefs; the difference a matter of 'nuance'. 'He'd be a bit more austere in spending,' Key later said, 'and I'd be more likely to say let's put some money into this.'

English gave newspaper columnists plenty to chew over when he remarked of his rival-turned-boss in 2009: 'I'm a stayer, he's a sprinter. I grind away. John just bounces from one cloud to another.' An MP who served under them both agrees that there is some truth to that. 'John couldn't have been the prime minister he was without Bill. But also Bill wouldn't have been able to do all the stuff without John. They were a really good team.'

English was stolid and steady, keeping tight control of the purse strings. Under his stewardship, the government partly privatised several state-owned energy firms and Air New Zealand, and delivered surpluses, while modernising the public and social services and reforming the welfare system. At the time, English was acknowledged as the deepest thinker the Right had.

Key ran front-of-house, the retail politician who bent with the public mood, and kept National's popularity up in those clouds. A polling junkie, he was so in tune with voter sentiment that he very frequently beat David Farrar, the party's pollster, in an unofficial bet they had on the weekly numbers. He successfully sold English's policy to cut income taxes by raising GST, even though he was initially dubious.

It helped that English is that rarity among politicians — without ego. Their dealings were cordial and easy, although they infrequently socialised. English would often lose track of time, wandering late into meetings at 'PMO', the suite of offices on the Beehive's ninth floor. Key was relaxed about the habit, but chief of staff Wayne Eagleson eventually warned English it gave off a whiff of disrespect to guests.

English's tardiness was legendary. Indeed, it had almost cost him his political career before it had even got off the ground in 1990, as he fittingly recounted nearly 30 years later in his valedictory statement. Mistaking the deadline to register as a candidate for the one-time seat of Wallace, he had just minutes to spare and no $200 deposit. Stranded in Gore, with enough signatures but not the deposit, nor a chequebook or car to come to his aid, he ran to his bank. But with no documentation, the cashier would not give him any money. Fortunately, his luck then turned: the manager, a member of the National Party, saved the day and New Zealand's political history was back on track.

Key and English remained tight until the end. They are still mates, texting occasionally, but don't live in each other's pockets. Key considers media misconstrued English's cloud-bouncing analogy. It simply and accurately reflected Key's multiple focuses. Key found English massively respectful: 'If he was doing something in the finance portfolio that was big, he'd ring and say, "Can I pop up?" and we'd run things through. There were never surprises of magnitude.'

They avoided any potential conflict over social issues that might offend English's strong Catholicism. Indeed, their respective philosophies — English is socially conservative; Key is extremely liberal — acted as a safety valve for opposing views in caucus. Key felt together they provided a very happy balance, and it probably helped that social issues were not their top priority when they had issues like the GFC and Canterbury earthquakes to deal with. To avoid conflict in the social arena, Key resisted enforcing party policy on issues such as ACT's member's bill on euthanasia, where he knew there would be sharp differences of opinion — Key remembers English saying, 'Hell will freeze over before I'll vote for that' — in favour of retaining a conscience vote. Key understood the public was weary of polarising social issues, debates that had raged through Clark's terms in office, including prostitution law reform, the establishment of same-sex civil unions and a ban on smacking children. A need to focus on the more pressing GFC and earthquake relief meant Key could push more taboo problems to the bottom of his agenda.

Key said the falling out between Labour Prime Minister David Lange and his finance minister Roger Douglas, over proposals for a flat-rate tax in 1987, made him acutely aware of how the working relationship can dissolve. 'Maarten Wevers was my first head of DPMC [Department of the Prime Minister and Cabinet: the policy and administrative nerve centre of Government] and he was foreign affairs [advisor] to David Lange. He used to tell me stories of just how horrendous it was between Lange and Douglas. The stories were exactly as were reported. They would just be writing to each other, and it was the definition of a dysfunctional relationship. We were so far away from that.'

But as Key had discussed with Obama, every political career has its 'Best before' date, and, as good a team as he and English made, Key could see his date approaching. So on his return from New York in September 2016, Key told English he was intending to step down. Momentarily stunned, English said there was no need to go: 'It's been a great Government, we're a great team.' In the blur of the weeks to come, Key can recall little of the conversation, only that English didn't try to force him out, saying 'it was almost the opposite'.

MP Nick Smith — part of the so-called 'Brat Pack' intake of young MPs in 1990, alongside English — spoke to English in the hours afterwards and confirms that the deputy tried to talk Key out of resigning. There has been speculation about the nature of the deal struck between the two men before they took control of the party. Did they have an arrangement similar to that agreed by Tony Blair and Gordon Brown when in Opposition in 1994, known as the 'Granita pact' after the London restaurant in which they supposedly hashed it out? Brown agreed to not run in the upcoming Labour Party leadership election, and Blair promised that, should he win, he would hand over the reins of power in his second term. Brown was to take charge of economic and social policy.

Key says the speculation of a similar agreement is not true: English was never going to get the numbers to win the leadership. The reason behind their deal was simply because, in their eyes, they felt they were the dream team. And there was an understanding that it was a time to avoid further division in the interests of unity. Others agree but add that as both men were still young at that time, English could well have calculated that he would get his own chance after Key had done five or six years. Although he would never have relied on it.

However, Key believes English had got to the point where he thought that if prime ministership was off the cards, he could go down in history as a long-serving, highly successful minister of finance. And this should not be seen as some placatory consolation prize. As Key points out, both the caucus and the media had enormous respect for English. 'Many of them would say I was "grip and grin" and he was the real intellectual core of the decision-making.'

As it was, in 2016, Key and English's conversation was brief and did not turn to succession. The two men and their Cabinet colleagues soon became consumed with the aftermath of the Kaikōura earthquake. They were also coming to terms with the surprise election of Donald Trump as United States President, and what that might mean for the country's economy and foreign policy.

A few days after the reality television star's astonishing presidential win, the USS *Sampson* was due in Auckland for the New Zealand Navy's seventy-fifth anniversary celebrations. The first US warship to dock in New Zealand waters in 33 years, it marked a major shift in diplomatic relations since the country was effectively suspended from ANZUS — the Australia, New Zealand, United States security alliance — over an anti-nuclear policy. On learning of the quake, the guided-missile destroyer redeployed to provide humanitarian relief to those stranded in Kaikōura. It was the culmination of a gradual improvement of defence relations under the Key administration, dexterously balanced with its more commercially oriented ties to Beijing.

Key also had to grit his teeth through Auckland's Mount Roskill by-election. Labour's Phil Goff was vacating the seat, held by Labour for 40 years, for the Auckland mayoralty. Key was curiously absent from National candidate Parmjeet Parmer's campaign, telling media in the final days that he thought she'd lose.

As the polls were closing in Mount Roskill, Mike Munro, Helen Clark's long-serving chief press secretary, was tramping in Kahurangi National Park in the northwest corner of the South Island. In the group with him was Nick Venter, English's chief press secretary, Labour's pollster Stephen Mills, and Brad Tattersfield, once an advisor to National Minister of Finance Bill Birch. They had all known each other for years, working on both sides of the political divide. On the Monday morning after the by-election, 5 December, they were descending from the glacier-scoured peak of Mount Owen when their cellphones simultaneously sprang into life. Venter received an urgent text message to telephone his boss and walked away to make the call. Enjoying lunch in the early summer sunshine, the seasoned political operatives thought little of it. When Venter came back he looked shocked, saying only that was there was going to be an announcement at 1pm. The group began speculating, but Mills was the only one to pick that it would be Key's resignation. The others scoffed at the idea: Key was well on track to win the election in 12 months' time.

Back in Wellington, Key and English's staff were preparing the ground for one of the most significant and shocking announcements in recent political history. There was no outward hint of what Key was planning. He'd dutifully attended the lower North Island National Party Christmas function in Palmerston North. On his way home on Sunday, he and Eagleson had dropped into Paraparaumu Beach Golf Club, north of Wellington, for a round of golf and a couple of beers.

Key spoke with Joyce at 6.45am on Monday. It was the usual rehearsal before Key's regular Monday morning media slots. He had cancelled the appearances in Auckland, opting to do the interviews over the phone. But he didn't tell Joyce what he was planning until a second call around 9am. Joyce spent the next few moments unsuccessfully trying to talk him out of it. After hanging up, Joyce immediately left his Wellington flat and hurried to the Beehive. Key and his chief of staff hit the phones: Eagleson using his ministerial telephone line to call each Cabinet minister; Key firing off texts. Ministers were invited, one by one, up to Key's office.

With a regular Cabinet meeting due to take place mid-morning, most assumed they were needed to discuss a proposed policy from their portfolio. The more suspicious suspected a reshuffle. According to Nick Smith, being summoned by text prior to a Cabinet meeting 'generally means one of two things.

You have a Cabinet paper on the agenda — I had five that day — and the prime minister is completely opposed and wants you to withdraw. Or you've screwed up somewhere.' Smith feared he was about to be sacked.

When Smith arrived, Key was sitting in his lounge, white shirt-sleeves rolled up, and wearing a silk tie in National's traditional blue. Smith sat opposite him on the leather sofa. Behind them, hanging above Key's desk, was a framed front page from the *Herald on Sunday*. It pictured Key on election night 2008, arms aloft, above the headline *VICTORY*. The last four letters — *Tory* — were outlined in blue. Below the newspaper cutting was a framed picture of the Queen.

'John said that he was pulling the pin,' Smith remembers. 'I had to ask him to repeat it, because when he said "resign" I thought he said he wanted me to resign.' Key explained his motivations, including that Bronagh was spending lonely nights in Auckland now that Stephie and Max had left home. For Smith it came as a bolt out of the blue. He had always felt Key was quite competitive with Helen Clark and thought Key would want to do something that Clark hadn't been able to achieve, 'to get the fourth term that had evaded others'. Smith says he had misread that part of Key's 'chemistry' and believes that actually it wasn't as big a motivator for him as family.

For some, there was an element of grief. A number of senior ministers knew he was tired and perhaps contemplating an end. He was known for being a real workhorse, and they acknowledged someone can only sustain that for so long. Nevertheless, many wanted him to stay on, to hang on. But it soon became apparent that he'd made up his mind and was not to be dissuaded.

Attorney-General Chris Finlayson arrived just as Health Minister Jonathan Coleman was leaving Key's office. 'I remember it very well,' Finlayson says, 'because Key rang me and said: "Hello, my little legal beagle. Would you come over and see me?" I thought: I don't think I've done anything wrong.' As soon as he was in the room, Key gave him the news: 'He said: "I'm out of here." I immediately had an "oh dear" moment. How few politicians get out while they are ahead? Unless you have the good fortune to die, most people fail in politics. John's a very special guy: it shows how smart he was, to get out while he's ahead and plan a new life.'

Each minister spent just a few minutes with their boss as he clinically told them what the deal was. Even though it had always been a possibility, it came as a shock.

For some, it brought down the curtain on their own careers. Months earlier, while recovering from surgery and a serious illness, Murray McCully had tied his political future to the prime minister, vowing to leave Parliament when Key did. Others saw it as an opportunity. Throughout his premiership, Key had been grooming the talent he saw in caucus. His post-2014 election ministry consolidated who was in the next wave of seniority, handing meaty portfolios to Nikki Kaye, Simon Bridges, Jonathan Coleman and Amy Adams.

Kaye had ousted Judith Tizard from the prized Auckland Central seat in 2008, ending a 90-year Opposition grip. She twice beat Labour's enskied Jacinda Ardern in the electorate. In 2013 Key promoted Kaye to Cabinet, and the following year she was handed responsibility for the complex state insurance scheme, as Accident Compensation Corporation minister. On leave from her duties to undergo breast cancer treatment in the later half of 2016, Kaye made an emotional return to Parliament to attend a caucus meeting the day after Key resigned.

Bridges was another electoral star, launching his political career aged just 32 by jettisoning New Zealand First from Parliament in 2008. Its leader, Winston Peters, had been trying to regain the seat of Tauranga, which he narrowly lost to National's Bob Clarkson in 2005. But Bridges, the Oxford-educated son of a clergyman and a school teacher, was young and energetic, with a solid-gold back-story in prosecuting criminals. He beat Peters by a whopping 11,742 margin, denying the old warhorse the electorate seat he so desperately needed to keep his party in Parliament.

Key rewarded Bridges quickly. He was appointed a minister-outside-Cabinet in 2012, moving into the Cabinet the following year with the hefty labour and energy portfolios. In 2014 he moved onto the front bench, pinching the transport ministry from Gerry Brownlee, and also becoming Key's deputy leader of the House.

Bridges attributes much of the stability of Key's government to the good job the PM did of cultivating a range of potential successors, employing the sort of succession planning adopted in big business. This meant that in Team Key there was a sense of assured continuity; as Bridges puts it, if one of the top guys fell under a bus, there was a plan in place. As a result there was no need for people to worry about succession. While in the background there was the inevitable consideration of who was up and who was down, it was not something the vast majority thought about.

Adams was also of the 'class of 2008': an influential group of MPs who were elected in the Fifth National Government's first term. A former commercial and property lawyer, she'd had a rapid rise, taking charge of the Finance and Expenditure Committee in the closing months before the 2011 election, always a sure sign of impending promotion. Adams was one of only a handful of MPs to boost their majorities, winning by more than 17,000 votes in the blue-ribbon Selwyn seat once held by one-time finance minister and economic reformer Ruth Richardson.

Adams held various portfolios, including environment, before being moved to the front bench as justice minister. There she made her mark with a liberal streak, wiping the convictions of men convicted of homosexual acts and raising the age of criminal juvenile jurisdiction to 18.

Once one of Australia's flying doctors, Coleman gave up practising as a GP to stand for Parliament in 2005. He was promoted in his third term, taking on defence. In 2014, Key handed him one of the most difficult jobs in politics: health minister. The role was made harder by being vacated by Tony Ryall, who kept the portfolio out of the headlines while implementing a large programme of centralisation and reducing waiting times even while budgets were constrained. Also picking up sport and recreation, Coleman rose from number 10 onto the front bench to be ranked number six.

Paula Bennett was at the front of the pack. A former beneficiary and a single mother, she was drawn into Key's kitchen Cabinet and given the challenging social development, climate change and associate finance portfolios. 'He called it the rounding out of Paula,' she says.

Bennett was one of the few Key told about his plan to back English to succeed him as leader. The reason he did so was because he believed she would make English an ideal deputy. Shocked at the suggestion, her focus shifted from thinking about English to herself 'pretty bloody quickly!'

Coleman had a similar train of thought. After the shock of being told of Key's departure, within a matter of seconds his thoughts raced to why it was happening and what was next. And then immediately: if there was going to be a leadership competition, he wanted to be in it. When he confessed his ambitions to Key, the outgoing prime minister replied that he was not surprised but added, 'Bill is the guy who I will be supporting.' Naïvely, Coleman thought he could overcome that.

Nick Smith takes a dim view of Key's overt succession planning. In fast-tracking talent like Simon Bridges, Amy Adams, Nikki Kaye and Paula Bennett, he believes Key 'inadvertently left a legacy where everybody thought they should be leader'.

Coleman thinks differently. To his mind, while Key wanted to create a pool of people who all had the potential to succeed, it could never be a detailed succession plan. This is because everyone in caucus has an equal vote, whether you are number one in the caucus or the last-ranking person. 'All a leader can really do is bring talented people in and give them the chance to shine. The rest really is up to them. And their ability.'

Another senior minister has observed wryly that history has shown that if there was succession planning, it was poorly done. While Kaye, Adams, Bridges and Bennett all ended up in very senior positions, all of them are now gone. 'And all of them absolutely blew it,' he believes.

Back on the morning of Key's bombshell announcement, the show had to go on, and Key chaired a palpably shell-shocked Cabinet meeting at 11am. Tearful staff and the leaders of United Future, ACT and Te Pāti Māori were also informed. The rest of the backbench MPs heard the news in a telephone conference at 12.15pm. A mysterious press conference was scheduled for 12.45pm, in the Beehive's Theatrette, stumping Press Gallery journalists who were expecting the normal 4pm post-Cabinet briefing.

At the press conference, it took Key three minutes to get to the point. 'I absolutely believe we can win the next election,' he said. 'But I do not believe that, if you asked me if I was committed to serving out a fourth term, that I could look the public in the eye and say yes.' Key wrote the speech himself, and at points in its delivery he was choked with emotion. The country's television and radio stations broke into scheduled programming with live updates.

Key said he would formally tender his resignation to Governor-General Dame Patsy Reddy the following week, once caucus had chosen a new leader. 'If Bill English puts his name forward then I will vote for him,' he added. It was an endorsement that divided opinion in caucus. Some felt he could do no less than offer his public support to English after a whole decade of partnership. Nevertheless, the degree of his open support was debatable. There were those who thought that if you are going, it is those who remain who have to live with the consequences and therefore you should respect them to make their own decisions. In offering such a strong, unequivocal endorsement, others would be hurt.

Sources say the one who was most hurt was Steven Joyce. A senior minister recalls that 'Steven was just very grumpy and going, "Why the fuck not me? I'm smarter than everybody else, I'm better." It was an interesting few days, that's for sure.' But those close to Joyce deny this, saying he wasn't interested in standing against English, and quickly made that clear to him. Even so, Joyce the strategist felt it was 'unhelpful' for the outgoing leader to interfere in a decision that should have been left to caucus.

Key says he felt boxed into a corner. 'I think Steven would say I tainted the process. One or two people were a bit angry, or disappointed, that I did that. And I get that. The leader is first amongst equals. If you are no longer the leader, you don't have any right to impose that. But I didn't have that luxury. If I didn't say, "I'm supporting Bill," I was, by definition, not supporting Bill. That's the inference the media would take. After a decade together, with us being hand-in-glove, if I didn't say, "He's right," then I'm actually saying he's not right. And I believed him to be right. And in politics, you have to wear your heart on your sleeve.'

*

By his own admission Key likes to be liked, and revels in the appeal of his down-to-earth ordinariness and breezy nature. He tells a story of trying to throw off the shackles of Parliament's very established hierarchy: 'Really early in the piece, two or three days after we got sworn in, we were at a kitchen Cabinet meeting. Gerry [Brownlee] was there, we were having a glass of wine and he said: "Will you pass me the wine, please, PM?" And I said: "Yeah, John will work." Gerry said: "Right, John: that'll never happen again".' And it never did. While Parliament is one of the most hierarchical of workplaces, and the prime minister is such a dominant character within it, at least at kitchen Cabinet Key wanted to embrace a degree of informality that would encourage open and effective communication.

And Key ran his government on those terms. Its centre of power was a late-night weekly meeting of his inner circle, where they'd mull over problems and map out strategy over a glass of wine. Often, they'd also get together in the hour before Monday Cabinet meetings. The blend of characters in the kitchen Cabinet was very good, but Key was nevertheless definitely the leader. English was number two, the deputy prime minister, with the mana that went with it. But also playing an important role was Steven Joyce. If Key needed someone to ring up, Joyce would always answer the call, no matter if it was 7am or midnight. It was felt that Joyce acted as a good coach, keeping Key on an even keel. Seven out of 10 times Joyce would moderate.

As transport minister, Simon Bridges was occasionally admitted into the inner sanctum, when policy discussions required him. Beneath a veneer of informality — which included chatting about New Zealand wine and golf shots and other bits and pieces — Bridges says it was a very tightly run kitchen Cabinet. There were serious discussions, and nothing important happened that wasn't talked through there. Bridges saw this as a good thing: 'You can't have too many chefs trying to stir the stew.' While there was debate and discussion at Cabinet level, and ministers had genuine power and autonomy in their area, those really running the show were in that tight circle. This allowed for a sense of direction and consistency.

Joyce and English kept an iron grip on what discussions filtered through to the executive. Joyce chaired the Cabinet Economic Growth and Infrastructure committee, or EGI, and English took charge of Cabinet's social policy committee. They are powerful forums, which essentially set the Cabinet agenda. 'It was a sort of a knocking system. I remember putting stuff up and getting annihilated,' Bridges says. 'Over time, I worked out that if Bill or Steven were being too conservative or, if I felt strongly, you could bypass them and go to John. But you wouldn't do that every week.'

Ben Thomas, a public relations consultant, worked as press secretary for the National Government. 'Joyce had this insane oversight,' he remembers. 'He got every MBIE-prepared briefing — that's something like 14 ministries. All of those ministers' briefings also went to Joyce. He fancied his economic policy nous, but really his role was PR. He would go line-by-line through government releases. He was the best chief press sec that John Key ever had.'

Another advisor says: 'Steven was very much a command-and-control kind of guy. A bit of the National Party culture came about by him being the campaign chair. You didn't argue with him.'

It is universally agreed that Wayne Eagleson was an integral part of the team. Eagleson had worked as a private secretary to Jim Bolger, headed up the party's research unit, and was campaign director in 1993. He was also a public affairs specialist. Working for Wellington powerbrokers Saunders Unsworth, he had lobbied for the mining industry against a bill to prohibit extraction on land in the Hauraki Gulf and the Coromandel. There was also a spell with Westpac bank, DB — one of the country's most recognised companies — and national grid operator Transpower. Brash appointed him chief of staff, replacing former newspaper editor Richard Long, in late 2005. Key kept him on once he assumed the leadership. Crucially, Eagleson matched Key's proficiency on the golf course.

'There hasn't been a chief of staff in Parliament like Wayne Eagleson,' Coleman says. 'He knew Wellington and the system inside out. He knew the party inside out. He had excellent judgement. The political management and support that Joyce and Eagleson gave Key was really absolutely crucial to our success.'

Eagleson dealt with problems before they reached Key. Other staff describe a man who, when approached, would remove his glasses and give a visitor his full attention. 'He could see the big picture really clearly,' Coleman says. 'He balanced out Joyce in that Wayne is just far better with people. You'd have to say Joyce is pretty ruthless, and that's in the best sense of the word. If you had a problem that needed a bit of humanity and a compassionate view, Wayne was the guy who could deal with that. Personal problems, difficulties in offices, difficulties between ministers. Joyce just didn't really have the skills to do it. And John was just too busy.'

All three men ran a regime of strict discipline. At the weekly caucus meetings, in plain language, Key would reinforce the message: 'If we can't run ourselves, they're not going to trust us to run the country.' Coleman says: 'He was so clear on caucus discipline and because he had the authority people would follow that.'

Key was also respected for swift decision-making. For some time, under Brash, the party had been kicking around the idea of repealing New Zealand's ground-breaking nuclear-free legislation. As leader, Key kiboshed the idea. It was an example of decisive, strong leadership. Often making a decision quickly is more important than the actual decision itself. Key's previous career on the trading floor had relied on fast decisions, making it unlikely to even occur to him to have a three-hour meeting to decide on a matter.

As a pressure valve, Key built meritocracy into the hierarchy. 'John would tell us: over time, most of you will be ministers. And that's a big prize for MPs,' Bridges says. Bennett says the first-term caucus was ready, and hungry for success after nine years in the wilderness. Having gone through a couple of leaders, Bennett says they saw in Key leadership that they could follow. 'He gave them hope. There was merit and loyalty and hard work, and everyone had a chance. He gave people a go and he thought quite long and hard about that.'

He ran his team like a chief executive, gave them yearly reviews, and expected key performance indicators, or KPIs, to be met. He was good at managing people: setting out what he wanted of them and his expectations.

But there are two sides to every coin. Good performance was to be expected and rewarded; that which fell below expectations was similarly recognised. Key's nickname, 'the smiling assassin', earned in the late 1990s when he fired some 50 members of his Merrill Lynch team, had resurfaced when he referenced it in a 2005 magazine profile. It was liberally applied by commentators when he dumped ministers Kate Wilkinson and Phil Heatley in a 2013 reshuffle. Finlayson inadvertently delivered the news to Heatley, who held the housing and conservation portfolios. 'Phil phoned me and said: "I've got to see the boss tomorrow. Are you going to see him?" I said: "No." He said: "There might be a reshuffle in the wings." And indeed, it was "see you later". Kate was pretty shattered. There was no inevitability to anything. You had to earn your stripes. And if you got into Cabinet and you weren't up to it, you would be moved. Key was tough. He had high standards. You could make a mistake once and he would forgive you. Make a mistake twice and you were gone.' Another MP says that once Key formed a negative opinion of you, it was hard to change it.

One MP who got on his wrong side was Hamilton East MP David Bennett. Despite being elected in 2005, he was never promoted under Key. Colleagues say it was because Key was dismayed by reports of Bennett's alleged late-night antics in the Beehive's third-floor bar, known as 3.2. 'John washed his hands of him. If you got offside with John, there's not a hell of a lot of belief in redemption.'

Key maintains that while the smiling assassin line is convenient, there was a far more mundane reason why people like Phil Heatley and Kate Wilkinson — and others over time —

were replaced. It was nothing to do with whether they were talented or hardworking or good — they were. It was more a matter that at any one time there were only really 19 slots, and maybe three of those would be taken by coalition arrangements. 'It's like a funnel: you're trying to get a lot of people through a relatively narrow gap. And eventually if you don't move anyone on, then no one else gets a chance.'

Ultimately, Key turned the assassin's knife on himself. 'I honestly thought I could win the '17 election. But what was going to be the stronger criteria for success of the party? My longevity? Or is it us refreshing and looking like we're not a tired third-term government, looking for a fourth? I thought if I go and Bill becomes the prime minister that means Steven Joyce will become minister of finance and there will be all these changes and movements. We might look just a little new. And it starts at the top. In the end I was prepared to do to myself what I was prepared to do to others.'

Key thought his careful political management meant National's brand could withstand the shock. But he had misjudged both the fragile unity and the shifting internal dynamics of his party.

3

THE PATIENT ENGLISH

A WEEK IS A long time in politics, as British Labour Prime Minister Harold Wilson once observed. And it was more than enough time for the National Party's legendary discipline to fall apart.

For a decade, Key's success had delivered him absolute authority over the caucus, and he expected a smooth transition of power, a mere formality, after he put the weight of his support behind his faithful deputy. But his exit left a power vacuum, and the fault-lines between the party's various factions began to open up.

With his gift of perfect timing, Key handed over the reins in the same week the government revealed the latest outlook on its financial accounts, known as the Half Year Economic and Fiscal Update (HYEFU). Even with a $3 billion bill for the Kaikōura quake repairs the books promised large and growing Budget surpluses, burnishing Bill English's bona fides as a competent manager of one of the fastest-growing economies in the developed world.

But instead of taking advantage of the moment, English was displaying a certain amount of apathy about taking on the role of party leader. He was coy and unsure when peppered by questions from journalists about his aspirations. Despite having had months to prepare, he didn't immediately seize the gauntlet, instead telling reporters he would speak to his family and National MPs before making a decision. Further, his insistence that he wouldn't stand if there wasn't strong caucus support for him hardly exuded self-confidence. Even a member of Key's kitchen Cabinet was unsure whether English would have stepped up, had it not been for Key's endorsement.

One obstacle was English's protective wife, Mary. The GP had bad memories of his last stint as leader as they juggled to bring up six young children. Her initial reaction was one of horror, and although she eventually got used to the idea, she hoped it wouldn't happen. In the end, she gave her blessing but with one condition: Wayne Eagleson, who had hoped to retire alongside his boss, must be persuaded to stay on as chief of staff. Eagleson agreed.

Key never had any doubts about his chosen heir. He says that although English had never pushed to take on the role, he wasn't reluctant to do so, being very confident in his own ability. And Key believed his successor had every reason to be.

The public were less certain. A snap Nielsen poll commissioned by Stuff revealed 39 per cent of respondents didn't know who they wanted to replace Key. (English was the clear favourite, though, with 37 per cent.)

The day after Key's resignation, the National MPs arrived at Parliament for a caucus meeting to decide the process for electing a new leader. As the governing party, National was in the caucus room on the second floor of Parliament House. (The third floor is traditionally the Opposition floor.) Portraits of former leaders line the polished timber-panelled walls, and when packed the room is often stuffy. Tradition dictates that the chair an MP takes for the first post-election meeting is theirs for the term. Mobile phones are surrendered at the door; discussions are meant to be confidential.

As they walk the red-carpeted corridor to caucus meetings, MPs run a gauntlet of Press Gallery reporters. This series of mini press conferences (known as 'stand-ups', as opposed to more formal seated press conferences) is known within Parliament's village as 'caucus run'. While English hesitated in the face of a barrage of queries, Jonathan Coleman was first out of the blocks, eager to fill the vacancy left by Key. The 50-year-old made a pitch for generational change; a reminder squarely aimed at ambitious and restless backbenchers that English had been in Parliament since 1990.

At the meeting, English came across as diffident and wasn't saying anything. Given that he'd known about Key's plans for weeks, it was surprising he didn't seem ready. Nevertheless, once the meeting had concluded, he publicly declared his candidacy: 'I'll be focusing on building the sort of support that will lead to a unified, cohesive caucus.' This public declaration did not entirely dispel the sense of indecision his fellow MPs had sensed in the preceding caucus meeting. As former Treaty Negotiations Minister Chris Finlayson put it: 'Typical Hamlet sort of Bill. And then he finally came around to it.'

By the day's end, he'd got the public backing of a host of MPs, including ministers Nathan Guy, Michael Woodhouse, Louise Upston, Nikki Kaye and Hekia Parata, and the leaders of the government's minor support parties. One senior MP says Coleman initially had a flurry of support, but it began to bleed away when Key and Gerry Brownlee started lobbying MPs, pushing for continuity.

There was another contender: Judith Collins. Until 2014, the former justice minister had been Key's most powerful female minister. However, when allegations of dirty political tricks in the run-up to the election surfaced, he had sacked her, only to reinstate her after an investigation concluded there was no evidence she had acted inappropriately. Some felt he had trouble dealing with very forthright women and could never really handle Collins. A colleague describes her as a 'very complex character' and suspects Key was a bit intimidated by her on a certain level.

Collins also resented being excluded from Key's kitchen Cabinet. 'She always had this chip on her shoulder about not being part of the [weekly] drinks with Key,' the minister reveals, adding that those meetings were for Key to be with the people that he could trust 'and he never had any trust in Judith right from when they were backbenchers'.

There was certainly no love lost between Collins and English. She revealed in her *Pull No Punches* memoir that English had urged her to resign at the height of the scandal. Collins reminded him of Jenny Shipley, who had carefully plotted to remove Prime Minister Jim Bolger in 1997, and English was said to be none-too-pleased when Key reinstated her. Collins would later admit, in 2020, that she just didn't think he ever liked her. She was probably correct. Collins was a protégée of Don Brash, and was part of the faction that rolled English in Brash's favour. Later, in a 2004 letter to Brash, English wrote that she had 'an unfortunately high estimation of her own competence'.

Collins objected to what she believed was a 'backroom deal' between English and Key. Her loyalty to Brash meant she disapproved of Key's own pathway to leadership, and she admits to stirring. But she also has ferocious political instincts and spotted a gap in the market: National's heartland MPs were spooked by a resurgent New Zealand First in the wake of the 2015 Northland by-election. Sticking a finger into the winds of change blowing after Brexit and Trump's election, she pitched at those already uneasy about Key's departure. She contended that the party was going to have to overcome any sense of complacency, 'any sense that it's steady as she goes, just more of the same'.

Key's plan to avoid a leadership contest had come unstuck. This wasn't to say that English would not win the vote: it was a matter of process. Some MPs felt there needed to be competition.

But an open contest, which could be destabilising and divisive, was the last thing many others wanted. In rode the Four Amigos: Mark Mitchell, Alfred Ngaro, Chris Bishop and Todd Muller. Journalists assumed they were a powerful alliance, who would play a crucial role in influencing the choice of 29 backbenchers. (There was a nice symmetry: English was one-quarter of the Brat Pack, the group of young thrusters instrumental in deposing Jenny Shipley.) That wasn't the case. The Amigos were all English loyalists, but they were worried about Coleman's 'change' challenge, and English's flat reaction. They paid English a visit at his seventh-floor Beehive office. The blunt message was: 'You've got to want it. Show us you want it.'

The Four Amigos did have other motivations. After five years in Parliament, Mitchell, a former police officer, and Ngaro, a pastor, were angling for promotions. Muller and Bishop were two of the standout talents of the 2014 intake. Although a relatively new MP, Bishop was a familiar face in politics, a protégé of both Brownlee and Joyce. Muller, an agri-business executive, was talked up as 'the next John Key' before he had even won an electorate.

Their entente had formed out of the wreckage of the Northland by-election, but they were by no means close friends, let alone 'players'. This was the impression inadvertently conveyed by Muller when, cornered by Newshub reporter Jenna Lynch, he clumsily blurted out the 'Four Amigos' nickname. This instantly had the effect of projecting the group into more of a thing than it was. The other three were furious. Nevertheless by then the damage was done, and the hype around the leap-frogging quartet irritated the caucus. 'They should learn to walk before they can run,' Finlayson snapped at a reporter when asked about their role.

But the Amigos weren't alone in their concerns. Gerry Brownlee, an English supporter, also dropped by. In his typically blunt way, Brownlee told his old friend he had overwhelming support and he shouldn't muck around. Nick Smith — English's best mate and one of the original Brat Pack — was also worried. He discerned a naïvety in the caucus, one which was particularly potent and dangerous after a very successful period of stable leadership, like that under Key. So while some colleagues felt that it would be refreshing to have a 'good open contest', Smith begged to differ. 'Actually, every time you have a vote in the caucus, particularly around those important positions of leader and deputy leader, you leave scars within the caucus and the party that will last a decade or two. A mature political party will have the internal capacity to be able to resolve questions of leadership by consensus, and are so much more successful when they do.'

By the close of the week, the caucus fell somewhat into line. A majority of 30 MPs confirmed their support for English, and Collins and Coleman withdrew their candidacy. English would be New Zealand's thirty-ninth prime minister.

Finlayson was one of those disappointed the race wasn't run. 'It appeared to me that it had all been organised over a cup of tea. Paula [Bennett] would move in as deputy, Steven [Joyce] as minister of finance, and Bill would go back to the leadership. I think that was probably a big mistake. That, for the sake of the party, it may have been good to have the great intergenerational debate there. That's not to criticise English. He had atoned for the errors in 2002, having been a very good minister of finance.'

Sensing there was an itch that still needed to be scratched, Finlayson and Brownlee approached Bridges. Neither man believed 47-year-old Bennett was the right fit to be deputy. 'We both got onto Bridges and said: "Why don't you go for the deputy leadership? You're the right generation." And so he publicly toyed with it for a few days,' Finlayson recalls.

The tussle between Bennett and 40-year-old Bridges was fleeting. Bridges exploited the power struggles within the caucus, emphasising that he, unlike Bennett, was not admitted into Key's inner circle. He would be the 'change and rejuvenation' married to English's 'strength and stability'. 'There's a real sense from our backbenchers that they want a champion, that they want to see after eight years in Government that we're listening, and I'm pledging to be that person that will strongly listen to them and be a champion for the backbench,' he pitched.

Speaking to the press pack assembled in Parliament's distinctive black-and-white tiled hall, Bridges also gave an intriguing glimpse into his future leadership style, appealing to those colleagues who wanted to climb politics' greasy pole. He explained how Key had plucked the young MP 'from obscurity' to make him a minister, and he wanted to offer the same opportunity to others. Bridges had some support. 'She [Paula] has got a lot of very positive attributes but being a behind-the-scenes operator was not one of them,' a former minister says. 'That was always going to be a problem,' it was felt, as the deputy's role is to hold the place together. Part of that involves sorting out any disgruntled members of caucus, a role which some felt did not suit her personality.

Bridges's support included Trade Minister Todd McClay, Muller, Clutha-Southland MP Todd Barclay, Wellington list MP Paul Foster-Bell, Invercargill MP Sarah Dowie, New Plymouth's Jonathan Young, Simon O'Connor (who would marry Bridges's sister Rachel Trimble that weekend) and junior whip Jami-Lee Ross.

Nick Smith believes Bridges was positioning for the future. Again, Smith felt that the deputy leadership was best arrived at by consensus rather than a vote. 'There's nothing wrong with being ambitious, but Simon Bridges was overly ambitious. And the fact that he would not take counsel and stood for the deputy leadership against Paula was partly because he's a good student of politics and knew we were moving into a post-Key era and it suited him to be defying the old guard.'

The manoeuvrings didn't work. By Saturday morning it was clear Bennett was the favourite, and Bridges pulled out. Finlayson recalls: 'He rang me and said: "Look, I've pulled my name out of contention. But I've done very well out of it." Well, that wasn't the purpose of putting him up, actually. He went from nine to four and unbelievably acquired all these other responsibilities. He was a classic case of the John Major-type person, he rose without a trace.'

Steven Joyce briefly weighed up a tilt at the job but quickly recognised the build-up of support for Bennett. A mother at 17, she had worked as a truck-stop waitress, a recruitment consultant and as Murray McCully's electorate secretary and later for his election campaign, before nudging her way up the party ranks. Don Brash had urged her to stand for Parliament, recognising the outspoken West Aucklander could shake National from its comfort zone. The TV series *Outrageous Fortune*, set in the area, was then at the height of its popularity. Westies were on trend. Bennett entered Parliament on the list in 2005.

When Key took over the leadership reins, he took the idea and ran with it, fast-tracking the self-confessed 'bogan' into the $20 billion welfare portfolio with only one term under her belt. Her Cinderella rise, vivacious character and love of leopard print made her one of the country's best-known politicians. But she was also polarising, with her hardline position on beneficiaries and controversial leaks to reporters seeing her attract vicious abuse.

Bennett was aware of what she had to offer: 'I got in there [to the kitchen Cabinet] because John was smart enough to know — and he would say it — that one in every second New Zealander needs to look at us and see something that they relate to. He wanted a contest of ideas. He didn't want that group to be Yes men or women. When he invited me in, he said: "This is my private group, Paula. I don't need a quota. I want you there because you think differently and we need to be challenged, and so you better go for it." It was a calculated moment. John used to say there will come a time when the party really needs you.'

In the Key years, Bennett went on to work closely with English on his social investment model. A bold shake-up of how social services were delivered, it eschewed the traditional conservative approach to welfare by spending generously to target socio-economic deprivation in the young.

So by 2016, Bennett and English not only had a proven working relationship, but Bennett's bubbly nature was seen as the perfect foil to English, who had a more dour, dry image. Thus Bennett became the country's first Māori deputy prime minister, and National's first woman deputy leader. Thanking her rival, she spoke of their 'sickening kind of mutual respect'. In another time, she said, she would have voted for Bridges and his 'awesome brain'. 'He's got a big role to play now and in the future,' she told reporters.

With Bennett in place as his number two, English had already made it clear Steven Joyce would be his finance minister. A refresh was badly needed; English had been an MP for 26 years and could hardly claim to be a new broom. But history was also weighing on his mind. Before him, Bill Rowling, Jack Marshall, Mike Moore and Jenny Shipley all failed to win an election after taking the premiership mid-term. English didn't want to risk taking National to the second loss of his career.

He had promised both stability and change, and his reshuffle was cautious. The leadership switch itself was dramatic enough without further spooking the horses. A handful read the room, with Statistics Minister Craig Foss and Local Government Minister Sam Lotu-Iiga swiftly announcing their retirement. McCully would also go, as earlier signalled.

Bridges and Adams won promotion, but English's front bench was largely unchanged. Recklessly, Collins was punished for her aspirations, demoted and stripped of the police and corrections portfolios she loved. She resented the snub. Old pal Nick Smith and English's apprentice in education Hekia Parata kept their jobs, which grated among those members who saw them as past their use-by dates. As one MP noted, in long-serving governments there is always tension between the old and the new and the less experienced. Some felt the traditionalist English, who is very conservative in National Party traditions, had placed too much importance on longevity. Rather than promote talent from the 2014 intake, people like Muller and Bishop, he mistakenly thought they could wait their turn.

To the incredulity of some of his colleagues, dairy farmer and accountant David Bennett finally won promotion (to minister for food safety and minister for veterans' affairs outside Cabinet), after entering Parliament in 2004 and having no ministerial role in Key's nine years. He wasn't the only one who looked as though they were being rewarded simply for long service; Jacqui Dean and Tim Macindoe, who had become MPs in 2005 and 2008 respectively, also became ministers outside Cabinet. A number of their colleagues wondered if this was the best image to project to take the government to a fourth term. English, they felt, missed a critical opportunity to change the shape and the feel of the ministry, showcasing 'new faces and more up-and-coming talent'.

Chris Finlayson, for one, thought little of David Bennett's abilities. 'I took on myself the task of trying to get MPs to think about members' bills, because the Labour Party was murdering us on that front. I needed someone to drive reform of the conflict of laws rules … I remember giving that to David Bennett. I thought: he's a lawyer. Well, I could have given him a cabbage.'

The rationale behind these selections was based on a number of factors. First, a belief in the need to project a strong sense of continuity with what had been a very successful government, having just lost the highest-profile member of the team. With no sense that the public was perceiving the administration as tired, any significant change amounted to change for change's sake. This risked upsetting sections of the caucus at the very time when projecting continuity was considered essential. And, in the lead-up to an election, a show of continuity provided a good point of contrast with the Labour Party, which was churning through its own people. There was a season for everything. After the election was won was the time for any 'refreshment'.

Certainly in the early days of English's administration there was little to distinguish it from the Key years. He kept the traditional weekly drinks with an inner circle, which included Joyce, Bennett, Bridges, Brownlee, Coleman, Adams and Eagleson. But one participant says the get-togethers lacked the joviality and energy of Key's meetings. 'It was throwing people together who weren't a natural fit. Whereas John was having a drink to decompress and kicking around some strategy in an informal setting, it wasn't very relaxed with Bill running it. And Bill was always one glass of wine and had to get home. It was all a bit serious. Key is far more of a party personality.'

Although he promised a policy stocktake, English indicated his priorities would remain infrastructure, supporting a strong economy and growing population, and the social investment approach to helping society's most vulnerable. In his first interviews, English noted Key had led through difficult times, and he hoped not to be hamstrung by natural disasters. Nonetheless, his first official visit was to quake-hit Kaikōura. Landing in a Defence Force helicopter on the lawn of The Store, a Kēkerengū café, he was met with dozens of furious locals, frustrated at progress in reopening State Highway 1. Putting his own stamp on the leadership was proving to be no easy task for English.

Only a week after Key's bombshell resignation, English was formally sworn in at a ceremony watched by Mary and their children. Following a celebratory afternoon tea, he returned to Parliament to watch John and Bronagh Key leave for another Hawaii holiday. National Party MPs formed a guard of honour down the granite steps, as the couple walked to a waiting Crown car. At the bottom waited the Englishes, who farewelled them with hugs. 'Trust your gut' was Key's parting advice to the new prime minister.

As they drove away, Key smiled at English's triumphant waving. His patient deputy was beginning his premiership on the same forecourt where his misery and failure had been captured all those years before.

4

JACINDAMANIA

A MID THE COMMOTION OF Key's resignation, another exit from Parliament achieved rather less attention, but it, too, would have significant implications for the political landscape. One-time Labour leader David Shearer was leaving to take up a high-profile post as the United Nations' special envoy to South Sudan. His resignation triggered a by-election in Auckland's Mt Albert. Former Prime Minister Helen Clark had held the seat before Shearer. Soon it would be occupied by another future premier: Jacinda Ardern.

Ardern was following on Key's heels, embracing her role as a celebrity politician with spreads in glossy magazines, breakfast television slots and cameos as a DJ. She had the dubious honour of thrice having been voted the country's sexiest politician. The 37-year-old was unapologetic about her profile, but there was plenty of sniping (within both parties) about her inability to land a punch in her shadow portfolios, particularly justice and children, and her unsuccessful record against Nikki Kaye in Auckland Central.

National chose not to run a candidate in the hurried Mt Albert race, and Ardern's main competition was Green MP Julie Anne Genter. Ardern was so well known her billboards featured only her first name. So far, the party had resisted promoting her to the deputy leadership. That would change after the February by-election when party doyenne Annette King was elbowed aside.

Within five months Ardern would also replace Andrew Little, as leader.

*

Bill English did not ease into the political year. By mid-January, he was in London to talk about the ramifications of Brexit with UK Prime Minister Theresa May. Then it was on to Berlin for a meeting with German Chancellor Angela Merkel.

The transition between prime ministers was smooth, with English retaining many of Key's staff. Those used to Key's designer watches and shoes were charmed by English's more down-to-earth style. For the trip to London he arrived at the airport carrying a battered, purple Kathmandu backpack — the luggage of choice for many a Kiwi's overseas experience.

English had thrown the Diplomatic Protection Service (DPS: the armed police officers, trained in hand-to-hand combat, who protect New Zealand's dignitaries) by opting to remain at his Karori family home instead of moving into the more secure grace-and-favour Premier House. Key was known to have hated the drafty and dated official residence, but successive governments have been loath to do it up, lest they be accused of domestic largesse by the taxpayer.

Although English had boundless energy, he often appeared over-tired on Mondays, slumping down into an armchair on arrival at his office. Eagleson soon got to the bottom of his fatigue: Mary, short on staff at her city GP surgery, was having him help scrub it clean on Sundays. It was also his job to cook the family roast.

'Bill had [earned] an immense amount of respect,' says one staffer who worked for both Key and English. 'But there was a settling-in period, as with any change, especially in politics. He is incredibly smart. Bill knew the public service, and had an innate understanding of which levers to pull to get the public service moving, and how it all fits together. But he was also open to advice and very honest about what he didn't know. He was almost earnest about briefings. He had an innocence about him.'

The long summer recess usually ends for parliamentarians on 6 February, when politicians of all stripes make the trip north to mark the signing of the Treaty of Waitangi, New Zealand's founding document. Although celebrated nationwide as a public holiday since 1974, there have been long-standing tensions surrounding the day, which is officially marked at Waitangi, where the Treaty was first signed in 1840, close to the town of Paihia.

As with Key before him, English had been denied speaking rights by the leaders of Te Tii Waitangi marae, the gateway to the Treaty Grounds, which traditionally held welcoming ceremonies for the celebrations. In 2016, Key chose to spend the day at the NRL Nines rugby league tournament in Auckland.

It was against this background that it was decided English would eschew the traditional visit to the Treaty Grounds in February, choosing to spend his first Waitangi Day in office with Ngāti Whātua Ōrākei at their marae at Takaparawhau, or Bastion Point. National's relationship with the iwi, or tribe, was vexed: in 1978 former prime minister Robert Muldoon sent 800 police officers to forcibly remove those protesting the Crown sale of their land. English's decision to visit was a thoughtful political calculation.

On Waitangi Day 2017, English celebrated the achievements of central Auckland's mana whenua, spoke of how government and iwi relations had improved, and mused on what a modern-day Treaty relationship should look like. In doing so, he nullified criticism that skipping the Waitangi Treaty Grounds commemorations showed a deep-seated racism. He also distinguished himself from Key, signalling what a very different prime minister he hoped to be.

As the incumbent, National started the election year with the advantage. English set the polling day for 23 September, announcing the economy would be at the heart of the contest. It was strange, then, that his scene-setting State of the Nation speech — the typical drawing of party battle-lines — focused on crime. Speaking at the five-star Stamford Plaza hotel, and hosted by Auckland's Rotary Club, English announced funding for 880 new police officers, the headline of a $503-million package to reduce offending. Law and order is safe Tory ground, but this was an acknowledgement of failure. Crime rates had been falling for half a decade, before rising again in 2014. Middle-class voters were especially frustrated with burglary rates. As finance minister, English had presided over a freeze on police budgets.

As opponents in Labour and New Zealand First crowed about a backdown (they had been especially vocal about funding cuts), English argued the crime surge was a symptom of a growing population. But this in itself was a problem for English: immigration had reached record highs in February 2017, with 71,300 more migrants arriving than leaving.

The government had successfully reversed the 'brain drain' to Australia, a promise that Key made standing in Wellington's

Westpac Stadium to illustrate that its 36,000-capacity was equal to the numbers leaving each year. That campaign ad helped National win the 2008 election. But many believed high levels of immigration were now crippling public services, stagnating wage growth and squeezing the housing market.

Winston Peters, long a staunch opponent of the post-war migration that fuelled New Zealand's economic success, was exploiting the jitters. As with elections in the United States and France, and with Britain's Brexit referendum, immigration became a lightning rod and a significant theme of the election campaign. As the year went on, Labour would take a more hardline approach, with policies aimed at slashing the intake of foreigners by tens of thousands. National responded by tightening access to skilled work visas to ensure Kiwis took jobs ahead of migrants.

The concern over immigration dovetailed with the other issue *du jour*: inequality. A defining question of the Left–Right spectrum for centuries, the disparities in wealth and income had once again begun to capture the debate among middle- and working-class citizens in Western economies. In the United States in November 2016, Donald Trump was elected by disgruntled blue-collar workers. The rising gap between the rich and everyone else had fuelled unrest across Europe, and had even featured in India's elections.

In New Zealand, opposition parties capitalised on a growing sense that National's focus on growth driven by high migration and the surplus had left too many 'ordinary Kiwis' behind, with worsening social outcomes. French economist Thomas Piketty's best-selling *Capital in the Twenty-First Century* became the summer beach read for Left-leaning MPs.

National was also on the back foot over the parlous state of water quality in the country's cherished rivers and lakes.

A booming dairy industry, with farmers encouraged to intensify and irrigate under National, was putting New Zealand's 100 per cent clean, green reputation at risk, with the water network now among some of the most polluted in the developed world. Environment Minister Nick Smith responded in February with a new management plan and 'swimmable standards', but these were largely derided as unambitious by experts and campaigners.

English had wanted the election to be fought on National's reputation for economic management. But, for the first time since 2008, the debate would not be on the party's terms. Labour, the Greens and New Zealand First had drawn their own battle lines: questioning just what the government's lauded economic management had really done for voters. As most measures of inequality had seen a rise under National, it became easy to argue that their free-market policies directed resources to those who were doing well and created an underclass who could never claw their way out of poverty. Images of shoeless children, and families sleeping in cars and collecting food parcels dominated the media discourse, along with stories of a worrying youth suicide rate. Instead of celebrating its economic policies, National was cornered into defending them.

Labour had no trouble recognising and articulating the zeitgeist. But under the unpopular and crabby Andrew Little the party could not capitalise on the voters' shifting mood. An earlier campaign built around Little's vision of the Kiwi Dream and closing the wealth gap between the baby boomer and millennial generations had fallen flat.

A trained lawyer, former trade union boss and party president, Little came to Parliament in 2011 by virtue of his high place on the list after failing to win the New Plymouth electorate. Accepting the poisoned chalice of leadership after the 2014 election, he was not the popular pick among MPs. Like David Cunliffe before him, he was foisted on the caucus by Labour's rules, which handed sway to the unions and membership: in this case, the union vote swung in behind Little and carried the day.

Eventually, Little won credit for uniting a caucus that had been riven by bitter infighting since it was dumped from office eight years prior. He had earlier earned respect by refusing to take a position in the internal tussles that accompanied a leadership contest between Grant Robertson and David Cunliffe.

As well as healing internal divisions, he'd also rebuilt campaign operations and party machinery, which were left 'a complete wreck' after the 2014 defeat. It would become known as his project. But he'd achieved peace by dumping Labour's most contentious policies — a specific capital gains tax, a rise in the pension age, a restructure of the wholesale electricity market — and appeared to be heading directionless into the election campaign. Little also had poor name recognition and could not throw off the 'Angry Andy' nickname dreamed up by National's strategists. An earnest man with deeply held principles, he simply did not have the appeal of Key's breezy charm, nor even English's dry, laconic calm.

The first 1 News/Colmar Brunton poll of the year showed voters were sticking with English. He was top of the preferred prime minister rankings on 31 per cent (Key had finished his tenure on 36 per cent). Winston Peters was on 8 per cent, with Little taking third place on a sorry 7 per cent. (It should be noted, though, that the poll did give an early hint of headwinds for National, with its party vote dropping four percentage points to 46 per cent. The opening two Roy Morgan Research polls followed similar patterns.)

With Key's departure — and then Annette King's — Labour was galvanised. Little and Ardern presented a fresh break from the Labour of old (neither had served under Clark). Little swapped his glasses for contact lenses and climbed into a Hugo Boss suit. Ardern was more attractive to women, youth and urban liberals, who had all drifted away to Key's National Party. Her tilts in Auckland Central also gave her some standing with the city's business community. The media were certainly excited at the prospect of a more competitive election.

But English had a trick up his sleeve. Within two days of Ardern's election to the role of deputy (with unanimous support from caucus), the prime minister dropped a bombshell. Overturning Key's promise not to increase the state pension age, English and Joyce announced that if re-elected the government would raise the threshold from 65 to 67 by 2040. The New Zealand Superannuation scheme (known as NZ Super) was forecast to grow unaffordable, with citizens living much longer.

Key's resolution had always made English uncomfortable. But he'd also been part of the Bolger–Shipley government and witnessed first-hand the backlash when they shifted the age of eligibility from 60. The manoeuvre was cleverly calculated, allowing English to step out from Key's shadow. It also boxed Labour into a corner. The Opposition could hardly argue NZ Super was now affordable, having campaigned on raising the age in the previous term. National's proposed policy trod a careful line, and, with a distant deadline and incremental rise, it did not risk alienating the powerful, older voting bloc. National's volte-face even had a get-out clause specifically designed to appeal to superannuant Winston Peters: the age could stay at 65 if potential coalition partners made their opposition a bottom-line.

Although seen as a contentious issue, the polls barely shifted. A Newshub-Reid Research poll put National on 47.1 to Labour's 30.8, which was actually a slight drop from the news channel's previous canvass in August 2016. A 1 News/Colmar Brunton poll a week later showed no change from January: National on 46, Labour on 30.

National had another weapon in its arsenal. Steven Joyce's first Budget was to be the opening salvo in the election-year debate. With a tax revenue take well ahead of forecasts, and fiscal surpluses predicted to hit $30 billion over the next four years, there was plenty of opportunity to offer a few sweeteners to voters before they went to the polls.

But although almost a decade of solid economic growth would allow the government to start writing cheques for election-year bribes, the Budget tip-toed on a tightrope of prudence and profusion. The centrepiece was a $2 billion package to bolster family incomes. As with the previous year's Budget, which raised benefits for the first time in decades, it made a daring raid into Labour territory by rewarding low- and middle-income earners.

Joyce thumbed his nose at the Opposition by building the package around Working for Families, an income-support scheme that Key had once labelled 'communism by stealth'. (He was also dangling bait: the changes wouldn't kick in until the following year, and only if the government was returned to office). Higher-income earners — National's traditional constituency — also benefited from rejigging tax thresholds, leading commentators to conclude it was a Budget with 'something for everyone'.

Overall, Joyce aimed to oil squeaky wheels. There was a state-run house building programme (which looked a lot like Labour's own KiwiBuild policy) to fend off criticism that National was ignoring a crisis of affordable housing. The accommodation supplement (frozen for many years) was also given a hefty boost, with the added bonus of staving off concern about rising levels of child poverty. Scrutiny of neglected mental health services was answered with a $224 million injection, part of an overall hike of $879 million for health (the biggest in 11 years). Close to $200 million would go on tourism infrastructure, to soothe worries about the pressure that a booming holiday industry was placing on local services. And the effects of the country's population growth spurt were tackled with an $11 billion spend-up on infrastructure.

As campaign manager as well as finance minister, Joyce had one eye on the optics, rolling out splashy announcements in a countdown to Budget Day, when the Budget was formally presented to Parliament. Labour was discombobulated. While Little refused to vote for the legislation, the Greens and New Zealand First fell in behind it, on the basis that any increase to low incomes was better than nothing.

Much was made by pundits about a lack of vision from a tired-looking administration. But the public didn't seem to mind that Joyce had opted for a business-as-usual approach. The first post-Budget opinion poll (from 1 News/Colmar Brunton) gave National a three-point boost, up to 49 per cent. Labour remained stubbornly on 30 per cent. A few weeks later, Newshub-Reid Research gave English's government a minute lift (just 0.3 percentage points), while Labour dropped more than four points.

*

New Zealand's election campaigns typically last four weeks, with the formal dissolution of Parliament setting the stage. That was due to happen in mid-August, but the 2017 general election would break all previous patterns.

As it turned out, the events that would shape the result kicked off a month earlier, at the Green Party's pre-election annual general meeting. In its earlier years, the party's conferences provided plenty of quirky material for journalists, defined for an era by television footage of Morris-dancing delegates. Now more corporate and bland, the best the Press Gallery had to hope for was the triennial scuffle about whether the Greens could ever enter into government with National. (Always unlikely.) Even that was a moot point. The Greens' fortunes were tied to Labour after signing a memorandum of understanding in 2016 to 'defeat' the National-led Government.

Bored reporters were shaken from their torpor when co-leader Metiria Turei used her keynote address to confess she had lied to claim extra benefits as a 23-year-old single mother. Turei told the social welfare agency Work and Income that she was living alone with her daughter Piu when she actually had flatmates. 'This is what being on the benefit did to me — it made me poor and it made me lie,' she said. 'It was a stressful, terrifying experience.' Turei's admission was designed to disrupt the debate and tap into a resurgence in left-wing radicalism led by US presidential candidate Bernie Sanders and British Labour leader Jeremy Corbyn.

She hoped to galvanise (and appease) the Green grassroots, which were apprehensive about her more moderate co-leader James Shaw and deeply uneasy about a flashy magazine cover that displayed candidates in a *Vanity Fair*-style spread. The revelation worked: in the next 1 News/Colmar Brunton poll, the Greens surged in popularity to 15 per cent, their highest ever, which would deliver 18 MPs. And then it didn't.

Turei's story began to unravel under intense media scrutiny. She then admitted enrolling to vote at an Auckland address where she was not resident in order to be able to vote for a friend running in the 1995 general election. The backlash was too great: the next round of polls saw the Greens slump below the 5 per cent threshold required for entry to Parliament. Turei resigned in August. She would be the second leader to quit that month. Her gamble had initially worked, but the upswing had only energised the Left, and seen voters defect from Labour.

When Labour's internal polling saw the party crash to 23 per cent support — worse even than the woeful David Cunliffe-led result of the previous election — Little began questioning his own leadership. 'Am I too damaged?' he asked his inner circle, which included Ardern, Grant Robertson and senior whip Kris Faafoi. There was certainly a sense of nervousness in the Labour camp. While no one thought there was a path to winning the 2017 election, the worry was that if it had another poor showing at the polls, this would make a 2020 win nigh-on impossible. Little had open and honest conversations about it. He said his only concern was duty to the party.

When the 1 News poll dropped shortly afterwards, placing Labour on 24 per cent, Little's inner turmoil intensified. The numbers were so dismal that Little, who was standing only as a list candidate, was dangerously close to missing out on a seat in Parliament himself, an unprecedented constitutional predicament for the leader of a party.

Little was due to be interviewed by 1 News political editor Corin Dann about the poll. Waiting in the network's green room, with his chief of staff Neale Jones and press secretary Jodi Ihaka, Little told them he was going to be upfront about his doubts.

Little told Dann that he had discussed resignation with senior Labour Party colleagues. 'I'd be lying to you if I hadn't thought that,' he said. 'They said we want you in the fight.' Honest displays of weakness are so rare in politics that it was assumed the remarks were a blunder. But his moves were calculated.

The poll offered a twinkle of hope. Jacinda Ardern had registered a steady 6 per cent in the preferred prime minister stakes in the last handful of polls. This was level with Little — but, eight weeks out from the election, surely she couldn't do any worse? It was becoming obvious that Ardern was the only viable option. If Little were to make the decision to move on himself, it could well avoid the negative implications accompanying other leadership changes where the knives were drawn. It would be seen as a positive, constructive move, not a sign of disharmony and panic. But it would take Little a full two days to reach the inevitable conclusion. In today's frenzied media cycles, that felt like an eternity.

The following morning, Little told Radio NZ's Guyon Espiner that at 24 per cent, even with minor party support, Labour couldn't credibly form a government. He spent the day with candidate Naisi Chen, launching her East Coast Bays campaign and attending events in the Chinese community. In the evening, Jones and chief press secretary Mike Jaspers joined Little for a beer in the lobby of Auckland's Stamford Plaza hotel.

Little was conflicted. If he resigned and Labour still lost badly, would Ardern be forever tarred by the defeat? Would it be better to allow her to rebuild support afresh after the election? His focus remained firmly on the best long-term interests of the party. If staying on as leader was best for the party in the long run, he could have stared down any panic and challenge from MPs. But doing so also threatened his 'project': the machinery and the culture of the party he had worked so hard to rebuild. He didn't want to burn it down. The gamble of changing leadership at this late stage would also be costly. He was featured in expensive campaign advertisements, which had already been filmed, and his face was on billboards, printed and paid for.

It was a late night of discussion. The team left the hotel at 5am to fly to Wellington. A morning interview with Radio NZ was cancelled. Ambushed at the capital's airport by reporters, Little said he wouldn't be resigning. Actually, at that stage he had not yet come to a decision.

On the 20-minute drive through the city to Parliament, he made up his mind. Jones hit the phone, first calling Ardern. 'He's going to resign and nominate you,' she was told. There were calls to Rob Salmond, Jones's deputy, who organised new contracts for staff to sign. Faafoi was tasked with calling a caucus meeting, and press secretary Phil Reid organised a media conference.

Ardern was elected unopposed. Changing leaders this close to an election was high risk. But it wasn't unprecedented: Labour had done it before. Just 59 days before the 1990 election, the charismatic Mike Moore, at 41, rolled bookish Prime Minister Geoffrey Palmer, when the polls promised a result that would slash the Labour caucus from 57 to fewer than 20. Ardern's succession would be more gentle. It was also infinitely more successful. Moore was installed to 'save the furniture' and stall an internal war. Ardern led Labour into government.

*

The election had been limping to a predictable conclusion. National stuck with its campaign to provide stability. Its warnings about flirting with the alternatives were underlined by the dramas that were consuming the minor parties on the Left.

But Ardern was a much more attractive candidate than Little. Youthful, likeable, photogenic, she drew immediate comparison with other progressive world leaders such as Canada's Justin Trudeau, France's Emmanuel Macron and even US President Barack Obama. The adulation would get its own name: Jacindamania. Her new deputy, Kelvin Davis, summed up the pageant perfectly when he described his role: 'I've got the easiest job in politics — I just need to kick back and bask in the glow of the Jacinda effect.'

Labour's campaign was revamped. The slogan became *Let's do this*. It was an easily repeatable tag-line that leveraged their cheerful underdog status. Donations began rolling into the cash-starved campaign coffers.

Within only a week, Labour's fortunes were transformed. The next Newshub-Reid Research poll saw Labour pick up nine points to rise to 33.1 per cent, although the votes were coming off the Greens. English saw a slight rise in his popularity (up 1.9 points to 27.7 per cent), but Ardern was now nibbling at his heels on 26.3 per cent.

There was a tendency within National to write Ardern off. Her reputation as a darling of the women's magazines and social media rather than a solid political achiever meant, one senior National MP admits, the party dismissed her as 'just a flake, it'll be fine'. Politicos accused her of being 'an inveterate self-promoter', but people liked her. And so from about 2015 some in National identified her as the biggest threat. 'If they changed to her, I thought we'd be in serious trouble,' the senior MP remembers. 'And then we were.'

Certainly, National's campaign initially underestimated Ardern's potency. The polling gave them confidence. They felt Ardern was a lightweight, with no gravitas, and that Labour had no policy. Against this was the legacy of the popular Key years, extended by English, and this was going to take them through.

'We had the record, we had the serious personnel, but we totally underestimated the celebrity element of it, which grew over time.'

But Key had seen the danger, thanks in part to his wife's observations, and had warned senior colleagues before he left. Bronagh — 'the voice of reason' — would watch Ardern go head-to-head with Simon Bridges on TVNZ's early morning political slot *Young Guns* and say to him: '"There is something about her, just tread carefully if she becomes the leader." She picked it.'

Joyce also recognised Labour's fortunes would change if Ardern took over. He saw that she shared 'a relaxed, common touch' with Key. Ardern, he feared, had the elusive X Factor.

Bridges recalls top-tier discussions about Ardern's potential. 'In the couple of years before her meteoric rise, Labour was doing so badly and Andrew Little was so hopeless, and there was a sense of hubris within some in the National Party that "we've got them". I remember seeing the senior heads, including John [Key], saying it could be quite different if they put in Jacinda. There was an understanding of that at some level; but they didn't see it coming the way it so quickly did.'

From her first press conference Ardern defied the critics. She had an instant chemistry with the media and the public. It struck fear inside National's campaign machinery, which was starting to crank into gear. 'The moment she was made the Leader of the Opposition, my sphincter tightened,' one insider recalls. 'I knew instinctively that she was going to be a star. She had gold dust all over her. The media went bonkers. In a similar way that they went bonkers for Princess Diana. Kind of crazy.'

National's campaign faltered. Joyce had always placed great faith in the persuasiveness of tax cuts, and so the jewel in the crown was planned to be a pre-election announcement of further cuts. But weaker economic forecasts put paid to that. Treasury's

Pre-election Economic and Fiscal Update (the PREFU) led English to conclude there was no headroom for immediate relief.

Four and a half weeks out from the polls, National was also wrong-footed by the retirement of Ōhāriu MP Peter Dunne. The internal affairs minister had served as a minister in both Labour and National governments, with his United Future party having bolstered National's majority since 2008. He'd held the Wellington suburb seat since 1984, helped by an explicit pact that the National candidate seek only the party vote.

In May, English had written to all his ministers asking if any intended to retire because he was planning a reshuffle. Dunne, who was thinking about leaving but wasn't ready to relinquish his portfolio, kept quiet. The birth of his first grandchild solidified his decision, but his U-turn blindsided National. It was likely the seat would go to Labour candidate Greg O'Connor, a former police union boss with a high profile. United Future disbanded. In the space of a few days National was robbed of both its best weapon in the campaign and its steadiest support party.

Then came another bombshell poll. With 23 days to run, Labour had overtaken National, rising six points to 43. National fell three to 41 per cent, its lowest point in a decade. As the ground shifted beneath him, English had to face Ardern in the first televised debate of the campaign. It was a cruel twist. The public were just beginning to appreciate English's achromatic style. Against Little, it would have been a contest of ideas espoused by two men perfectly matched in their drabness. But just as English emerged from Key's shadow, he was faced with his predecessor's female equivalent: smiley, relaxed and with a magnetic attraction to voters. The campaign had to recalibrate.

National had brought in media trainer Janet Wilson to prep English. The respected former broadcaster had long-standing links to the party and had polished Key's performance ahead of the 2008 election. In a bid to zhuzh him up, the campaign team had English record an excruciating video of his exercise regime (a walk-run up the capital's Te Ahumairangi Hill), along with unforgettable social media snaps of his homemade pizzas, topped with spaghetti and pineapple. Voters instinctively identify inauthenticity, and English was worse than most politicians at faking it.

Wilson's main goal was to get him to relax and be himself. She recognised she needed to draw out his best qualities: his passion to lift people out of poverty and his ferocious intellect. There were hours of rehearsals, with Wellington Central candidate Nicola Willis pitted against English. A former researcher, Willis had badly rattled Key when she played Helen Clark in 2008. She reprised her role as Leader of the Opposition, making a convincing Ardern. Chris Bishop — a university debating champ regarded as one of Parliament's sharpest orators — was also drafted in to hone English's performance and to craft zingers.

The team were anxious that English would pitch the wrong tone and come across as patronising to the younger woman. 'It was hard,' an insider says. 'His view of her was that she's just an idiot and doesn't know what she's talking about. And that did come across a bit in the debates.'

In the first clash, a relatively staid discussion moderated by TVNZ presenter Mike Hosking, English retorted: 'People can't go shopping with your values.' A week later, at *The Press* Leaders Debate in Christchurch, he dismissed her with the opening remarks: 'Now the stardust has settled, you're starting to see the policy ... as an alternative to a successful New Zealand, you're being asked to vote for a committee.' Ardern bit back: 'This stardust won't settle.' It was a memorable exchange that neatly summed up the generational differences in thinking.

By then, National's campaign team was worried. Ardern went into the debate with momentum: the latest 1 News/Colmar Brunton poll saw Labour maintain its lead on National. The Christchurch newspaper's town-hall style debate was always a much longer and rowdier affair than the formulaic televised clashes. And the city's residents were exasperated by a lack of progress in the post-earthquake rebuild. As National expected, the anger boiled over within the Riccarton auditorium; according to an insider, some in the audience 'turned feral'.

English, apparently haunted by the ghosts of 2002, retreated into himself. As Ardern toured the country and was mobbed for cellphone selfies like a pop star, his performances seemed increasingly lacklustre.

The election appeared to be ebbing away from National, and a ripple of panic went through the ranks of senior MPs. 'There was quite a bit of concern that Bill was Bill,' said one minister. Suddenly English's strengths of substance trumping style, and eschewing the more superficial attention of politics for rolling up the shirt-sleeves, were beginning to be seen as liabilities.

Another former minister agrees. 'Even though he'd been in politics for years, he found the attention of being leader a bit difficult to deal with. He is much more comfortable talking serious policy. He didn't seem energetic. It was almost like a member of the royal family who has to step up when there's an abdication and never really wanted to be the king.'

Others saw the problem as wider than a single individual, pointing out that the campaign format was tired. In 2017, it was the same as it had been in 2008. As one former staffer says, 'Steven Joyce got up and said: "I'm the conductor, we've got the orchestra and we've got very good at winning elections." But they didn't do any renewal. It was incredibly dangerous, after nine years of power. It means you're in danger of having an old product.'

Jonathan Coleman was also frustrated by the campaign. English had wanted to make him foreign affairs minister, but with two young children Coleman asked to remain in the health portfolio. Behind the scenes he had battled against under-investment in the sector, never getting in Budgets the amounts he knew he needed. When English became prime minister he was determined to continue this fiscal strategy, and new finance minister Joyce was 'extremely dry'. Coleman's frustration and battles behind closed doors continued. As well as not serving the sector well, Coleman believes the leadership team made a strategic error in consistently under-funding health. 'It was quite obvious if you want to knock a government over, knock them over on health. And we probably needed another $200 million. They just did not understand that, now that we'd got back into surplus, the public, including people that voted for National, wanted more investment in health and education.' After the election, English would tell Coleman: 'Maybe we should have given that extra $200 million. We probably would have had a few extra points.'

Simon Bridges agrees. 'A part of the problem was [that] John, Bill and Steven were so much in that GFC, Canterbury earthquakes mode, where you had to pay down debt and have everything tidy economically. With the benefit of hindsight, we didn't put sufficient weight on the social issues like housing, environment. The '14–17 term was a time to open up the till a bit and do some social spending.'

As campaign chair, it fell to Joyce to rally English, his star. A source says, 'Steven had to go and put it to him: "You're in this. You can't get out of it. So, you just need to fire up." And he did.'

Joyce had another trick up his sleeve that would again switch the tracks on this rollercoaster of a campaign. Summoning journalists to the Beehive's seventh floor, he passed spreadsheets and papers down the long boardroom table that dominated his office. National had discovered a gaping $11.7 billion hole in Labour's calculations, he said. Grant Robertson couldn't afford the campaign promises he was making. In the fallout, there was much debate about who was right. But that was almost beside the point: Joyce had cast doubt on Labour's economic credibility.

English was galvanised — this was territory he knew well. It was a play National had used before: during the 2011 *Press* debate John Key had questioned how Phil Goff would finance his policies, challenging 'show me the money'. Three years later, David Cunliffe was flummoxed by National questioning how Labour would pay for a 'baby bonus' package for new parents.

English impressed his team in the closing stretch, becoming more confident, more authoritative. Instead of buckling under the baggage of the 2002 defeat, English went the other way. 'It was a real credit to Bill,' one of his aides says.

A former MP also believes English ran a really good campaign. 'The team around him was unified, there were no factions or egos getting out of control. The messages were clear: don't put it at risk, we are strong economic managers. The only thing I regret is that his idea of social investment wasn't communicated more clearly, and in a more marketable fashion.'

English also had his own amulet: to the dismay of his team, Mary was to join the campaign trail. 'There was a lot of nervousness inside the camp about Mary,' the insider says. 'During 2002, she'd been a nightmare, a de facto head running the campaign. [Staff] largely blamed her for having too much say and so when she came back in there was a lot of nervousness about her role, and what she was doing. They didn't want her getting in his ear all the time, particularly before the debates. She could throw him. She is such a strong personality. Sometimes it could knock him sideways. I don't think anything was said [to the couple]. They managed it. She was kind of quietly pushed off to one side.'

Largely, their worries were unfounded. English's mood lifted when his wife was present. 'They hired a penthouse [at] the Parkside Hotel, in Auckland, ahead of one of the debates. And he had the whole family there, nearly all the kids. There was a lot of anxiety about that. But he was more centred when she and his whole family was around. He's such a family guy. That's when he was at his most relaxed.'

Unrelenting attacks on Labour's vague tax policies also began to pay dividends. There was certainly a plethora of new taxes for National to get their teeth into: a regional fuel tax, and a $25 levy on international tourists, for starters. Then critics managed to frame bringing agriculture into the emissions trading scheme as a tax, and a plan to put a small charge on bottled and irrigation water brought protesting farmers into the streets of Ardern's Morrinsville hometown. Labour also intended to extend a 'bright-line' test, introduced in 2015, which was essentially a capital gains tax aimed at property investors.

Ardern and Robertson were deeply frustrated at what they called a campaign of spin, lies and misinformation. But Ardern had created a rod for her own back. Under Little, the party had proposed a tax working group to scrutinise the system for any inequity. He had promised any proposals would be put to the electorate, pushing any likely changes beyond 2020. Ardern overturned the requirement for a mandate. She wanted the flexibility to introduce a capital gains tax to address the housing crisis. But her captain's call painted her into a corner.

At every opportunity, English and Joyce hinted at the prospect of anything from a capital gains tax to land, asset or inheritance taxes. Ardern, in her inexperience, had forgotten the two golden rules of New Zealand politics: property is king, and change must be incremental. National's assaults began to grind away at Ardern's 'relentlessly positive' strategy. Labour was tied up issuing denials or complicated clarifications of their intentions. And as everyone knows, in politics, explaining is losing.

Just as advance voting opened, National had seized back momentum. The next poll, from Newshub-Reid Research, put them on 47.3 per cent, a huge four-point bump. Labour panicked. Nine days from the polls closing, Grant Robertson hastily called a press conference at Parliament to announce a U-turn. There would be no new taxes from Labour after the election, he insisted.

The final two public polls of the election put the result on a knife edge. National was still the largest party, but under the mixed-member proportional (MMP) election system there would be no outright victory.

National had made another miscalculation in trying to avoid 'the curse of MMP'. In a proportional voting system, mainstream parties often burn off their smaller coalition partners. The minor parties fail to prosper as they lose political distinctiveness and are tied to unpopular Government decisions. By 2017, United Future had disbanded and ACT and Te Pāti Māori were moribund. 'National had basically sucked up the entire centre-right,' a former staffer says. Party strategists developed a fixation with hoovering up the lost vote. 'Their obsession was winning this two per cent through a turnout game.'

To do so they imported sophisticated voter-tracking technology from America, which was used by the Republican Party. Known then as the Voter Vault, it would be renamed the

GOP Data Center in 2019. The program uses marketing data and information culled from other marketing sources, such as retailers and subscription services. That allows grassroots activists to track and target voters based on their address, professional interests, or even favourite brands and hobbies. But, as it turned out, the party's strategists overestimated the high-tech edge it gave them.

The voter model National used was based on a Key profile. However, turnout was already high among the older demographic, who tend to vote National. In New Zealand the profile of those who don't vote tend to be people under 30 who are low-income, and are often disengaged and don't like politicians. Given that if they do vote it is highly unlikely to be for the Tories, spending time trying to turn them out was a waste of resources.

Moreover, National failed to appeal to the younger generation. A first-time voter at the 2017 election would have been in primary school when John Key was first elected. The National Party in power is probably all they could remember, and there was nothing new on offer. So when Ardern came along with the promise of a bright new future, young people responded and identified with the avowedly youth-adjacent alternative on offer. The media began to call it a 'youthquake'.

There was no jubilation at either election night party, although after a tense campaign there were moments of levity. Holed up in Auckland's Pullman Hotel, English took delivery of a spaghetti pizza. Ardern's partner Clarke Gayford passed out sausages, and a fish he'd caught himself, to reporters stationed outside their Point Chevalier home. Inside, Ardern watched the live coverage in her slippers.

By the end of the night, National was 10 points up. But there was muted enjoyment of the red wine and canapes on offer at the party's SkyCity Convention Centre event. The feeling was flat. Getting a win was far from certain.

National could count on the support of ACT, with leader David Seymour returned to Parliament. But Te Pāti Māori faced wipeout, with both co-leaders Te Ururoa Flavell and Marama Fox losing their seats in emotional scenes. The combined Labour–Greens vote was within a whisker of National's vote. The result was a hung Parliament.

As it was in 1996, the first election held under MMP, neither Labour nor National held enough seats to govern without New Zealand First. After a decade of being the dominant force in New Zealand politics, National could rely on only one electoral certainty: to keep power they'd have to make a deal with the devil.

Two hundred kilometres north, celebrating in the bar of Russell's Duke of Marlborough Hotel, Winston Peters was back in the driving seat. And he was going to take it slowly.

5

QUEENMAKER

THE LAST TIME NATIONAL had tried to negotiate with Winston Peters, it didn't go well.

The 2005 election delivered a cliffhanger, after a close-run, hard-fought campaign. Labour was trying to salvage power by stitching together a government. Helen Clark held a one-seat majority and needed at least two minor parties to form a government. But squabbling had broken out between the Greens and Peter Dunne's United Future. Peters, now without a seat, was refusing to give a definitive answer on whether New Zealand First would support a Labour–Greens coalition.

Don Brash, who had picked up substantial ground for National, clung to hope. He called a clandestine meeting with Te Pāti Māori co-leaders Pita Sharples and Tariana Turia, ACT's pertinacious leader Rodney Hide, and Dunne. Brash and deputy Gerry Brownlee slipped out of Parliament and across the road to Wellington's Bolton Hotel. It was a somewhat reckless choice — the hotel is a popular coach-stop for MPs when Parliament sits.

Theirs was an unlikely grouping but not an impossible one to form a government. With 57 seats in a 121-seat Parliament, they would need support from Peters. Despite Peters's assertions he would first negotiate with the party with the largest vote, the leaders decided to make a tentative approach to the taciturn autocrat.

Brownlee had served his first term in MMP's inceptive and tumultuous National–New Zealand First coalition. He thought the group was deluded. Dunne was also reticent, particularly worried that Brash was prepared to concede too much to Peters. (Brash had suggested making New Zealand First MP Ron Mark minister of police and giving the education portfolio to Brian Donnelly.)

After the experience of '02 to '05, United Future was not 'wildly keen' to go with Labour again if it could be avoided and was curious enough to talk to Brash. Dunne recalls: 'My gut feeling was United Future, ACT, Māori Party, Winston and National: it's going to be a mess to put together, but let's go through the process. I could not get over his [Brash's] ineptitude in negotiating. I told him: "The moment you start offering he'll [Winston] come back and ask for more."' The meeting was short — Hide had to leave early to attend rehearsals for TVNZ's *Dancing with the Stars*.

The call was made to Peters. He agreed to see them on 11 October in his office in Bowen House, the 22-storey building joined to the Beehive by a tunnel. Peters said little, letting Brash do most of the talking. Dunne wasn't present. Brash followed up by sending a one-page written proposal, penned by Dunne's chief of staff Rob Eaddy, by courier. The letter went unanswered. Within a week, Clark struck a deal to give Peters and Dunne ministerial posts outside Cabinet in return for a confidence and supply agreement.

A looser arrangement than a coalition, support parties will back the government on key legislation such as the Budget. In return, the lead party advances specific policies. The deal left the Greens, Labour's natural allies, out in the cold.

Peters bristled at criticism he was 'seduced by the baubles of office', a reference to a pre-election speech in which he promised not to be motivated by status. National would misunderstand this about the shrewd demagogue to their great cost.

*

In 1996, following New Zealand's first election under MMP, with 13.5 per cent of the vote, New Zealand First had held 100 per cent of the power. Now, 21 years later and with around half that support, Winston Peters was again the kingpin.

Over a 40-year career in politics, sharp-tongued Peters has had an antagonistic relationship with the media. In successive campaigns since MMP was introduced, he has particularly revelled in a 'will he, won't he' guessing game with reporters — and voters — remaining vague about which party he favours as a coalition partner. And in 2017, he was once again outwardly playing his usual coquettish games and holding court for the cameras stationed outside the Duke of Marlborough on the morning after the election. A keen fisherman, he talked about spending the afternoon on his boat. No one knew how seriously to take him.

But despite his Delphic pronouncements, Peters already had a meeting in the diary. When he and partner Jan Trotman drove south on Sunday, most reporters assumed they were heading for their coastal property in Whananāki, Peters's childhood home. In fact, Peters was going to Wellington for a 7pm meeting with

Bill English. The caretaker prime minister had deliberately, and publicly, wooed Peters in his election night address. Ardern, too, had made an overture — but said her first call would be to the Greens.

'I want to acknowledge the strong performance of Winston Peters and New Zealand First,' said English, speaking past supporters gathered at SkyCity and directly to Peters's vanity. 'Voters of New Zealand have given New Zealand First a role in forming the next government. In the next few days we will begin discussions with New Zealand First in finding common ground and most importantly forming the kind of government that will allow New Zealand to get on with the success.'

When English and Peters met on the Sunday night, Peters was 'very keen to get straight out of the blocks', says a senior MP. The two men, along with Gerry Brownlee and Rotorua MP Todd McClay, talked in a ministerial meeting room on the second floor of the Beehive. Peters had first come to Parliament as a National MP and served alongside McClay's father, Roger, who later became his advisor. The drab grey office, with its walls tiled with Tākaka marble and its floor-to-ceiling windows, would be the room where Peters conducted all of his post-election negotiations in the coming weeks.

National's most senior figures were 'encouraged' by the meeting. They thought they were definitely into a discussion at least, but 'there was an edge' to the atmosphere, which could be attributed to Peters's long and choleric history with National.

Peters was first a minister in National's Fourth Government, appointed Māori affairs minister in 1990 by Prime Minister Jim Bolger. He lasted only a year. Bolger was forced to sack him from Cabinet after he openly and repeatedly criticised the government's economic policies. Peters was especially disenchanted by Ruth

Richardson's 1991 'mother of all Budgets', which slashed welfare and introduced 'user pays' to public services. As a backbencher, Peters continued to be outspoken, and eventually the caucus expelled him. English seconded the motion.

He went on to form New Zealand First, and in 1996 went into government with National, appointed deputy prime minister and treasurer. It lasted almost two years before he was sacked. The fallout almost destroyed his party.

In 2008, a year dominated by a scandal over financial impropriety and undeclared electoral donations to New Zealand First, John Key said he would not work with New Zealand First in government. 'The appointment of a minister to Cabinet has to be done on the basis that as prime minister I can look that person in the eye and have confidence that I can rely on their word. In the case of Winston Peters, I'm just not confident I can do that.'

Voters rejected New Zealand First too, and many assumed it was the end of Peters's career. Peters, deeply sensitive to any disrespect, never forgave Key.

Nine years later, he was also incensed by English's strategy, late in the 2017 campaign, to urge the public to 'cut out the middleman' — to rob Peters of his decision-making power. Peters also blamed National for a leak to the media revealing he was overpaid on his pension for over five years. He returned the amount — nearly $18,000 — as soon as he was made aware of the error. In the days following the election, it emerged Peters had served court papers on nine people, including Bill English, Steven Joyce, Wayne Eagleson, Paula Bennett, social development minister Anne Tolley and campaign communications manager Clark Hennessey. (His legal action would ultimately fail.)

Losing his Northland seat to National MP Matt King had done nothing to ease Peters's antipathy towards National. Veteran

Labour MP Annette King recognised, and took heart in, the rancour. She was confident Peters would go with Labour. 'I just felt it,' she is quoted as saying in her 2019 biography. 'The way he was treated [by National]. The way [Parliament's Speaker David] Carter treated him in Parliament … The way they insulted him and the way they kind of tried to destroy him, tried to destroy him out of his seat and did. I felt within a year of the election the way things were going that if we had a chance Winston would go with us.'

A former National minister concurs: 'There was no courting. Was it possible to get a different outcome, post the 2017 election? Yes, there was. But by that stage, my colleagues had done so much damage to any relationships that existed that there was no prospect of him going with us. He knows how to carry a grudge better than most people that I've ever met. And if you're gonna belittle him and insult him in the House, which is what some of our people did, then there's a consequence for that. [If we treated him with] the respect that is deserved by someone who has his longevity and experience, then it would have been a much harder decision for him to make.'

But, encouraged by the initial English–Peters meeting, Steven Joyce, suffering from a virus, checked out of Auckland's North Shore Hospital and headed for Wellington. Joyce had wanted to be a part of the negotiating team, and English had decided it was time to get him on board. Paula Bennett decided to head to the capital too.

The expansion of the negotiating party was a mistake, many in the caucus now believe. And it is hard to disagree, especially with regards to Bennett's presence. At the time it was public knowledge that Peters was unhappy with both Bennett and Tolley, blaming them for having misused the system to get his

Super overpayments into the public arena during an election cycle. Another MP puts it more bluntly: 'The thing that really stuffed it was putting all the people that Winston hates into the coalition negotiating team.'

There was to be a pause for two weeks while 'special votes' were counted. Making up 15–20 per cent of the final count, these include the votes of those who cast their ballot overseas or outside their electorate. One curiosity is that the special votes tend to skew Left. In 2017, that cost National two seats, which went to Greens and Labour, and with that its advantage in the negotiations.

Labour and the Greens had used the hiatus to thrash out their own deal, the terms agreed over a series of meetings on the second floor of Parliament's Old Buildings.

Two of National's most senior staff, advisor Cameron Burrows and press secretary Michael Fox, were tasked with working through New Zealand First's election manifesto to try to divine what Peters's bottom lines might be.

On 5 October, the horse-trading got underway. Peters met with National in the morning, for just 30 minutes, and Labour after lunch. That set the pattern for the talks. Everyone involved signed non-disclosure agreements.

Peters brought with him MPs Tracey Martin, Shane Jones and Ron Mark, chief of staff David Broome and old friend Paul Carrard. Carrard, also known as 'PC', was an oddity to the other negotiating parties, who noticed his preoccupation with the piloting of drones over Lake Brunner, a trout-fishing mecca on the West Coast. Rarely interjecting, he also clearly had Peters's ear.

Joyce and Bennett joined English, Brownlee and Eagleson for the talks. Eagleson had formally resigned but agreed to stick around while the shape of the government was formed.

Labour deployed Ardern, Robertson, deputy Kelvin Davis and, crucially, Annette King, who knew Peters well from their time together in the Clark Government. Also in the room was chief of staff Neale Jones, former finance minister Michael Cullen and Mike Munro, Helen Clark's advisor. They tried to use King's knowledge of Peters to their advantage. For example, before the Labour team went in, she made the point that the negotiation was all about respecting him. Earlier, she had reminded them how important dressing properly was to Peters and so requested that all the men wear a shirt and tie to their meetings.

Their first meeting with Peters lasted 27 minutes. Ardern took her own copious notes.

Peters kept his cards close to his chest, bar one detail. He wanted negotiations wrapped up by 12 October, with the return of the writ, a formal order setting out the successful candidates. Perhaps also Peters enjoyed marking the anniversary of the 1996 election, after which he kept the public waiting two months for a decision. Few believed his deadline, less than a week away, was possible.

It was assumed that curbing immigration would be on the table. This — and developing a plan to recover the bodies of the 29 men lost in the Pike River mine explosion — would be easily met by Labour. But Peters was against implementing royalties for water for irrigation and bottling, one of Labour's campaign pledges. David Parker, the policy's earnest architect, was agreeable for Ardern to trade it away, removing the problem.

It was assumed the Greens' desire to legalise recreational cannabis would be a stumbling block for the more conservative Peters. In fact, during talks with Labour it was he who proposed a referendum. It was felt Peters thought a referendum would fail, and so wanted to deal with the issue that way. With Greens co-leader James Shaw knowing Labour didn't want to take on decriminalisation, he was happy to accept the referendum as a vehicle. Labour was left caught in the middle, not even really sure they wanted one.

When it came to ministerial positions, the commentators — and National's negotiating team — assumed wrongly that Peters was chasing 'the baubles of office'. In the negotiations with Labour, the issue was not even discussed until the last 48 hours. Even then, the conversation was held between Ardern and Peters alone to avoid any embarrassment.

Conversely, it was one of the first topics National's team raised. Peters later told colleagues he thought it was 'disingenuous' and he was offended by the crassness. As it turned out, National's final offer was more generous than what their rivals eventually agreed to.

Labour also learned quickly how not to upset Peters. The phrase 'the Greens' was banned from the room. He refused to have any communication with them, which complicated the negotiations. Ardern got around the problem by occasionally telephoning Shaw to give vague outlines of any contentious issues. Labour also asked Shaw for a list of redlines: New Zealand First policies that his party could not sign up to. Greens staffers dutifully scoured the New Zealand First manifesto and cross-checked all Peters's campaign announcements. There would be one that would later catch them out, and sorely test inter-government relations: an electoral law change that would allow parties to expel rebel MPs from Parliament. As the so-called party-hopping, or waka-jumping, bill hadn't been mentioned, the Greens assumed it had faded into history and weren't expecting it to make another appearance.

Ardern and others would occasionally bring gingernut or chocolate biscuits to share. Peters never provided treats. But Labour felt it was about their showing respect and hospitality.

Again, National took a different approach, and in doing so got the tone all wrong. 'I thought Steven and Paula were incredibly patronising of Shane Jones and Tracey Martin. It was terrible,' an MP recalls. 'I have known Shane Jones a long time, and when he started referring to Steven as Steve, I thought, Ah. The EQ was zero. I could see the look in the [New Zealand First team's] eyes sometimes. They'd always be the minnows, a bit-player. They thought they would have to battle on everything, and that we'd be the big National Party that rules the roost.' Another negotiator says Joyce treated Martin, once the party's deputy leader, 'like a secretary, to take the notes'. However, a source close to Joyce disputes this, saying he and Peters enjoyed cordial relations and that Shane Jones would often phone outside of the formal meetings. 'There was no rancour.'

One sticking point was Peters's demand for a regional economic growth fund to invest in local projects to boost jobs. Joyce's response was to deliver a lecture on the economy. He offered smaller, individual initiatives for Peters to announce, effectively, as one negotiator recalls, telling Peters he was 'going to be playing second fiddle' to Joyce's initiatives.

Labour had no problem caving to demands for what would become known as the Provincial Growth Fund, to be run by Shane Jones. New Zealand First had asked National for $1 billion over three years; Labour ultimately invested $3 billion. Labour knew the fund mattered to New Zealand First and so set about finding a way of making it work. Ironically, it was Joyce who had given them the kernel of an idea of how to make that happen. Peters had campaigned on giving goods and services tax revenue earned from international tourism back to the regions where it was raised. Joyce had dismissed the idea, arguing that the money was largely returned in the form of infrastructure investment anyway. So Labour's economic advisor Craig Renney was tasked with trying to work out whether or not that was true; to a degree it was, thereby enabling them to construct a way to give them what they wanted. National circles believe Labour was in an easier position: being in Opposition they weren't tied to Budget commitments.

National also refused to cave on Peters's demands to reduce net migration. New Zealand First's election policy was to cut it to just 10,000. National had already changed the immigration laws quite a bit, and Immigration Minister Michael Woodhouse was confident these changes would deliver Peters's desired reduction without any further adjustments to the settings. Peters was unconvinced. After all, they were just projections. It would have been easy for National to be less dismissive and make an actual commitment; that they didn't was just another example of poor negotiation. The incoming government stuck with Labour's proposals for a reduction to between 20,000 and 30,000 per year.

National noted Peters's strange fixation with events of the 1990s. It was as though he wanted to relitigate that decade, even down to re-creating the Forestry Service. It was an apparent preoccupation with what National would do if there was a world economic crash that offered the clue. 'We were scratching our heads thinking, We had the GFC: that's what we did,' an insider recalls. 'It took us two meetings to twig that his entire frame of reference was Jenny Shipley. It was as if 2008 to 2017 had never happened. And then we had a problem. I don't know if it was grudge [against National] or he really did believe that that's when the world went to hell in a handbasket.'

English and Joyce also would not countenance a keystone of Peters's election campaign: moving Auckland's port north to Whangārei. Labour easily agreed to commission a report. It was yet another difference between the ways the two major parties approached the negotiations. Labour included on its team former colleagues of Peters, like Annette King, who understood him and knew how to communicate with him. They were also genuinely seeking to give him what he wanted. On the other side, it was felt that National came to the negotiations with an attitude that one small party was holding the country to ransom and it wasn't going to work.

Key's strong sense of self-confidence had seeped into the party, but power made its senior figures arrogant. They assumed New Zealand First would be bound by convention and align with the highest polling party. That meant they had no clear strategy for dealing with Peters. They neither embraced nor shunned him in the lead-up to the election, gifting him the balance of power. The presumption to be the natural party of government also saw them overlook the bad blood between Peters and the negotiating team.

But one negotiator had read the tea leaves from the very first meeting. 'We went back up to Bill's office and they were all saying: "We think it's going well." I thought: You guys are fucking mad. Can't you see how they've reacted to us?'

Other MPs shared the trepidation, again tellingly revealing a generational divide in the caucus. Everyone agreed that whatever deal Peters put to them would be sure to come at a very high cost. The difference was that newer MPs were a lot more ambivalent than the likes of English and Joyce about paying Peters's price. A more junior minister of the time sums it up: 'For them it was the last time in government. For the rest of us, a significant number in caucus, there was a sense that we can't sell ourselves for 30 pieces of silver.'

A significant part of this disconnect went down to who would actually be paying the price of a deal with New Zealand First: it would be National's newest and prospective ministers. Another MP describes 'real mixed feelings' about the potential arrangement. 'I remember when [English] announced the shape of the deal for us. He said: "We've given them five Cabinet positions." We were sitting in the caucus room and you could see [the faces of] the people who had just been made ministers. They were the jobs that were going. Last in, first out: so Jacqui Dean, [Tim] Macindoe, [David] Bennett — no longer ministers. And I remember thinking: if New Zealand First goes for this, I won't be a minister.'

By 11 October, Brownlee urged English to cease negotiating. 'Pull us out before Winston does it to us,' he advised. The circus dragged on. Day after day, Peters and his coterie would pass the gaggle of reporters stationed in the Bowen House's polished-stone foyer. In the increasingly febrile atmosphere, the interactions with media grew more and more tetchy. Bored journalists, hyped-up on caffeine and 'lolly cups' from Parliament's Copperfield's Café, were reduced to reporting what Peters ate for lunch that day.

In the Beehive, bored staffers alternated between watching the coverage and *The Chase*, and learning new MPs' names. National was the caretaker government, meaning staffers had to show up to work, but they were completely removed from the negotiations. With no meaningful work to do, an advisor says, 'you could actually change channels, so you could have a game show on for the full eight hours'.

On the day of New Zealand First's self-imposed deadline, Peters announced the negotiations had concluded. But that did not mean a decision had been made. With Peters's characteristic guile, he outlined further steps to his process. First, an all-day caucus meeting, to chew over ministerial positions on offer. Then the party's board would assemble to discuss the proposed deals. This came as a surprise to many, who assumed the final say rested with Peters. Journalists scrambled to find out more about this anonymous, unelected group who would hold the country to ransom for at least another four days.

Commentators had a field day lampooning the convoluted party processes, which were temporarily delayed by a funeral and a flight schedule. Barry Soper, of radio station Newstalk ZB, wrote: 'It could be Maud from Mataura or Doug from Dargaville who'll be deciding who's going to govern us for the next three years.'

When Decision Day dawned, it came with a flurry of activity. The board had wrapped up their two-day meeting on Wednesday afternoon without making a call. That night, Peters went into final, secret meetings with English and Ardern. English went first, back into the negotiating room at 5.30pm. He would later tell a senior MP that the meeting was punctuated with lots of long silences.

Ardern followed, taking a different route to the room from usual to avoid the media pack. She offered him the role of deputy prime minister. While the feeling for many in Labour was that Peters was always going to go with them, offering him the deputy's role right at the end was significant; perhaps even a clincher.

Still in the dark, English scheduled a Thursday caucus meeting to outline the offer to MPs. Mid-morning, Joyce's phone rang. It was Peters's chief of staff, Broome, asking for an extra ministerial post. Joyce got a 'stony response' when he returned the call. A senior MP remembered, 'Steven said to me: "I've got a bad feeling about this."' By early afternoon there was a distinct drop in temperature in relations, which made the Nats nervous.

Peters also called Ardern, with the same demand. 'Winston, that will just look silly,' she told him, 'if all of your caucus are in the executive.' Instead, it was agreed to extend a parliamentary under-secretary role to Fletcher Tabuteau. But that then required a call to Greens co-leader James Shaw. Shaw had earlier had to disappoint his MP Jan Logie, who had her heart set on being minister for women. This new offer would make her an under-secretary with responsibility for domestic and sexual violence issues, a cause she had championed for years.

Shaw, still without a co-leader, hastily called a meeting with his seven MPs to outline the revised deal: ministerial posts, which would go to Eugenie Sage, Julie Anne Genter and himself, and an under-secretary. In his excitement, he'd forgotten to tell Logie. 'Is that me?' she asked him in a whisper.

The final deal would have to be agreed to by the Greens' membership, a complicated exercise which involved a long teleconference and a vote. It can be a fractious body and is much more radical than its caucus. But Shaw had mitigated the risk they would reject the deal by forming a reference group, which included respected former co-leader Jeanette Fitzsimons, to provisionally advise the party. That group would recommend whether to accept the terms at a special meeting, so Shaw could offer some assurance to Ardern, who could then do the same for Peters. After two weeks of twiddling their thumbs waiting for Peters, suddenly the Greens had to activate their process and get their membership to sign off on the deal. This, even though they couldn't release the deal until Peters had made the call. The tension was enormous.

Shaw, who had just endured a hellish election campaign in which his co-leader and two MPs resigned, said the negotiation period was the 'most stressful experience of my life' for a lot of reasons. 'It was the first time the Greens got into government. But the blind negotiation, especially after the horrendous campaign we'd just had, [and] needing to honour the party's values and vision and hopes and dreams — [all] under less than ideal circumstances. And also a team that was pretty shattered.'

By the afternoon, the phones fell silent. Labour had been expecting a call mid-afternoon, and with no one from New Zealand First talking to them, they thought Peters had decided to go with National. Labour's most senior heads feared Ardern had blown it by sticking to her guns on the immigration cap. Shane Jones, once a Labour minister who had only recently joined New Zealand First, was urging his former colleagues to soften their stance.

As it turns out, the impasse was actually due to a miscommunication. 'There was a bit of misunderstanding about who was going to call who between Jacinda and Winston,' King explains in her memoirs. 'So we were sort of waiting for them to have their last talks, thinking Winston was going to ring Jacinda and they thought Jacinda was going to ring Winston. And I sent a text to Shane saying, "All ka pai [good]?" And he phoned me and said, "She hasn't phoned, she hasn't called." So I said to Jacinda, "Winston's waiting for you to call." So she called, talked to him. I'm not sure what they said. He didn't tell her he was going with her. I think he asked some questions and then a few minutes later, maybe it was minutes, sometime later he came through Bowen [House].'

It was expected Peters, ever the showman, would time the announcement of his decision to make the 6pm news bulletins.

Around 4.30pm, Paul Carrard and Marco Marinkovich, an advertising executive with a long association with Peters, were dispatched to assess the podium set-up in the Beehive Theatrette, usually the venue for post-Cabinet press conferences and significant ministerial announcements. There was much excitement when a burst of applause came from Labour's floor. Staff were cheering at quiz show *Family Feud*, it was quickly clarified. Media outlets began setting up and journalists took their seats, but the allocated time-slot came and went.

Just before 6.30pm, a brief statement was emailed to the Press Gallery: Peters would speak soon. At 6.50pm he took his place at the podium. Neither Labour nor National knew what Peters planned to say. After eight minutes, in the final line of his speech and 26 days after New Zealanders had voted, he put the country out of its collective misery. 'We've had to make a choice, whether it was with either National or Labour, for a modified status quo or for change. In our negotiations both National and Labour were presented with that opportunity ... We choose a coalition government of New Zealand First with Labour.'

At 37, Ardern would be the country's youngest premier in 160 years, and its third female prime minister. As English stood on the Beehive's ninth floor watching the TV coverage, he learned his fate at the same time as the New Zealand public. Mary and youngest son Xavier were by his side.

English called Ardern to offer congratulations, and then gracefully waited for her to give a press conference before speaking to waiting reporters. Flanked by Mary, and with Joyce, Bennett and Ōtaki MP Nathan Guy behind him, English said he accepted the result. The statement was live-streamed by most media outlets, the picture framed with an exit sign over his head. 'We will be by far the strongest Opposition party that the

Parliament has seen,' he said. 'From here the National Party will regroup, we'll have a caucus meeting next week to discuss the outcome.'

Bennett organised a party in her office. English, standing on a desk, gave an emotional and gracious speech. By the end of the night, Bennett was dancing on the tabletop as Joyce played DJ. 'There was heaps of red wine. McCully turned up with some bottle from 1996 or something that was undrinkable. People drank it anyway,' one MP, a supporter of English, recalls. 'Ministers were emptying the cellars: "We don't need this anymore." It was a pretty depressing night because there was a real sense that it was a good government and [there was] unfulfilled potential with Bill.'

As in 2003, English was most concerned with reassuring stricken staff. Again, how English handled defeat was a mark of the man. 'There were a lot of tears. It was heartbreaking, because it wasn't his fault,' one advisor says. 'He thought it was his fault, but that's the nature of him. He's a really decent man.'

Watching from Los Angeles, former Cabinet minister Maurice Williamson thought Peters's decision was so inevitable he'd been prepared to place a bet at the TAB, New Zealand's sole betting agency. An MP since 1987, Williamson had known and worked alongside Peters for years. But he'd retired at the election, immediately flying to the United States to take up a consul-general post. 'I always said Winston will go with Labour,' he says. 'He had twice gone with a third-term, dying government. He did that in '96 with National. And then he did it in 2005 with Labour and was wiped out again. If he went with National again, he could guarantee a wipe-out at the next election and be gone. Whereas if he went with a brand-new, fresh face, he could at least have a chance at a second term.'

Williamson thinks the animosity is overplayed. 'There was that hatred as well in '96. Bolger and he had such a falling out, and such vicious venom. I'd go up to the ninth floor some nights to have a drink with Bolger and he'd say, "That bloody little arsehole and cheat." And then we got to do a deal and become a coalition government. A few nights later, I went up and he and Bolger were having a whisky together and telling jokes.'

Labour believed the match-up was inevitable too. 'When you actually listen to what he said on the night it is exactly what he said to us in the first meeting we had,' a Labour source says. 'About the failures of capitalism and the need to do things differently. If I were being a bit more cynical, I would suggest Winston was also looking at a sunset industry and a sunrise industry. I think that probably dominated a bit of his thinking.'

National MPs were devastated, not just at the loss but at English's personal disappointment. One MP, a supporter of English, gives insight into this, and into just what a lost opportunity he believes Peters's decision may have been. 'Bill was a different guy to John. He had different drivers, and those drivers were where the public was at: worried about housing, the underclass, poverty. He had comprehensive and substantive answers on all those issues. He had the opportunity to reshape, to really put his own stamp on it. He could have spent his first nine months as prime minister defining the terms of engagement for National in 2017. But Labour defined the terms of the election. It is a tragedy really, a lost opportunity.'

6

KNIVES OUT

I N ONE OF THE most famous campaign exploits of English's political career, he stepped into a boxing ring. Dressed in a National-party blue vest, the Opposition leader duked it out in a fundraiser for the prevention of youth suicide. With only seven weeks to run until the 2002 polls opened, it was also a stunt to raise his profile. He lost the fight … and the election.

Fifteen years on, *The Dominion Post* retold the story of 'Raging' Bill's performance for the newspaper's Flashback history series. 'I'm a firm believer in testing yourself and giving things a go,' the then prime minister said. 'But I also believe that if you do that and you discover you're not much good you should cop it and move on — hence you haven't seen me in a boxing ring since and you won't again.'

Few in National believed English would stay on as the party's leader. As outgoing ministers cleared out their Beehive offices, English refused to be drawn on his political future. It is English's habit to slowly turn things over in his mind — a demoralising defeat would not change that.

Nonetheless, shell-shocked colleagues urged him to stay. They were wary of recent history repeating. Helen Clark had resigned on election night, plunging her party into instability and a series of leadership challenges that had dragged on for nine years until they finally settled on Jacinda Ardern. They also believed English had earned the leadership, capturing a 44.5 per cent share of the vote. In the MMP era, only John Key had done better.

And no one really wanted the job, up against a celebutante prime minister enjoying a first-term honeymoon. English was accordingly advised not to go, even though he naturally wanted to. He was encouraged to stay, because he had been a good prime minister and his time would come to beat them in three years. National considered Labour hopeless, incompetent. A coalition with both New Zealand First and the Greens was never going to work; given time, they could be beaten.

Ardern had handed New Zealand First a regional economic development portfolio, super-sized with the Provincial Growth Fund. They also had responsibilities for foreign affairs, primary industries such as forestry and fisheries, infrastructure and defence. The Greens had a proportionate number of positions but outside Cabinet. It was assumed the deep contradictions in their manifestos would lead this 'three-headed monster' of a government to break down, riven with dysfunction and intractable ideological disagreements.

The complex union would be a first. New Zealand First had defied history and the will of half the electorate — nearly one in two voters had wanted National. Peters's own support base would also have preferred he enthrone English — by a large majority of 44.5 per cent. Ardern, a relatively inexperienced leader, would have to work hard to keep onside not just her support parties but a chary public.

Although reeling from the loss, National were confident. They were by no means a spent force: entering Opposition with 56 MPs, and thus more resources than when their opponents had been in opposition, including five press secretaries.

English was re-elected unopposed at the first caucus meeting of the term. Paula Bennett remained as deputy and Steven Joyce agreed to stay on in finance. The front bench was relatively unchanged, with the exception of Chris Bishop, who was handed the police portfolio, with Anne Tolley nominated Deputy Speaker. English told reporters he didn't believe the 'sober but positive' caucus was looking for generational change. 'I am confident in the discipline and focus of the caucus … I'm sure my performance will be under scrutiny just like everyone else's is.'

Thirty years in politics gave English that foresight; but for now he was safe. The early signs were encouraging. At the opening of Parliament, National humiliated an ill-prepared government. Labour MP Ruth Dyson had nominated Trevor Mallard for the role of Speaker. But several MPs were missing from their benches, including Winston Peters and trade minister David Parker, both travelling to Vietnam for an Asia-Pacific Economic Cooperation (APEC) meeting.

Detecting an uncertainty in the novice government, parliamentary past-master Gerry Brownlee leaned across and urged Shadow Leader of the House Simon Bridges to raise a point of order. Brownlee, whose mastery of Standing Orders, the rulebook of Parliament, rivals only that of Mallard, was making mischief. Nonetheless, National demanded a clarification about whether absent MPs, who hadn't yet been sworn in, had a vote. Bridges revelled in the shambles. 'Where's Winston when you need him?' he yelled across the chamber.

Fearing Anne Tolley could end up as Speaker, Labour panicked and offered concessions to National. Bridges and Leader of the House Chris Hipkins cut a deal to increase the number of MPs on select committees from a proposed 96 to 109. National was triumphant, even more so when the pictures of Bridges playing hardball with Hipkins were splashed across the front of the following day's *Dominion Post*.

Labour were starting from scratch after nearly a decade in the political wilderness and it was shambolic, from back-office administration right up to the running of the House. National exploited its institutional knowledge, running rings around the government. Ardern was unsure of herself, National felt, and no one knew how Peters was going to go. Against this was English, who was a strong parliamentary performer. 'In the first Question Time we had eight questions, and something like 45 supps [supplementary, or follow-up, questions],' an MP says. 'We were hammering them every day. [The former] Ministers knew where all the bodies had been buried and they knew where all the mistakes had been made. And we came out swinging.'

The strategy was great for morale — as was opinion polling. The final 1 News/Colmar Bunton poll of the year put National on 46 per cent to Labour's 39. They also dominated in the closing three Roy Morgan Research polls of the year, at 46 per cent but falling to 40.5. Insiders say this matched the results of internal polls, not publicly released. But the political cycle was entering summer barbecue season, and English was losing his grip on the leadership.

Away from the whips and the sharp eyes of the Press Gallery, restless politicians are more prone to gossip and plot over a backyard beer. It was slowly dawning on National that Opposition is a very hard place to come back from. Many of the old guard were struggling with the loss of the advantages that come with a ministry: a Crown car, prestige and countless officials ready to do your bidding. English alluded to adjusting to his new status as Parliament rose for the Christmas break: 'I found myself, actually, on the way to the Chamber here, outside the door without my fob to swipe and I saw one of the DPS [diplomatic protection service] staff over there and I was waiting for him to come and do it for me, but he didn't do it.' Joyce was seen leaping out of a taxi at the British High Commission's annual glitzy Christmas ball, hastily followed by the driver through the doors of Homewood, the elegant Karori residence. So used to being transported in Crown limos, Joyce had forgotten to pay the fare.

Nick Smith said the realities of the move into Opposition were 'utterly demoralising'. 'There is a huge reduction in resources. And when you're a minister and you say the sky is blue, there are newspapers that will give you a story. Suddenly, you're in opposition and it's quite difficult to get press unless you say something stupid. And you have the normal chemistry that occurs with a change of government: the new government has got the megaphone, claims anything that happens that is good as its own work and anything bad as the fault of the previous lot.'

One MP noted how the appointment into the shadow Cabinet of most of the outgoing ministers, such as Nikki Kaye and Jonathan Coleman, was 'both a blessing and a curse'. Reports emerged of Kaye complaining that Parliament's IT was not swift enough in fixing her computer. Former trade minister Todd McClay was said to have kicked a photocopier in frustration. 'They knew their portfolios really well but they also acted like they were still ministers,' the MP said. 'They just didn't have 20 staff wandering around helping them.'

The reality really hit when it came to voice: no longer would any pronouncement they made automatically get media coverage.

The metamorphosis from minister to Opposition frontbencher took some adjusting to.

In the large caucus, ambition soon bubbled to the surface, with those who had been on the cusp of being ministers hungry to show their stuff. Among them were Todd Muller, Chris Bishop and Andrew Bayly. The latter, a wealthy merchant banker with a penchant for adventure, was a former Territorial Army officer and a member of the British Parachute Regiment that dragged a sled to both the North and South poles; he also scaled Aoraki/Mount Cook, New Zealand's highest peak, and four mountains in Antarctica. In the previous term he had been on the Finance and Expenditure Committee and was keen to make a contribution. He was just one of a number who now appeared fettered and under-utilised.

Self-doubt also began to creep in as Labour found its feet. By mid-December, Finance Minister Grant Robertson had delivered a 'mini-Budget' that promised free tertiary education and replaced National's promised $2 billion tax cuts with a $5.5 billion 'Families Package' to slash child poverty. He also committed to raising the minimum wage and to resuming contributions to the Superannuation Fund, which invests to fund the state pension. National had ceased deposits at the height of the global financial crisis.

Significantly, Robertson committed to delivering surpluses, and directed ministers to review spending in their portfolios. The 'coalition of losers' was starting to shape up as a government that wasn't as transitory and shallow as critics on the Right had first assumed. Ardern's popularity also continued to soar, almost 10 points ahead of English in the 1 News/Colmar Brunton December poll. On 19 January, Ardern shared news of her pregnancy on social media, posting a picture of three fish hooks.

It was an obvious reference to her partner Clark Gayford's passion for fishing — he hosts the *Fish of the Day* television show — and a nod to the Māori symbol of fertility. The news brought a whirlwind of international media attention and an outpouring of support for Ardern. A cover story in *Vogue* followed in February. By the time her daughter Neve was born in June, Ardern's celebrity had eclipsed Key's.

National's assumption they would likely be back in government at the next election was beginning to look shaky. As the summer holidays drew to a close, reality began to bite. New Zealanders tend to give governments a second term so long as they are not making a complete mess of things, and the Labour-led Government were looking far from hopeless.

The two largest parties typically congregate for a caucus retreat before Parliament resumes. For years, Labour favoured Brackenridge, a hotel and spa in Wairarapa's wine country. Key used to bring his MPs to Premier House, the official residence a stone's throw from the Beehive. In 2018, English opted for Tauranga, the provincial city in the Bay of Plenty, home to both Simon Bridges and Todd Muller. In the week leading up to the retreat a series of news reports had surfaced suggesting some were agitating for change. The tensions were centred on Bennett and Joyce.

As MPs came to terms with their loss, their ruminations led to some disquiet about the handling of the coalition negotiations. There was a feeling that Key's hurried anointing of a somewhat reluctant Bill English, while a tidy solution in the heat of the moment, could well have cost them a fourth term. A natural moment for refreshing and renewal had been lost. For National to win the election, change was needed, not more of the same but without Key. And when it came to post-election coalition negotiations, Winston Peters was never going to support the guy who had seconded the motion to expel him from the caucus.

The blame game had begun. With plenty of time to think over the summer break, MPs began to question whether the party's leadership had done enough to build a relationship with Peters throughout the preceding term. And they wondered whether the negotiators were the right choice to be at the table with Peters. What would the post-English leadership look like? they mused.

The knives were out, particularly for Bennett, with some refusing to accept her firm assertions that she was not responsible for leaking Peters's pension details. (In 2020, Peters was ordered to pay her costs after his failed court action). Some were also irritated by her informal, peppy approach to party business.

Bennett, who had returned to Parliament with a dramatic new look having undergone gastric band surgery, said she'd heard no rumblings about her position. 'I just don't think we are looking for scapegoats ... each of us wants to do the best we can,' she said. English also moved to quell the rumours, and Anne Tolley called the reports 'scurrilous gossip'. But the conjecture overshadowed English's State of the Nation speech at the end of January 2018.

Stepping up to the podium at Wellington's InterContinental hotel, English attempted to laugh off the story. 'A bit of leadership speculation certainly turns out the journalists,' he chuckled. But he was clearly frustrated. The address, to a business audience who paid $90 to attend, began with a thinly veiled warning to his caucus: 'Opposition is naturally a robust, adversarial role ... But despite the political jousting, most MPs are there for the same reason. We're there because we all want to make New Zealand a better place.'

While lines lampooning the government's approach as 'a nostalgic belief in trees, trains and trade unions' were well-received by the Business NZ crowd, the press conference following the event was dominated by questions about English's leadership. He told reporters that he wouldn't be 'derailed by a bit of gossip'. He defended Bennett as robust. 'She's used to not being liked by some people,' he said. But it was in vain.

Flanked by several MPs, including Amy Adams and Chris Bishop, he said: 'These are ambitious people who want to change the way the world works and see politics as a way of doing that. So I wouldn't be at all surprised if there was some talk. But I have to say the conflation of that into some kind of threat to my leadership, I think, is ridiculous.'

However, as he closed the stand-up, English admitted he had considered resigning after Peters chose Labour. Within two weeks, he would do just that. The decision was made over the summer break, on holiday at the family homestead in Dipton.

In the dark about his intentions, English's team was disappointed by the reaction to his speech. It was supposed to set out the party's vision and underline how National's performance over nine years had delivered the strong economy the new government was now enjoying. He also launched a campaign to 'Protect NZ Jobs' — an attack on planned industrial employment law changes — and a new website. National was still riding high in the polls: a Newshub-Reid Research poll in late January put National on 44.5 per cent, to Labour's 42.3. But English's personal ratings were slipping, more than 12 points behind Ardern.

In-house, the jostling had started. The leaks to the media about unrest with the leadership began and their timing felt deliberate. Some believed the most likely culprit was Simon

Bridges. Another MP recalls the 'unsettled feelings'. 'It was Simon and Todd McClay. I am very confident it was. [Newstalk ZB political editor] Barry Soper ran all those stories. Barry and McClay are quite close.'

Bridges denies this. 'I certainly wasn't actively doing anything. But there's no doubt things were warming up by around that Tauranga retreat. Because [change] was probably coming. And we needed to be thinking about what was next.'

The two-day retreat kicked off with a barbecue at Bridges's home. There was plenty to talk about. The cracks in National's celebrated discipline were growing deeper. Although the discontent had not crystallised into any formal moves, the stage was set for uncomfortable and frank discussion. While there was no outright positioning to be the leader, there was an assumption that English wouldn't be leading the party into the next election, which signalled a change of leader at some point.

Nick Smith was 'cross and frustrated' at the agitators. He traces the faltering in discipline back to the lack of consensus on choosing the new leader and deputy leader and the subsequent need to put it to a vote. After that, tensions grew, and were clearly noticeable by the time of going into the February 2018 retreat. 'The caucus that had been so watertight began leaking and once it starts, it is so difficult to plug.'

The unusual step of including the next five candidates on the party list in the retreat — Maureen Pugh, Nicola Willis, Agnes Loheni, Paulo Garcia and David Hyatt — fuelled speculation there would be resignations among the old guard. A planned caucus photograph was also postponed, which was taken as another sign of potential change.

The retreat, as with all caucus meetings, was held behind closed doors. MPs, assembled in the conference room of the waterfront Trinity Wharf hotel, enjoyed panoramic views of the city's harbour. Outside, during meal breaks, they mingled with Gallery reporters who had also made the trip from Wellington. There were vociferous denials about disunity. English joked he was 'apparently' still leader, insisting a vote on the top jobs was not on the agenda. Bridges pledged 'full confidence' in Bennett and English. 'I think we're energised and excited, that's not to say we can't learn lessons about how we've done things in the past ... we'll need to evolve with the times. But I think we can definitely do it with our current leadership.'

Jonathan Coleman claimed to have left his ambitions in the past. 'We've got to have a team approach that gets us into the best position to lead in 2020. Bill's had a great mandate from the public and he's doing very well as the leader and we're all right behind him.' Steven Joyce, Chris Finlayson and Nick Smith all committed to serving another term.

In front of reporters the atmosphere was relaxed and cheerful. Behind closed doors, it was anything but. A party staffer, with a long history in the party, says tensions were stirred with gossiping and back-biting: 'Simon and his crew were agitating, almost undermining Bill. I detect quite a bit of bad blood about the way Simon almost elbowed out Bill.'

The caucus malcontents wanted accountability. The leadership triumvirate were not about to deliver. 'Certain people had a chance to present, under their portfolios, a few ideas and talk about what went wrong in that election,' an MP recalls. 'The majority of the caucus felt like we didn't show enough heart. [Ardern had] personability and approachability. People were sick of our corporate style.'

Some debated whether National should have done more to acknowledge problems such as the housing crisis, inequality and gaps in health services. Everyone had a chance to have a say. However, Steven Joyce's displeasure was evident in his body language, repeatedly shaking his head as MPs spoke. 'We were getting right to the end of that meeting,' an MP says, 'and Joyce got up and he was very defensive. He was taking all of this constructive criticism and then blatantly dismissing it. It was very much the kitchen Cabinet still making all the decisions.'

New MP Lawrence Yule, a former mayor of Hastings elected to represent the Hawke's Bay Tukituki electorate, along with a group of MPs wanted to champion a four-year parliamentary term. While most politicians, of all stripes, favour extending the government term by a year, they are loath to formally propose it, lest they be accused of self-interest. A majority of the caucus were in favour, but English shut down calls for a ballot, saying they didn't hold votes. Yule acknowledges that as a new kid on the block he got a bit ahead of himself but says the message from English was clear: 'we manage the politics'.

However, there were hints that English's heart was no longer in it. 'We could tell Bill wasn't really enthused,' one MP recalls. 'He was a bit disinterested, going through the motions. Paula, as deputy, did a lot of leading the discussions about what went wrong in the election and what a new National was going to look like.'

Nevertheless, he delivered a strong rebuke to the disaffected. 'Bill was really strong in that caucus — he still had that mana,' a staffer says. 'Bill had that steel about him. And he gave this really great speech to caucus, telling everyone that if you want to stay in Opposition, start leaking. Everyone got the message.'

Having stared down his challengers, English was ready to retire. 'He was clearly unnerved by the leaks, as the pent-up ambition of those who wanted to lead started to perpetrate into the media,' Smith says. 'There was talk "from caucus sources" that "National needs a fresh start" which is blunt code that the knives are being sharpened. Bill came to a conclusion: they're going to get me eventually down the track. Better to make a clean break.'

Like John Key before him, English was going out on his own terms. He told the caucus of his decision on 13 February. Joyce, Bennett and Key had been in the know for about a week. Finlayson learned when English sent a text asking: 'Where's a nice place to take the family for lunch? I'm resigning.' Finlayson recommended MariLuca, an Italian restaurant famed for its saltimbocca and a short stroll from the parliamentary precinct.

In his typically casual way, the caucus meeting was 20 minutes in before English made clear his intentions. Having served his first year in government alongside Robert Muldoon, he was signing off after 10,000 days as an MP. 'I've decided to stand down, you need to find a new leader,' he told MPs. His words were met with shocked silence. 'You could have heard a pin drop,' one MP said. 'It was surreal.'

English reiterated his warnings from Tauranga, cautioning MPs about factionalising. He emphasised there was a process to follow, and candidates needed to manage themselves carefully so that caucus wasn't disrupted. Tearing down the stability built over a decade was a 'recipe for staying in Opposition'.

The Press Gallery had intuited his announcement when he was 20 minutes late to the meeting and then left early. Almost all 55 MPs joined Bill and Mary English for the official press conference. 'Now is the right time,' he said. Unlike Key, he did not endorse a successor. 'National's two-day caucus meeting last week confirmed to me that our team has the talent, the ideas and the energy to return to government in 2020,' he said. 'It's important that National's new leader has the time and the best possible opportunity to achieve that.'

When Key left, English had seemed the natural replacement, as deputy, finance minister and party elder. When it was his turn to leave, though, there was no clear follower. So for the first time in a decade, National's leadership was in serious contention.

Despite English's counsel, the jockeying began almost immediately. On Valentine's Day, the first contenders began wooing their colleagues. National had two weeks to choose a leader, with English's resignation effective from 27 February.

Judith Collins was the first to express interest in the job, in a tweet. 'I'm announcing my candidacy for Leader of the NZ National Party. We're going to need strong & decisive leadership if we're going to win in 2020. I'm that person,' she wrote at 8.22am. The tweet received 337 'likes'.

On Radio NZ's *Morning Report* show, she claimed to have a plan to secure 61 seats in the 2020 election. 'I'm one of the few people in our caucus who's had any experience in Opposition and it is not going to be easy but we do need to do that,' she said.

Bridges followed, returning to his previous pitch for generational change. He held a press conference on Parliament's black-and-white tiles. 'I'm 41. I have a young family. But I've held a raft of senior portfolios, from energy, labour, transport and economic development to communications and others besides,' he told reporters. 'All of that gives me the experience, the acumen, and the drive to do this job very well.'

Amy Adams then called a press conference, standing on Parliament's forecourt in the bright summer sun. She emphasised her experience, having held 10 ministerial portfolios. Economically conservative and socially liberal, the Selywn MP spoke of appealing to both urban and rural communities. She was accompanied in support by Nikki Kaye, Chris Bishop, Maggie Barry and Tim Macindoe. They all denied seeking the deputy-ship. Absent was Todd Muller, who mysteriously broke his promise to show up.

Adams stressed the internal battle would not become nasty. 'Our focus is not going to be on the petty skirmishes along the way,' she said. However, the manner in which she announced her candidacy raised eyebrows. Publicly lining up supporters was not how National did things. Adams assumed Bridges didn't have much support because he did his press conference by himself, but she miscalculated. Her decision to make her own announcement with people behind her also backfired, because, as a fellow MP puts it: 'She picked the wrong people ... hardly heavy-hitters.'

Nick Smith says it showed a lack of discipline. 'If you publicly identify yourself with Amy, what happens if Amy doesn't make it? You're taking a hit and so is party unity. You end up in a position where the party and your electorate openly knows you didn't support the newly elected leader. You're saying actually, the caucus has made the wrong choice — or I've got it wrong.'

Yule agrees it was a 'fatal mistake' and was exactly what English had warned them to avoid. 'He used to say every time we talk about ourselves, [it's] another percentage off the polls. And he's right. Labour was like that — for nine years, they did exactly the same thing. Some of those people [who supported Amy] then found it difficult when Simon was elected.'

Mark Mitchell hired Clark Hennessy, the staffer embroiled in Peters's pension privacy lawsuit, and declared his campaign 'to win'. His was the ritziest of all the stump speeches, held at Ōrewa Surf Life Saving Club. Staff re-positioned the camera crews so they could capture a rescue boat and Whangaparāoa Peninsula behind him. He was greeted by *The Bachelor* reality TV star Zach

Franich, who was also a coach at the club, and was supported by wife Peggy Bourne, the widow of rally legend Possum Bourne.

Mitchell dismissed the need for generational change: 'When you're the leader of a country, you lead for all generations,' he said. He revealed colleagues had approached him about leadership three weeks before English's resignation. In doing so, he laid bare the fissures the party was so desperate to conceal.

Steven Joyce remained undeclared for a full week. Unbeknown to his colleagues, this was do-or-die for the father-of-two. With his young son Tommy diagnosed with autism relatively late, Joyce was increasingly torn between politics and his family life in Auckland. After talking it over with wife Suzanne, Joyce concluded he didn't want to die wondering but decided to retire if he didn't win the leadership.

The canny publicist chose the top-rated breakfast radio show hosted by Mike Hosking to confirm he was in. 'I've been approached by a lot of people over the last few days, both inside and outside the caucus, and considered it carefully and then made the call,' he said. Joyce had joked he had a 'goodly' amount of support. But what he didn't say — or perhaps did not know — was that a considerable amount of resentment had also built up against the shadow finance minister and campaign director.

The seeds of this discontent were sown from the early days of government when Joyce had assumed the role of 'message disciplinarian'. A downside to being the 'yes or no guy' was that any displeasure was always more directed at him than at the leaders, Key or English.

An advisor says: 'He wasn't collaborative. He wasn't as worried about culture and feelings. In politics, you need to bring people with you. And although he was making all the right calls, they wouldn't feel like they were part of it.'

A former minister agrees. 'Steven obviously had carried a huge amount of the political management load. He would have been disappointed that he wasn't seen as a potential successor [to Key] and was probably even more disappointed when after Bill left he didn't carry a significant group of the caucus behind him. That was simply because of his management style. He's very smart and doesn't suffer fools gladly, and was pretty assertive in managing both ministers and colleagues. I don't think he understood until it was too late that he was diminishing any prospect of enjoying support as a potential leader.'

Finlayson says: 'Steven, frankly, could have been a very good leader. But there was one thing he lacked: he never walked along the corridors chatting to people. He was not clubbable. [Robert] Muldoon did that when he wanted to roll dear old Jack Marshall. Jack would go home to Bolton Street for dinner; Muldoon would have dinner with the chaps.'

Another MP adds: 'He was nine times out of ten right. But he was dogmatic ten times out of ten. It's not his fault the caucus was over him. But it was time for a change.'

Smith supported Joyce. 'Steven was just a phenomenal worker within Cabinet. He brassed me off when he stomped on some of my pet projects, but I never held it against him because I knew how important it was to have someone within the team who was constantly looking at the big picture and making the hard choices on what ideas we would run with. In my view, Steven got quite a rough deal.'

Bridges, supported by McClay, Jami-Lee Ross and his 'numbers man' Brett Hudson, exploited the pique. 'He worked really hard with the Jami-Lee Rosses and the Todd McClays to nurture the disgruntled middle benches, having drinks, nurturing their grievances and building support,' Smith says. 'Simon was very deliberative about it.' He believes Bridges had been plotting for some time. 'Simon put a huge amount of political effort into building a power base within the caucus. He was very strategic, and you have to admire that. But it was strategic in the sense of benefitting Simon. Whereas, in my view, if Steven had adopted the same strategic approach, he probably would have become leader. But instead, he was far more focused on looking after Brand National than Brand Steven.'

Whatever the reason, Bridges was at the time the favourite. It was only natural to put himself forward and to give it his best shot. His pitch was very much to the MPs elected in 2014 and 2017, promising that Joyce's days as kingpin were over; Joyce would have no real role under Bridges. Caucus responded to Bridges's promise to talk more about the environment; perhaps they were tired of Joyce keeping everyone on message all the time, even though it had won them three elections.

Bridges was also getting favourable media coverage. *New Zealand Herald* columnist Steve Braunias declared him 'an obvious pick': 'Simon Bridges ... famously had Labour MPs running headless and clueless within seconds of the swearing-in ceremony. I hope he becomes National's next leader. I've always liked his company. The Leader of the Opposition ought to operate as satirist-in-chief and Bridges is sharp, prosecutorial and very funny.'

Seasoned commentator John Armstrong, writing for 1 News, wrote: 'The Tauranga MP is not everyone's cup of tea. He has made no effort to hide his ambitions in the wake of National's removal from power last October. Bridges can be overly abrasive ... But no-one else who is likely to seek election as leader has the competence, experience, freshness or drive necessary to stop the political juggernaut that is Jacinda Ardern from cleaning up at the 2020 election.'

A *Dominion Post* editorial asserted that all the possible leaders had 'striking flaws': 'The most plausible is Simon Bridges: he is youngish, ruthless, and embarrassed the Government early with a swift tactical triumph in Parliament. He might be able to appeal to centrist voters as well as the hard-right core of National.'

Left-leaning website The Spinoff 'power ranked' him their favourite. 'He's young, he's Māori, he shows flashes of wit,' wrote editor-at-large Toby Manhire.

Bridges's people were certainly adept at working the media and creating spin. But behind the scenes, the team was less subtle, a fellow MP maintains. 'You've got Jami-Lee cracking skulls and bullying people. The way [Bridges] got it [the leadership] was terrible. He had Jami-Lee really strong-arming people. He got there in the end. But the way he got there created all the problems for him.'

Smith was horrified. 'Simon was back playing the old game, trying to drive the leadership from the public debate. "I can win, just if people think I'm winning." He was gaming the caucus, in the sense that nobody wants to be on the side of the loser.'

He, too, had a visit from Ross. 'Jami-Lee Ross turns up in my office and says he's heard that I was talking to Steven. And if I don't support Simon he is going to destroy me. It was just awful. I'd been through the leadership contests between Bolger and Shipley. I was [thinking]: "Oh no, how are we allowing this to happen?"'

Shaken, Smith rang Bridges, telling him to 'rein in his dogs'. 'You're not going to get my vote by sending your henchman to threaten me,' he said. Smith says he wasn't the only MP who was paid a visit. 'It was a very threatening tone that Simon tolerated from Jami-Lee. Jami-Lee was a nasty piece of work. But the black mark for Simon was that he tolerated it.'

Ross came on so strongly with the class of '17 that Yule asked him to back off. 'We were being absolutely hard-lobbied and we didn't like it.'

Others were sweet-talked with promises of promotion. 'There was an awful culture that became acceptable as we bounced from one leader to the next through that first term of Opposition, of prospective leaders promising portfolios, horse-trading for votes,' Smith says. 'A successful political party needs to punish that behaviour. Because you actually want the caucus applying their very best judgement. To orient the team on the very best. Not self-interest.'

Bridges doesn't see the contest in the same way. 'I don't perceive there was particularly bad blood. It was straightforward. Three of us had been in the kitchen Cabinet together at the end. And I don't know if there was massive horse-trading. There was still a sense that this was, if not the party of John Key, still having the culture.'

The lobbying went right down to the wire. Because the vote was to be held in progressive rounds, with the lowest polling knocked out at each stage, the candidates were also courting the second votes of the supporters of their rivals.

The caucus duly met on 27 February. Each hopeful was to give a five-minute pitch. To win they needed to secure 29 votes, but Bridges was just a few votes shy. Mitchell withdrew his nomination, aware that Bridges shared his desire to see Paula Bennett retained as deputy. Mitchell had quite a few supporters in the new intake, so when he stood up and endorsed Bridges 'for the good of the party' many of those votes went to Bridges and put him over the top.

The deputy leadership was decided immediately afterwards. Collins pitted herself against Bennett, and the voting went to two rounds. Bennett was re-elected. 'She was the right person,' Bridges says. 'She provided balance to me and kept the broad church of the National Party broad.'

Bridges immediately promised a reshuffle. Joyce would have a 'strong role' but Bridges refused to say if he would retain his finance portfolio. 'We can't go into the election with the same plans we've had, we can't do the same things. We have to modernise,' Bridges said at the press conference following his election.

Bridges chose to hold the press conference in the rimu-timbered hall of Parliament's Legislative Council Chamber, which once housed Parliament's upper house and is modelled on Westminster's House of Lords. With lush red carpet, upper galleries, backlit stained-glass windows and Italian marble pillars, it is an impressive setting in which to address the media.

Bridges and Bennett were photographed leaving the meeting, both grinning widely. Bennett was striking in a dress shaded in National Party blue. The party tweeted the picture. In the background, just over Bridges's right shoulder, was a smiling Jami-Lee Ross.

7

THE YOUNG AND THE RESTLESS

WHEN JAMI-LEE ROSS ENTERED Parliament he knew he was meant for great things.

Born to Lisa Helmling, a teenage mother, and a father who Ross described in Parliament as 'nothing more than a faceless name that never stepped up to life's responsibilities', he was raised by his grandmother 'Nana' Sharron Martin. They lived from week to week in a small flat in Papatoetoe while Martin cared for her own frail mother.

Ross was sent to Dilworth, a boys-only private boarding school that offers scholarships to pupils from 'good families of limited means', set in sprawling grounds in the affluent Auckland suburb of Epsom. Numbered among its old boys are former prime minister Mike Moore and former minister and historian Michael Bassett.

Maurice Williamson, a battle-scarred National MP first elected in 1987, was delivering pamphlets on Fisher Parade in Auckland's Sunnyhills when an elderly Martin struck up a conversation with him over her garden gate. 'Don't worry about us, we're National,' she told him, waving away the literature. Her grandson dreamed of being an MP, she explained. What should he do? Williamson said to make an appointment with his local office, and he would offer advice. 'Oh, but he's here,' Martin told him.

'This 12-year-old kid was standing there in the garden,' Williamson recalls. 'That was Jami-Lee Ross.'

Taken aback at the ambitious child's youth, Williamson told the family to look him up in 30 years' time. But Martin was insistent, so they agreed to get in touch once Ross reached adulthood.

On leaving school at 16, Ross, who was a keen swimmer, became a lifeguard without formal qualifications. Then shortly after his eighteenth birthday, he duly arrived at Williamson's electorate office, in Auckland's eastern suburbs, full of his dreams to get to Parliament. 'You are too young,' Williamson said. 'You've never had a job.'

Undeterred, Ross said he planned to stand for Manukau City Council. 'You won't have a show,' Williamson told him. 'Those votes go on name recognition, and we've got people like [Olympic runner] Dick Quax in this ward.'

Despite his contention that it was a lost cause, Williamson eventually agreed to help Ross, thinking it would be a good lesson for him. The senior politician invited Ross to accompany him to the Howick markets, and supplied him with flyers and business cards printed by a friend. 'He bloody did it brilliantly,' Williamson says. Ross knocked on every door in the electorate, something Williamson himself had never achieved in two decades of his own campaigning. 'Bang. He got elected — twice.'

Ross won a seat on the Manukau City Council, in the Howick ward. Fiscally conservative, in 2007 he joined a band of councillors to veto a mercy mission by city planners to Nuku'alofa. The Tongan capital had been razed by rioters. (Manukau City had long had a large Pasifika community.)

Ross also displayed a zest for the cut and thrust of partisan politics. As councillors campaigned for election to the new Auckland Council — the amalgamation of eight local bodies into a supercity — Ross had left-wing mayoral candidate and front-runner Len Brown in his sights. He challenged the Manukau mayor over personal spending on his official credit card, including $59 for a family Christmas ham. Ross's fellow councillors turned on him over his campaign to have Brown officially censured. He was accused of 'disgusting' antics and dragging the local body 'into the political gutter'.

His stance of moral superiority over expenses came back to bite him when Labourites used freedom of information laws to reveal Ross had claimed $14 for the mileage to drive to an Anzac Day ceremony.

Others accused him of racism when he called for a ban on flying the Tino Rangatiratanga and Kingitanga flags from municipal buildings. Ross says he is of Ngāti Porou on his father's side.

Although he stood as an independent, Ross was aligned with the Citizens and Ratepayers. He was elected co-leader of the Right-leaning local political outfit with the promise to secure at least half of 20 seats on the new supercity. They won five, including his own seat, representing the Howick ward.

Ross had also joined the National Party in 2003. A decade later he would enroll his two-year-old son Henry in the Young Nats, proudly tweeting a picture of the membership card. 'Start 'em early,' he wrote. As a councillor, Ross worked 12 hours a week in Williamson's Pakuranga electorate office. 'He worked really hard,' the former MP says. Ross still had his sights firmly set on a national-level political career.

By 2010, Williamson was a minister in Key's government. He planned to fight one more election before stepping down in 2014. By this time, Ross had established himself as the popular MP's heir-apparent in a safe blue seat. 'He was on my electoral committee, my campaign committee — they all loved him,' Williamson says. 'Pakuranga was going to be his seat in three years.'

But Ross was impatient. In December, the neighbouring Botany seat became vacant when Cabinet minister Pansy Wong resigned after breaking taxpayer-funded travel-perk rules. Ross had no qualms about abandoning the local councillor position to which he'd been elected only a year earlier, even though the resulting Howick by-election would cost ratepayers $150,000. 'No one ever said democracy was cheap and I didn't know Pansy would be resigning,' he said.

Nevertheless, his selection was far from a foregone conclusion; the competition to be National's candidate was heated. Maggie Barry, the popular host of an eponymous television gardening show, was among the field of 13. She'd joined the party only a few days earlier and granted a rare waiver to stand. 'He was ahead until Maggie Barry entered the race,' Williamson says. 'Then it tipped.' Ross was short 14 delegate votes, and Williamson offered to rally support. Over three weeks Williamson lobbied delegates in their homes, over many cups of tea.

By the time of the selection meeting in late January, the contenders had been trimmed down to Barry and Ross. Thanks to Williamson, Ross beat the television star by one vote. Barry would follow him to Parliament after the 2011 election, as MP for the North Shore. But she would continue to resent Williamson for the intervention that cost her Botany.

Ross's campaign launched at the Pakuranga Country Club. The Botany by-election received little attention, however, taking place as it did just 11 days after a magnitude 6.3 earthquake had struck Christchurch, killing 185 people and reducing much of the city centre to rubble and ruin. It did not help that the field was also reduced, with the Greens candidate, Richard Leckinger, failing to register after getting stuck in traffic on Ti Rakau Drive. Ross comfortably beat Labour's candidate Michael Wood.

In a profile interview conducted during the by-election, Ross described *The Hollow Men*, the 2006 political book by investigative journalist Nicky Hager, as 'essential reading'. In his 2014 work *Dirty Politics*, Hager would reveal the involvement of Cameron Slater — a party member who ran a vicious right-wing blog — and his friend, shadowy strategist Simon Lusk, in Ross's campaign. 'Besides advising him, [Slater and Lusk] used personal attacks to smear the other National Party hopefuls for that electorate and thus cleared the way for Ross. It was they who made him MP for Botany … Ross shows all the signs of being an apprentice of their destructive type of politics,' Hager wrote. Slater travelled to Wellington to watch his 'old mate' give his maiden speech.

At 25, Ross was the youngest MP in the House, a self-confessed fan of TV musical *Glee* and caramel frappés. And although Ross's campaign to enter Parliament may have flown under the radar, his inaugural speech did not go unnoticed. Quoting Ronald Reagan and Margaret Thatcher, two of his political heroes, Ross also called for a referendum to abolish Māori seats, upsetting National's Māori Party coalition partners. Shane Jones, then a Labour MP, quipped the speech would have made the Tea Party movement's Sarah Palin proud.

Ross was granted spots on the social services and transport and industrial relations select committees. At the general election, a few months later, he increased his majority.

But he was not satisfied. A National Party advisor recalls a conversation with 'the baby of the House' shortly after Key announced his second-term Cabinet. As the pair were walking into a function in Parliament's Grand Hall, Ross told the advisor he was not happy: 'I didn't make Cabinet — I'm a bit disappointed about that.' The advisor was astonished by Ross's sense of entitlement after only eight months as a backbencher. 'He was delusional.'

In Parliament's unsparing hierarchy Ross was so lowly that Trevor Mallard, first elected in 1984, referred to him only as 'the one with the three first names'. Fellow MPs noticed his expensive taste, though, and wondered how he could afford tailored suits and shoes on a new MP's salary.

He hero-worshipped Key. 'He was spending hours doing things for John Key,' Williamson recalls. Recognising that Key's time at Parliament was on a countdown, wily Williamson advised Ross not to hitch his wagon too tightly to that of the leader. But Ross's reasoning was that as prime minister, Key decided on Cabinet positions, and so the relationship was worth cultivating. 'He was nowhere near a Cabinet position,' Williamson says.

Ross did eventually earn promotion when National appointed him a third whip, the first in Parliament's history. Senior whip Louise Upston and junior whip Tim Macindoe displayed riding whips outside their offices; staff joked Ross should be given a fly swat. His successes at Parliament were not notable (a controversial strike-busting member's bill was vetoed by Peter Dunne). But this should not be given undue weight, as Government MPs outside of Cabinet are expected to be seen and little heard.

However, in 2015, Ross attracted some attention — albeit of the unwelcome variety — when he became mired in a 'cash for favours' scandal that had earlier cost his mentor his job. A distraught Williamson had resigned his portfolios in May 2014 after journalist Jared Savage revealed Williamson had telephoned a senior police officer about the arrest of wealthy Chinese-born property developer Donghua Liu, who was facing domestic assault charges, which were later dropped.

Four years earlier, Williamson lobbied colleagues to grant Liu citizenship against official advice, and also asked Key to open Liu's proposed hotel development. The company of which Liu was director subsequently made a $22,000 donation to the National Party in 2012. Liu also gave $25,000 to Ross's election campaign through a local 'Cabinet Club'. National's so-called Cabinet Club scheme offered access to ministers in exchange for cash, the party arguing the practice was innocent and also necessary in the absence of state funding for political parties. (When the Cabinet Clubs became tainted by scandal, National rebranded them as the Platinum Club, operating with more discretion.)

Liu's donations came to light in 2015 as electoral returns were made public; Key was dragged into the controversy. (It should be noted that Labour and the Māori Party also received donations from Liu.) The gift to National was made after Key attended a private fundraising dinner at Liu's multi-million-dollar Auckland home. Key and Ross were photographed smiling alongside Liu and his family.

Ross eventually returned the money to Liu but not until after the election and Williamson's resignation as minister. The young MP acknowledged the donation was to be used in his Botany re-election campaign but said it hadn't been spent.

When Williamson retired from Parliament in August 2017, Ross attended a farewell party in his office and was the last to leave. He and Williamson never spoke again.

The donations row certainly impeded Ross's own career. Although he was promoted to junior whip he never made it into Cabinet, unlike Barry. He had learned no lessons, though. In 2016, he visited China on an all-expenses-paid trip as a guest of milk formula manufacturer GMP Dairy. The Chinese-owned, Auckland-based company had earlier made donations totalling $25,400 to the National Party, Labour MP Damien O'Connor revealed.

Four years later, donations from Chinese businessmen would land Ross in trouble once again. Only this time he would find himself in the dock of Auckland's High Court, facing charges of deception.

*

It isn't altogether clear when Ross's behaviour became Machiavellian. Or harmful. In the fallout over the *Dirty Politics* revelations, and given his associations with Lusk and Slater, it was assumed Ross was aligned with Judith Collins. As Hager revealed, Collins had approved of the trio's verbal assaults on Ross's rival for candidate selection in 2011, former Auckland councillor Aaron Bhatnagar. The son of a wealthy retail entrepreneur, Bhatnagar was a party member, having joined in 2002 and holding internal office, including chair of the Epsom electorate and its Remuera branch.

But Collins showed no party loyalty. She wrote to congratulate Slater on his attacks on a fellow party member in 2011: 'Loved the utu [blog] post … Frankly I wd be out for total destruction of Aaron if I was JLR [Jami-Lee Ross]. But then again I've learnt that to give is better than to receive.' As a whip and younger member of caucus, Ross was seen as Collins's likely 'numbers man' in any post-Key leadership contest. So there was mild surprise when he seemed to be performing the same role for English, Collins's rival, in the 2016 race. 'You had Jami-Lee Ross playing games all over the place,' remarked the staffer who had earlier been startled by Ross's overconfidence.

Fellow MPs say he was a good whip, generous with his time to new entrants. 'He helped a lot, gave templates for letters, how to run a morning tea — simple things that you don't know how to do until you have done it,' one rookie recalls. Ross was also an effective electorate MP 'until he got other notions'. But he had allies rather than close friends. The rookie MP describes him as odd. A staffer confirmed that he did not trust him and avoided Ross's attempts to make conversation.

Around 2015 Ross began to hold small drinks parties on Wednesday nights at his Bolton Street apartment, a stone's throw from Parliament. One former minister described 'Jami-Lee's very uncomfortable soirées' to which selected senior people would be invited. 'There was a very weird atmosphere. It felt like a weird kind of audition.' It appeared Ross was creating a power bloc that could fall in behind a future leadership contender.

Ross told a minister that some backbenchers were yearning for Opposition 'so we can get ahead'. He constantly had a chip on his shoulder. 'He hadn't got the interests of the National Party foremost. It was all about his personal advancements.' Ross and his wife, Lucy Schwaner, certainly seemed to see themselves as an emerging power couple.

In 2016, Schwaner ran to be chair of Howick Local Board, a body within Auckland Council that makes decisions on services at a community level. Katrina Bungard, a board member and teacher, would later allege that 'manipulative' Ross led a campaign of harassment against her. She revealed that she had to seek medical help and was concerned for her family. 'I had phone calls where he was "going to war" with me and my family,' she told *The New Zealand Herald*. Bungard said she was pressured to support Schwaner by Simon Lusk, who promised her a career in politics. 'You know it's not a good day when you're getting calls from Simon Lusk,' she says. Lusk said he could only help if she was in a 'good place' with Ross. 'If you fall out, I can't do anything,' he told her. Bungard, also a National Party member, asked the party for help. Ross had her barred from a party morning tea.

David Collings, the board's chair, also complained to National Party general manager Greg Hamilton about Ross's behaviour. 'It got very nasty,' Collings said. He alleged Ross had used Bungard's aspirations to be a National MP to manipulate her.

Schwaner, elected to the board but defeated in her quest to be chair, dramatically quit minutes after being sworn in. In doing so, like her husband six years earlier, she forced another costly local body by-election on ratepayers. Schwaner later claimed it was a 'toxic environment' and took out a full-page ad in the *Eastern Courier* newspaper attacking Collings.

'It was like *House of Cards*,' Bungard said. As it turns out, Ross is in fact a huge fan of the political thriller, whose central character is a vengeful and merciless politician. The New Zealand MP favoured the earlier British version, built around ruthless Conservative Party chief whip Francis Urquhart. (An American version was remade with Kevin Spacey starring as Frank Underwood, a secretly gay Democrat who rises from majority whip to President.) Colleagues say Ross had a keen recall of the plot details and dialogue.

Ross also had another unlikely hero: his cellphone ringtone was the sinister-sounding 'Imperial March', the musical accompaniment to *Star Wars* arch-baddie Darth Vadar. 'I think he had a Walter Mitty view of himself as Darth Vader,' says Chris Finlayson. 'Sometimes his voice would get very low and he'd say "You can't cross me and get away with it." He was basically in a dream world.'

Sarah Dowie, a bright young MP who now deeply regrets an extramarital affair with Ross, recalls a conversation in which he revealed a disturbing view of politics. They were talking about their reasons for entering Parliament. Dowie wanted to make the country a better place. He responded: 'Don't be silly, Sarah. It's all about power and control.'

*

When National lost the 2017 election, Ross realised his desire to hold office was out of reach. But other goals were viable, now that Simon Bridges was elevated to leader.

Bridges nursed his own hopes: he wanted to be New Zealand's first Māori prime minister, ideally at the next election. In the early weeks of his leadership, he relished the honeymoon. There were family photo shoots with women's magazines, which pictured a beaming Bridges with 12-week-old daughter Jemima in his arms. He played ping-pong with columnist Steve Braunias in a leaders' challenge. And he returned to his former school, Rutherford College in Te Atatū, for his first major speech as leader. Principal Gary Moore remembered his former pupil's competitive nature: Bridges never liked coming second.

The new leader put in place his new team, and his inner circle was well rewarded. For all his talk of rejuvenation, there was little fresh talent on show. Sarah Dowie made it into his shadow Cabinet, taking conservation, but many of the same faces remained. Mark Mitchell got justice and defence. Todd McClay was happy with the foreign affairs portfolio, stripped from Gerry Brownlee who was also demoted from the front bench. In a bid to keep Collins close and preoccupied, Bridges ranked her fourth and set her against Phil Twyford, Labour's flailing housing minister.

But Jami-Lee Ross was unhappy. While Bridges had promoted him to the front bench, with the grunty infrastructure and transport portfolio, he was denied the position of Shadow Leader of the House and being in charge of the party's polling. He lost the whip to Barbara Kuriger. Those positions would have handed him far too much power, and influence even greater than deputy Paula Bennett.

Unknown to Bridges, Ross was now nursing a grudge. He began secretly recording their conversations. Ross also disliked Bennett, and she was no fan of him. One MP even confronted him for carrying out a 'character assassination' of her during the leadership contest.

In the shadow Cabinet reshuffle Steven Joyce was not offered finance, which went to Amy Adams, and quit before Bridges could formally announce his reshuffle. MP Nick Smith says it was 'an awful error of judgement' on Bridges's part. Smith suspects Bridges considered Joyce a threat, but the loss of Joyce from the team was 'absolutely huge', and the assuaging of any insecurity would come at a high price. 'We lost our message centre and one of the key players in holding the discipline together.'

The impact of sidelining Joyce was felt immediately, a senior MP says: 'We were adrift. We didn't have direction.' It wasn't clear what Bridges wanted to achieve. 'His narrative was "Labour are hopeless and we are better." That works as long as people remember the last government, but the best people had gone. Bill went. Steven left.'

But an MP in Bridges's camp says it was a question of fairness and simple demographics. 'Amy [Adams] secured the second-most votes and was a woman.' She also offered a contrasting liberal perspective to Bridges's conservatism. 'He was trying to do the right thing.'

In April, it was decided Bridges would embark on a 12-week nationwide tour of 70 venues to introduce himself as leader. The town-hall meetings would be advertised on billboards. Bridges also wanted to have an aggressive push on social media.

After making a speech to business leaders in Auckland criticising Labour's economic intervention, he would visit New Plymouth. The powerful oil and gas sector in regional Taranaki was noisily protesting Jacinda Ardern's dramatic ban on new exploration. As a former energy minister who had cleared the way for more prospecting, Bridges would be warmly welcomed in the blue electorate. From there he would take in small towns on the Coromandel Peninsula and in Waikato, before moving south.

National's polling was holding up. By April it had a slim lead over Labour (44 to their 43 per cent). However, no one was seeing Bridges as an alternative prime minister; he was trailing Ardern by 27 points. The electorate needed to get to know him. But roadshows and social media ads are expensive, and not all of the costs could be covered by the party's taxpayer-funded allowance. According to a long-serving board member, Bridges and Bennett asked party president Peter Goodfellow for $100,000. The board felt the tour would go over well in rural provinces because people 'were hungry to hear from Simon'. But the source says the request was declined by Goodfellow. 'Guess who stepped in?

Jami-Lee Ross said he'd raise the money. Beware of unintended consequences. It caused so much angst.' That angst is still playing out in the High Court, with Ross and three others accused of deception over six-figure donations to the National Party.

The donations scandal actually began, ironically enough given Ross's past obsessions, with a row over expenses. In August 2019, Newshub carried a report about Bridges's inflated parliamentary travel costs. Over three months he'd racked up $113,973, of which $83,693 was spent on travel in the Crown limousine, a BMW.

The expenditure was put down to his leadership roadshow. In the same period a year earlier, Labour's Andrew Little had spent roughly $35,000 less. Controversy about MPs spending large on hotels, flights and road travel is not unusual. Press Gallery reporters scrutinise the quarterly release of all spending. As stories go, it wasn't that damaging. However, it was a baptism of fire on press secretary Rachel Morton's first day. She had returned to the party after previously working for Bennett and Joyce in government. National was able to offer up an easy defence to the media: Bridges lived in Tauranga, whereas English and Little were both Wellington-based, which cut down on their travel. And holding town-hall meetings could not be portrayed as an egregious or lavish abuse of funding. 'It was such a small thing,' a staffer says. 'It shouldn't have spiralled.'

But something set this case apart: the source. For the figures did not come from the official quarterly reports but from confidential documents that had been leaked a week before they were due to be reported to Parliament. Bridges was furious. He blamed the Labour Party and Speaker Trevor Mallard, and demanded an inquiry. Mallard agreed to appoint former solicitor-general Michael Heron QC to investigate.

At first, no one suspected any unrest within the National Party. The last three opinion polls consistently put National at 45 per cent, ahead of Labour even after the birth of Ardern's daughter. In June it held the Auckland electorate of Northcote in a by-election triggered by Jonathan Coleman's resignation when he was head-hunted for a role in the private health sector. While Bridges didn't have Ardern's popularity, there were no obvious cracks in his leadership. But Mallard knew the leak could only have come from someone within National because of the form in which the data had been given to Newshub. Ardern said none of her MPs had access to the information.

Bridges could not accept it was one of his own. At one point Ross, together with other MPs, was asked by reporters about the leak. He said he 'doubted' the breach was internal, adding that he had absolute confidence in his leader and that the party was unified. But Ross was secretly dissembling. An anonymous letter was written to the party giving false information to try to divert attention away from caucus members.

Mallard called off the inquiry a week later after receiving a text message claiming to be from a National MP, who confessed to the leak and claimed to have mental health problems. The text included details of a caucus meeting, confirming it had likely been sent by an MP. Bridges also received the same text, and Ross was in the room when he received it. National's leader refused to accept that one of his MPs was behind the leak. And because Bridges trusted Ross, the latter 'was able to play this weird, complex game of chess, several steps ahead', an MP close to the leadership says. 'It's always easy looking back to say [Bridges] should have known.' But clearly he didn't. Bridges's attacks on Labour and Mallard continued.

In late August, the National Party commissioned its own investigation by consultants PricewaterhouseCoopers and law firm Simpson Grierson. It dragged on for weeks, producing more and more damaging headlines. By now some in the caucus suspected Ross. Winston Peters gave the first hint of the treachery during a general debate in the House on 19 September. Always attuned to parliamentary gossip, Peters enjoyed mischievously repeating rumours in Parliament, where statements are covered by privilege and can be made without the fear of being sued. Drawing attention to Ross's empty chair, he claimed to know who was responsible. 'Mr Bridges needs to reveal who the leaker is or I will.'

Nothing more was heard of the matter for the next fortnight, beyond the occasional headline and gossip in the corridors. Then, on 2 October, in what at first was presented as an unrelated move, Ross issued an abrupt statement saying he was standing down from the front bench, relinquishing his portfolios and taking a few months' medical leave. Colleagues, including Nikki Kaye, publicly fell in behind Ross, offering sympathy and support.

But tongues soon began to wag, especially as punters began to join the dots back to that inquiry-halting text, which had specifically cited 'mental health issues'. The rumours had to be addressed. At a subsequent press conference in Auckland, Bridges tried to stem them, saying he took Ross at his word that he was not responsible for the leak. 'It's a very separate matter from his personal and wellbeing issues.' Bennett scolded reporters for the speculation. National was backing Ross who was going through a traumatic time. 'We ask the same of the media ... we don't do speculation that's unhelpful, unnecessary and untrue.'

But the pair weren't being totally upfront with reporters. While the new inquiry into the leak hadn't yet concluded, National had been approached with complaints about Ross's behaviour towards female staff and party members. Four women had made allegations of bullying and harassment, details which would later be revealed by Newsroom.

By now Ross's relationship with Dowie had ended acrimoniously, and she, too, raised concerns. She felt groomed, and that he had exploited her loneliness away from her two young children. He had also encouraged her to sleep with other colleagues. Another woman said he targeted her for a relationship. She claimed he had narcissistic tendencies, was controlling and exhibited 'incoherent rages', and said the sex was 'brutal'. An anonymous woman said Ross 'intimidated, threatened and abused' her over two years. 'He is a master manipulator and a deceitful liar,' she said. A staffer felt so undermined she sought medical help for stress and anxiety. 'He destroyed me as a person. It makes me shake just thinking of him.' One of these women had complained to the party 18 months earlier, and the matter was raised with Ross. Goodfellow later said the issues 'were dealt with at the time'.

Bridges was sucker-punched by the claims. An MP close to him says he was somewhat blind to Ross's worst flaws and 'had a degree of naïvety' about his former friend, to the point where he had wondered whether Ross was gay. The MP says Bridges should have had more guile. 'Rightly or wrongly, [he] tended to take people in a straightforward way.'

Bridges and Bennett, accompanied by National's imperturbable chief of staff Jamie Gray, confronted Ross. Given the number of damaging accusations mounting up, and especially against his background of self-confessed mental fragility, they told him to resign his portfolios and take leave until after the summer recess. Bennett told him it was 'the lightest possible way out of this'.

Bridges promised Ross he could 'get through it' and even work towards a promotion off the backbenches. 'There are downsides for me, letting you off what you've done … But if you take the [media] statement [prepared] for you, and your behaviour subsequently is good, I will never refer to the matters we've talked about.' There was no contrition, however, with Ross rejecting the allegations as 'the worst'. He left the meeting, which he had secretly recorded, and then demanded a one-to-one conversation with Bridges. Ross also taped that call, which was later played to Newstalk ZB. In what he believed at the time to be a private conversation, Bridges said he believed the women's allegations. 'I think it happened. Honestly, Jami-Lee, if I gave you natural justice on these issues it wouldn't be four or five [allegations], it would be 15,' he said.

Ross took leave. But the investigation findings from PricewaterhouseCoopers and Simpson Grierson arrived over the weekend. They pointed, conclusively, to Ross. Bridges and Bennett visited Ross at his home in Dannemora, Auckland. They told him the caucus would be voting on Tuesday on whether to suspend him. He didn't give them the chance to even get back to Wellington before he fired off a volley of tweets. 'Later today Simon Bridges is going to attempt to pin his leak inquiry on me,' he wrote. Some months ago he'd fallen out with Bridges, he continued. 'I have internally been questioning leadership decisions he was making and his personal poll ratings which show he is becoming more and more unlikable in the public's eyes.'

Then came the bombshell. Ross accused Bridges of unlawful activity that could be proved by his secret recordings. 'When I started to become expendable I confronted him with evidence … Working on his instruction, he asked me to do things with election donations that broke the law.' He claimed the leader had forced him to take leave in order to gag him. In a final tweet, he pledged to speak publicly in the coming days.

Flummoxed, Bridges and Bennett faced the media at Parliament. Although Ross hadn't elaborated on his allegations, Bridges said they were wrong and that his MP was lashing out.

The PricewaterhouseCoopers report pointed to Ross being the sender of the anonymous text message, Bridges said. He was not satisfied with Ross's explanation. And there were other 'matters concerning his conduct' that suggested a pattern.

Rather than waiting for a flight, Ross embarked on the nine-hour drive to the capital, sleeping in his car. He called a press conference for 11am. It was timed to coincide with the caucus meeting that was voting to expel him. Ross walked out to use the lectern that reporters had set up for Bridges. For close to an hour he spewed bile about his leader and former friend. He claimed to have had a mental breakdown and would later be admitted into care.

Most damning were his allegations around party finances. Ross claimed Bridges had asked him to collect a $100,000 donation from a wealthy Chinese businessman, Yikun Zhang. The pledge came after both men attended a dinner at Zhang's home on 14 May, he claimed. Ross would later tweet a photograph of Bridges taking tea with Zhang.

In order to keep the gift below the threshold over which the donor's name would have to be declared, it was to be split into smaller amounts. Ross said these were put in the name of different donors. This was unlawful. Ross claimed he had proof, a taped conversation with Bridges, that he would take to the police. 'I believe Simon Bridges is a corrupt politician,' he said. With breathtaking sanctimony, he added: 'Simon is a flawed individual, without a moral compass and without any underlying principles, except power.' Bridges strenuously denied the claims, and the tape did not subsequently offer the proof Ross claimed.

After a 10-month Serious Fraud Office investigation it was Ross, not Bridges, who was charged. The case relates to two $100,000 donations: the one highlighted by the MP and another in June 2017. His co-accused are Zhang, Shijia Zheng — a prospective National Party MP also known as Colin Zheng, and also Zhang's business partner — and Hengjia Zheng.

The explosive claims re-ignited debate about Chinese influence in the political system. During the 2017 election campaign National list MP Jian Yang faced allegations about his ties to the Chinese Communist Party. He and Labour MP Raymond Huo would resign within days of each other in 2020, amid rumours of security concerns. Zhang had also been pictured with Jacinda Ardern, Phil Twyford and Auckland mayor Phil Goff. ACT's David Seymour said the businessman repeatedly asked to dine with him. Seymour declined.

University of Canterbury professor Anne-Marie Brady had long raised concerns about the reach of the Chinese government. Politicians believed they could take the money and maintain independent foreign and domestic policies, she told Radio New Zealand. 'But it's very clear that the money comes with strings attached and that was revealed in that conversation that Jami-Lee Ross played to us.'

The scandal did lasting damage to National's brand. Pollster David Farrer says the impact can't be understated. Disaffected and vocal MPs are normally on the outer. 'This was a frontbencher, who had been promoted by the leader to the front bench, and was probably one of the two closest advisors.' There are two ways to look at it, he says. 'If you believe Jami-Lee, the leader is a criminal. Or you think Jami-Lee's gone mad. But how did he get to be so high, and why was he so close to the leader? Either way, it wasn't good for National.'

An MP close to Bridges says Ross was put into positions of leadership and power by John Key and Bill English. 'Obviously, his influence grew under Simon's leadership.' The MP believes the party should have intervened. 'I don't know why they step back and let these car crashes unfold.'

Initially, Ross threatened to quit and force a by-election in Botany, which he said would be a referendum on Bridges's leadership. But in the end he backed out and stayed on as an independent, teaming up with a conspiracy theorist Billy Te Kahika to unsuccessfully fight the 2020 election.

National went on to win Botany with a new candidate, a former chief executive of New Zealand's flag carrier airline and a protégé of John Key, named Christopher Luxon.

8

A TRAIN WRECK

OST OF NATIONAL'S CAUCUS now agree that the messy and
embittered Jami-Lee Ross saga was the prelude to the end
of Simon Bridges's leadership. However, the perfidious MP had
been right about one thing: MPs were starting to have doubts
about their leader's weak personal poll ratings.

After Ross's spectacular self-immolation the caucus united
behind Bridges. No one wanted to inherit the mess he'd created,
but, behind the calm reassurances about unity, the party was in
turmoil. Some felt Bridges didn't deserve their trust after Ross's
secret recordings revealed their leader's true feelings. This largely
concerned a discussion the pair had had on how to satisfy donors
by bringing in more than one ethnically Chinese MP. It sounded
as though they were auctioning off list places. 'Two Chinese MPs
are better than two Indians,' Ross said. Discussing a 'mercenary'
cull of sitting list MPs, Bridges referred to Maureen Pugh, the
low-ranked West Coast MP, as 'fucking useless'. David Carter
and Chris Finlayson, who both had given the party long service,

and Christchurch-based Nicky Wagner were also mentioned as potential exits.

Others were deeply troubled about their leader's anaemic popularity. Until the Ross fiasco, the party's polling had held firm, usually coming in above Labour; but voters were not warming to Bridges. In the aftermath, National fell behind Labour, with a two-point drop to 43 per cent. Bridges's preferred PM ratings also dropped by three points to 7 per cent. Nipping at his heels was Judith Collins on 5 per cent.

With not even a year under his belt, Bridges was heading into barbecue season with a question mark hanging over his head. Although the lion's share of blame lay with Ross, many MPs wondered about his handling of the problem. He had doggedly prosecuted the leak of his expenses. Better to have let sleeping dogs lie, some concluded. Many who had seen the dark side of their former whip also recognised that Bridges had tolerated his attack dog before he was bitten. There was also disquiet that Bennett had allowed the allegations about bullying and harassment to become public.

One advisor, close to both Bridges and Bennett, says the doubters in caucus were too quick to judge. 'The backbench had never had to deal with anything on that scale, and they wouldn't have known what the hell to do either. Everything was unravelling at a million miles a minute.' Calls had to be made, the advisor says. But the caucus expected Bridges and Bennett to have all the answers. 'Should she have done that? Probably not. But he [Ross] was trying to take us down, and there is no rule book for that. It would have come out anyway.'

Bridges struggled to rejuvenate the party. His front bench line-up was bolder than English's but it lacked clout. Amy Adams failed to fire in the finance portfolio. 'We lost Steven and Bill;

Amy became finance and our core equity went out the door. We never made any inroads in the finance portfolio, which is the real strength of the National party,' another senior party advisor says.

Finlayson is typically caustic about Adams's abilities. 'She'd been overseas on a Speaker's tour. When she came back, she came into caucus and said to me: "Are you still here?" Grant's [Robertson] first Budget was coming up and she'd swanned off overseas. So I said: "The bigger question is, are you still here?"'

It didn't help that Labour had neutralised National's most powerful weapon to fight the 2020 election campaign: a capital gains tax (CGT). Early in 2019, National gained traction with stinging attacks by raising the spectre of greater taxation of residential rental investment properties.

The matter of whether or not to introduce a CGT was Labour's Achilles heel: Ardern had a personal commitment to the introduction of the tax, but the public was deeply opposed. After the CGT policy was scrapped a week out from the 2017 election, the government essentially threw the hot potato to a team of consultants appointed to review the system. The Tax Working Group recommended the introduction of a CGT, allowing National to again roll out the criticism and the attack ads it had deployed in the election campaign. It had the same result. By April 2019, Ardern had promised no tax. Bridges half-heartedly declared a win, but in reality it was Winston Peters who played the veto. 'We've heard, listened, and acted: No Capital Gains Tax,' he tweeted. Adams would announce her retirement in June.

The Opposition landed some punches through 2019, most notably in opposing the immigration minister's decision to cancel the deportation of Czech drug smuggler Karel Šroubek. The party's base also liked Bridges's hardline views on the Ihumātao dispute, which concerned a sacred site in south Auckland seized by the Crown in 1863 and sold to private developers in 2016. 'Time to go home,' he said of the protesters who had occupied the disputed land for close to half a decade. 'We are already home,' they responded.

In May, National's leak of documents from Labour's much-hyped 'well-being' Budget was excruciating for the government and a welcome morale-boost for Bridges and his team. Security around the Budget is normally extra-tight — any advance knowledge has the potential to move markets. The Treasury Secretary, Gabriel Makhlouf, called in the police, rashly claiming IT systems had been 'deliberately and systematically' hacked. In an embarrassing twist, it emerged National's clever apparatchiks had simply used the website's search function. They gleefully entered economic terms over 2000 times, producing a treasure trove of supposedly secret information. It became known as the Budget Smuggling Incident (a play on Antipodean slang for men's tight swimwear). It was point-scoring gold for Bridges over Finance Minister Grant Robertson, each as tribal as the other.

But maintaining the momentum and keeping the government on its toes was an uphill battle. The role of the Opposition is an important one for democracy and scrutiny: to question and criticise the government, to highlight their mistakes and misjudgments. One of the best in the business was Judith Collins. For months, she'd kept the government on its toes on housing and infrastructure. A one-woman attack machine, she was crucifying beleaguered minister Phil Twyford, who was struggling to get KiwiBuild and his Auckland light rail 'ghost trains' off the ground. Ardern would relieve him of the problem in June, demoting him from Cabinet. Collins expressed sympathy for the man she'd spent months criticising. She had her eye on another scalp.

As Bridges reeled over Ross's betrayal, the end-of-year polls had put Collins neck-and-neck with her leader. Come February, as MPs were returning to Wellington after the summer holidays, she had overtaken him. Two weeks shy of Bridges's first anniversary as leader, his favorability ratings were halved as Collins's accelerated. 'Next to no-one wants him as PM,' said Newshub, reporting the results of their poll. The more the public saw of Bridges, the less they seemed to like him. A leak of a UMR Research presentation to clients revealed the brutal truth: a word cloud (a visual representation of phrases) made up of perceptions of Bridges was almost wholly negative. The graphic representation featured 'untrustworthy' prominently alongside other derogatory language. UMR chief executive David Talbot said the message was striking. It was the lowest net favourability of any leader since Jenny Shipley. 'Clearly, people are having a sort of quite deep negative emotional reaction to him.'

To rub salt into the wound, the party had shown its worst result in more than a decade of the Newshub poll's history. On 47.5, Labour had overtaken National, and it would stay in front for the next six months. But Collins's leapfrog of Bridges wasn't a catalyst for change. She dutifully did damage control, giving an interview to Radio NZ's evening *Checkpoint* show. 'We don't want to have years and years of chopping and changing like Labour did,' she said. 'We are working very well as a team and leadership is always an issue for caucus and they have made their decision. I'm just getting on doing my job.' But Collins is a master of apophasis. Confident she was the public's favourite (a UMR Research poll had confirmed her as such in the 2018 leadership race), she was sending a message to her caucus, the arbiters of the top job. '[Caucus has] made their decision,' she repeated. Few of her colleagues bought her fealty.

As police minister, she'd earned the nickname 'Crusher' for a policy that saw boy racers' cars pulverised. Although she later claimed to hate the name, it perfectly encapsulated her approach to politics. Her career was littered with casualties. Unhappy with police culture, she purged its senior ranks, including commissioner Howard Broad and deputy Rob Pope. As corrections minister, she questioned the leadership of her chief executive Barry Matthews after a string of scandals. He retired a year later. And she led the charge against Labour minister David Benson-Pope over allegations he assaulted pupils while working as a teacher more than two decades prior. Police investigated. He was not charged, but he eventually resigned over other misconduct. In 2004, she caught Immigration Minister Lianne Dalziel's office leaking a letter about the deportation of a sexually abused Sri Lankan girl. Dalziel had to resign. Even Collins's entry to Parliament was cut-throat. As part of new party president Michelle Boag's drive to clean out the old guard in 2002, Collins swept aside Warren Kyd, an MP who'd held the largest majority at the previous election. She was unapologetic about her reputation. 'You can't make an omelette without cracking an egg.'

The youngest daughter of Waikato dairy farmers, she grew up a Labour supporter, even interning for David Lange. But a run-in with trade unions when she ran a restaurant converted her to National. Under Key, she rose steadily through the ranks. As a tax expert, her field of discipline in law, it rankled that he never awarded her an economic portfolio. Collins enjoyed the respect if not the friendship of her colleagues. In private she could be a tough critic. Some were downright nervous of her vengeful streak, including Paula Bennett, Amy Adams, her justice ministry successor, and Anne Tolley who followed her as police minister. Collins and Tolley couldn't have been more different. Crusher displayed a (disarmed) police Taser in her ministerial cabinetry. Tolley's contained her impressive collection of stilettos.

Collins drew the veil from her own character when she wrote to cruel right-wing blogger Cameron Slater about utu, a Māori word often defined as revenge. 'You know the rule — always reward with double.' She added: 'If you can't be loved, then best to be feared.'

When she became embroiled in the scandal sparked by the *Dirty Politics* exposé, Key had few options but to sack her. She believes she was a scapegoat, sacrificed to save National's 2014 election campaign. A shadow had already been cast over her career earlier that year, because of her ties to Chinese milk company Oravida. Revelations about a friendship with Slater and a smear campaign against Serious Fraud Office director Adam Feeley were the final nails in her coffin. She was resurrected by Key in 2015, after an inquiry found she was associated with those trying to undermine Feeley but not directly involved. Her notoriety only boosted her profile. The name recognition translated to popularity. For much of the decade, she was in the frame as a serious contender to lead National.

Collins modelled herself on her political heroine Margaret Thatcher. She loved the former British prime minister's uncompromising style and mourned the death of the 'highly intelligent, brave, formidable woman' in 2013 with an official statement. At the age of 60, she regularly featured in preferred prime minister polling, and her name was frequently mentioned in any speculation about a coup. There was no sign she was being actively disloyal to Bridges. But from her early days in Parliament, Collins had cultivated the media, and his supporters suspected her of being behind gossip fed to the Press Gallery. They identified at least one leak from a policy analyst who would later be hired as one of her closest advisors. The resignation of a press secretary, for personal reasons, dominated a media stand-up when it was leaked to journalists. 'It had nothing to do with anything. And we had stuff to announce. It was such a waste of a media opportunity,' one former staffer says. Others harboured suspicions.

Some caucus veterans were members of an informal group that called themselves 'the Orphans', named because they were the few survivors of their intake. Among them were Brownlee, Smith, David Bennett, Waitaki MP Jacqui Dean and Collins. 'We would rotate drinks in our offices,' one of the Orphans says. 'And Judith would just take delight in leaks that occurred.' On at least two occasions when information damaging to Bridges was leaked, the Orphan had first heard it from Collins. 'My instincts said that was where it came from.'

In April, Newshub reported dissent among the ranks. Bridges was branded 'incompetent' and a coup was predicted in the coming months. Allegiances, it said, were shifting behind Collins. That wasn't true, and possibly says more about the motivation of those doing the whispering. 'No one trusted Judith,' an MP says. 'She would have been lucky to have three votes in caucus. David Bennett, Harete Hipango, Matt King — and maybe Andrew Bayley. That's probably about it.'

During Labour's time in Opposition, a band of MPs opposed to the leadership of David Cunliffe became known as the ABC or Anyone But Cunliffe club. National had its own ABC club — Anyone But Collins — and most of the caucus were in it. She assiduously courted the unrequited backbenchers, but she had more enemies than allies. Her supporters were not influential. 'Her constituency is playground losers,' a former staffer says. 'There was always a kid like Collins in every school who was king of the outcasts. The Maureen Pughs, the Cameron Slaters.'

Sensing Collins didn't have the numbers for a challenge, Bridges called her bluff at a caucus meeting. He convinced senior colleagues to confront her, and MPs including Brownlee, Tolley and Maggie Barry upbraided her for her behaviour. He had another thing in his favour: National was still polling in the forties. She was vanquished and Bridges temporarily shored up his own support. The reprieve did not last. There was a fresh round of leaks in May and again in June. Details of private discussions reached journalists even before caucus meetings had wrapped up. With phones banned from the room, Bridges's inner circle blamed MPs wearing Apple watches.

Occasionally, Bridges handled the frosty rivalry clumsily. He allowed Collins to find out from the media that she'd lost the infrastructure portfolio to Paul Goldsmith in the wake of Adams's resignation. Goldsmith, a list MP, also leapfrogged her ranking into finance. Trying to pour cold water on the fire, Bridges told media he was on such good terms with her that they'd dined together on the evening of his reshuffle. This wasn't quite the case. Collins waited a couple of days. And then she paid back double, letting slip on a radio show the pair had merely crossed paths as she left and he arrived to eat.

Each round of polls that placed Bridges ahead of Collins sparked a fresh round of gossip that he was about to be rolled. The media scented blood in the water. 'There was just this hunger to take Simon down. Particularly from Newshub. I've never seen anything like it,' an advisor to Bridges says. But Collins wasn't the only problem. The leadership was being steadily destabilised by the damaging leaks, and Todd Muller was also in the frame.

Bridges's team suspected the leaking came from a band of three young staffers, who support MPs with both advice and administration. The 'smart arse' trio became known within the leader's inner circle as 'The Ratfuckers', a slang term used by Richard Nixon supporters to describe the dirty tricks they used against their opponents. One particular pointless and nasty saga unnecessarily humiliated press secretary Rachel Morton and cost another advisor his job. In the hours following the 15 March mosque attacks that cost 51 lives in Christchurch, a petition was removed from the National Party website. It concerned a UN migration pact, which was at the centre of a far-right misinformation campaign and was referenced in the terrorist's manifesto. Brian Anderton, who had worked for the party for six years, deleted it. Bridges's team believe it was The Ratfuckers who urged him to do it and then leaked it to the media. He would become known as 'the emotional junior staffer'.

Morton mistakenly told reporters it was routinely archived — an error that was quickly revealed. Bridges then had to explain that. He said the deletion was unsanctioned and blamed Anderton's state of mind. To the public, National looked duplicitous and focused on trivial matters in the wake of a national tragedy. Anderton would later resign, sparking yet more headlines. He apologised to Bridges's staff on his final day. 'I've been used by a Member of Parliament,' he told one.

The team felt ground down, constantly fighting fires lit by their own MPs. 'We had this massive opportunity to make Labour a one-term government,' a staffer says. 'Some of us were working really hard towards that. And others weren't.' Bridges had a coterie of MPs in his corner: Mark Mitchell and former ministers Paul Goldsmith, Louise Upston and Michael Woodhouse. One supporter, who initially had reservations, grew to respect Bridges's leadership. 'He showed an enormous capacity to absorb pressure. He's a very good Opposition MP and could do negative politics.' Bridges kept the party relevant. 'And he kept our numbers up through what was a very difficult time.' The downside was Bridges didn't present well on television. 'A big chunk of the public took a position against him.'

There were obvious divisions. And because National had a large caucus, MPs on the margins were increasingly worried about their job security. Groupings formed based on the year of entry to Parliament, and gripes were fomented at Wednesday night drinks parties. Once the House rose around 10pm they would meet, alternating offices each week. 'It is really good for each of their classes, but it becomes really competitive,' a staffer says. 'The class of 2014 felt they should be higher up and [treated] better than the class of 2017. None of it was based on merit. The class of 2017 was huge and they were arrogant.' A former minister agrees. 'They'd come together as a bunch of newbies, and suddenly, because they've got numbers, they feel they're influential. They used these drinks sessions to wield power and influence.'

Amid the boozy bitching sessions a culture of entitlement developed. 'Under Bill [English], everyone was given a portfolio,' the staffer says. 'So someone running a portfolio next to someone who had been a Cabinet minister felt they were on an equal footing. It just didn't work. There needed to be some hierarchy there. It became a competition rather than adjusting and learning.' A former MP refers to the class of '17 as 'the bane in National's life', responsible for 'nothing but leaks, a sense of self-entitlement and real arrogance'.

Another issue was the politicisation of MPs' staff, who usually stay neutral. An insider says some began agitating. 'They got involved in the games,' the senior staffer says. 'We saw things that you never saw before, especially things getting leaked.' For those who had served the party under Key, it was frustrating to see the party machine and discipline eroded. 'Egos got in the way,' the aide says. Bridges felt alone and under enormous pressure: 'I always lived knowing that, were there a bad TV poll, the small camps in caucus around Todd Muller and Judith Collins would become larger.' His leadership, he felt, 'was damned and doomed'.

The disloyalty was 'one of the hardest things' about Bridges's tenure, another advisor says. 'The Jami-Lee thing is not the thing I look back on as the worst thing that happened in his time. Simon was just being white-anted by everyone. It was everything he did.' The internal machine that was oiled with unity and discipline began to break down, and without that discipline staff became worried about who they could trust. Some felt the party was drifting. 'We lost direction and experience,' one staffer says, 'and there just became a bit more noise than strategy.'

That wasn't altogether fair. Under Bridges, the party had established a plan to write policy led by the meticulous Nick Smith. The caucus was divided into groups dictated by their portfolio focus and would meet weekly to exchange ideas. Eventually, they would be tasked with writing discussion papers that would form the basis of the 2020 campaign. In mid-2019, Bridges also launched a 'Have Your Say' campaign to crowd-source ideas. He toured the country, delivering speeches to different groups. 'The policy process was set up really well,' a staffer loyal to Bridges says. 'Nick Smith has a lot of faults, but his drive and getting people organised was outstanding.' MPs and staff felt they had a focus and something to work for.

Staking out policy ground and differentiating your party from opponents is a tricky balance to strike in Opposition. Revealing too much policy detail too early is tactically inept. It makes it easy for the incumbent government to respond, either with criticism or by stealing ideas. National did try to articulate a clear choice with an economic paper released at its annual conference. It offered to repeal the ban on oil and gas exploration, heralded a cut in taxes, promised a regulations 'bonfire' and issued a warning to unions. It was red meat for the centre-Right, but other ideas fell flat. Some were distinctly Trump-like. A war on gangs was ridiculed for its Strike Force Raptor, an elite police force mirroring one in Australia's New South Wales. After Bridges proposed an idea to fine the parents of school drop-outs $3000, one commentator pointed out the party's own Paula Bennett who left without qualifications at 16 would have attracted the penalty.

There were plenty of own-goals. A bizarre witch hunt against Corrections for spending $1 million on 200 slushy machines to keep overheated staff cool in summer was widely ridiculed. There was a strange episode where Bridges gave Alfred Ngaro licence to explore the establishment of a religious coalition party.

Bridges drew ire when he called Ardern, a new mother, a 'part-time' prime minister following a visit to Tokelau, a dependent island territory of New Zealand in the Southern Pacific. It was the first visit of a prime minister in over a decade. Critics argued the jibe was too personal and carried sexist overtones. He was polarising and could not get the public to warm to him. For a time his MPs consoled themselves with Australian Prime Minister Scott Morrison's surprise victory in May. He, too, was unpopular but beat back Labor on cost-of-living issues.

But the caucus could only kid themselves for so long. 'I never thought we would win the election under Simon,' a disillusioned MP says. Although Bridges kept polling in the forties, the caucus sensed the public were not going to vote him in as prime minister. Bridges's pugnacious style resonated badly with a public who were still in love with their 'relentlessly positive' prime minister.

That was only emphasised when she reached superstar status in the wake of the tragedies that befell New Zealand in 2019.

'They are us' Ardern had written on a A4 sheet of paper on learning of the attack on Linwood Islamic Centre and Al Noor Mosque. She repeated it later that day in a speech that perfectly encapsulated New Zealanders' feelings of horror and solidarity. In the days following, pictures of her wearing a head scarf while consoling members of the Muslim community went around the world. An image of her, taken by photographer Hagen Hopkins, was beamed onto Dubai's 828-metre-tall Burj Khalifa skyscraper. Her government acted swiftly to implement an immediate ban on all military-style semi-automatic guns. (Bridges, too, earned praise for supporting the required law changes.) In the weeks following, her approval rating rose to its highest level since taking office. She climbed seven points to 51 per cent in the 1 News/ Colmar Brunton poll. Labour's party vote got a three-point bump to 48 per cent, while National's rating dropped to its lowest since September 2017, at 40 per cent.

Ardern would earn further affection for her handling of another catastrophe: the eruption of Whaakari, or White Island. Early in December, the offshore volcano exploded into blue skies. It killed 22 of the 47 people exploring the island's strange, moon-like landscape. Many of the casualties were passengers on a visiting cruise ship, and included tourists from Australia, the United States, Britain, Germany, China and Malaysia. Ardern remained on the ground in the Bay of Plenty for two weeks. She was photographed hugging emergency service workers. Her response saw an outpouring of affection from overseas. In the coming months she would be named one of the world's most powerful women, mentioned as a potential candidate for the Nobel Peace Prize and profiled in international media, including the cover of *Time* magazine. Remarkably, National stayed ahead of Labour in the main opinion polls between June 2019 and February 2020, reaching 47 per cent in October, seven points ahead. However, Bridges struggled for relevancy. At one point his approval ratings fell to 4.2 per cent. That would worsen with the outbreak of the coronavirus pandemic.

During the course of his leadership, National had been driving a combative social media strategy. It had mixed success. In August 2019, then associate Minister of Transport Julie Anne Genter proposed a car 'feebate' emissions scheme. 'We were down on our luck polling wise,' Bridges would later write in his memoir, *National Identity: Confessions of an Outsider*. 'I spotted an opportunity. I instructed the team to go all guns blazing on social media against the car tax.' Bridges says the effect was 'rapid', pushing polling up 'by several percentage points'.

A number of campaigns followed — on gangs, KiwiBuild, and a contentious series featuring Labour MP Deborah Russell that earned a rebuke from Speaker Trevor Mallard, who objected to the use of edited Parliamentary TV footage. 'Some in the team were squeamish,' Bridges wrote. 'They wanted "Kumbaya" with the Government (and still do). The mainstream media … were in full moral panic mode … In addition, the left weaponised the Advertising Standards Authority.' Complaints began flooding in. Bridges was bullish about the approach. He believed the campaigns were keeping National's polling in the forties and occasionally delivering a three- or four-point bump. Facebook was his friend, until it wasn't. He now partly blames social media for his downfall.

New Zealanders were proud of their response to the outbreak of Covid-19. As infections grew around the world, Ardern closed New Zealand's borders in mid-March 2020 and the country entered lockdown soon after. Her 'Be Kind' motto and unflappable leadership endeared her and Director-General of Health Ashley Bloomfield to most of the population. There were only 25 deaths during the first wave. Her government was celebrated by the World Health Organization as well as Anthony Fauci, the face of America's fight against Covid-19, and Britain's former PM Tony Blair, for whom Ardern had once worked.

Early on in the pandemic, MPs were unsettled by Bridges's leadership of a special select committee set up to scrutinise the Covid response while Parliament couldn't sit. It was established by Brownlee, as Shadow Leader of the House, and his equivalent in government, Chris Hipkins. The pair have a mutual respect and it was a positive example of cross-party co-operation in a time of crisis. 'Simon just ruined it,' the senior MP said. 'The prime minister was going to keep doing these stand-ups [a daily 1pm televised briefing to the nation]. You either have no voice or you have a complimentary voice. A contrary voice is not going to work.' Bridges filled the committee with his strongest supporters, including Woodhouse and Goldsmith. One confrontation with Sir David Skegg, a respected epidemiologist who was advising the government, particularly jarred. 'He set it up as adversarial,' the MP says. 'He got people offside. He was looking all the time for this to be a failure, and it was just a disaster.'

With flights grounded, Bridges opted to commute the 500 kilometres from his home in Tauranga to Wellington, driving there and back each week. This went against official advice not to take long trips. He defended the decision, variously claiming his internet connection was poor and that he needed to be close to the Press Gallery. The public, locked up at home, didn't like it. 'Simon was travelling badly,' an MP says. 'It's very hard, but he just kept making mistakes and our numbers tumbled.' MPs began to fear a 'massive loss'. Lawrence Yule says no one paused to take a deep breath. 'Jacinda got the headlines, managed it. Simon adopted an adversarial approach. There's no playbook.' Yule thought Bridges was putting people offside, when the country was focused on unity. Both Gerry Brownlee and Nick Smith appealed to Bridges, asking him to take the offensive down a notch. Smith told him the country was facing a crisis akin to World War Two. Bridges's 'aggressive' approach was misreading the national mood. 'By the time we got to April, May, the party and the public were really anti it.'

Bridges's caustic commentary on the government's reaction struck entirely the wrong note. It looked like carping when compared with Ardern's calm compassion. On 20 April 2020, when Ardern extended the country's strict lockdown measures for five days, Bridges responded with a Facebook post. 'The decision for New Zealand to stay locked down in Level 4 shows the Government hasn't done the groundwork required to have us ready,' he wrote. 'The public has done a great job of self-isolating and social distancing. The entire country has made huge sacrifices to ensure the four week lockdown was effective. Unfortunately the Government hasn't done enough and isn't ready by its own standards and rhetoric.' With hindsight, many of his points criticising testing-and-tracing and the availability of personal protective equipment were valid. But the country, comfortable in the cocoon Ardern had provided, wasn't ready to hear them. The backlash was enormous. The post received more than 25,000 comments, with much of the negativity directed at Bridges. The caucus was unnerved. Throughout lockdown they had watched Bridges's flailing performance with dismay. 'It was a train wreck,' one senior MP said.

The badly received 342-word Facebook message was the final straw for a rattled caucus who saw their hopes for an election win drain away with every Ardern press conference. It 'might be viewed as the beginning of the end for me as boss of National,' Bridges would later admit in his memoirs. 'The circling wolves got the chance they'd long been waiting for and a spill was on.' Initially, it was assumed Paula Bennett or Mark Mitchell would step up. 'People who were on his front bench were shaping for a change,' a senior MP says. 'Paula and Mark were thinking about it. There were constant conversations.'

The caucus was nervous because for some time Bridges had refused to share internal polling. Rumours suggested they had dipped into the thirties. 'I'm sure this happened in Labour,' Yule says. 'The leader doesn't want to release it because it reinforces a negative narrative. And then the caucus thinks things are going wrong.' Success brings discipline, power and loyalty to the leader, Yule says. 'When you're on 45 per cent, MPs step out of line at their peril. But when you're 28 or 29, your colleagues — listees or seats — are at risk.' It was hugely tempting for the opposing forces in caucus to leak bad results, he says. 'Because of that lack of discipline we could never have an honest conversation. Most people wanted Simon to succeed, but there wasn't a safe forum to say we need to change direction. It's hard to fix because it's a trust thing.'

Beleaguered, Bridges fought on. He took on the government over the legality of its Covid measures and won a review of the law. When the Budget was delivered, offering a $50 billion Covid spend-up, his criticism was muted and he supported some measures, opting not to call for the traditional vote of no confidence. Two disastrous polls were his death knell. It was worse than National's MPs had feared: in the Newshub-Reid Research poll the party vote fell to 30.6 per cent — a staggering 26 points behind Labour and the worst result in more than a decade. To those in the know, the internal polls were even bleaker. A senior MP says they plummeted as low as 22 per cent, and the rumour mill cranked into gear. Bridges could not edge past 5 per cent in the preferred prime minister stakes. On those numbers it would be near impossible to win an election head-to-head with Ardern, and at least 16 MPs would lose their jobs.

The spill was on. In an email leaked to Newshub, a constituent wrote: 'Time to roll Simon. Landslide loss in September otherwise.' David Bennett replied simply: 'Yeah, working on it.' A vote of no confidence was slated for the following week's caucus meeting.

It was Todd Muller who stepped into the breach. 'There was a period of time when the Muller camp was quite candidly talking to the Bridges camp,' a source says. Collins was seen as the bigger threat, and Team Bridges would rather a challenge from Muller than Collins. 'Even the party members, who are normally the most loyal, were so negative,' the source says.

The two men's careers had always run on a strange parallel. In 2008, Muller had declined to put himself up for selection in Tauranga, the seat that Bridges went on to win. Although they now held neighbouring electorates, they weren't friends. A former MP says there was always a rivalry between them. 'There was resentment that Simon had been made a minister and his career was on the up. Muller has always seen himself as leadership material. Quite frankly, he saw himself as something special. I think Muller was jealous and thought he could do a better job.'

Muller began calling on MPs. 'He came to see me, said he was doing it,' says one. 'I advised him not to. I thought he should wait. There was no point: we were heading for a bad result, an absolute shocker.' Over a coffee, Nick Smith also told Muller to hold off. But, egged on by Amy Adams and his prospective deputy Nikki Kaye, Muller did not heed the advice. As torchbearers, they championed his abilities to fellow MPs and eased his private doubts. Chris Bishop and Nicola Willis, the whip-smart leaders of the party's liberal wing, were also pivotal in drumming up support. An MP says the caucus was worried that there was no clear direction from Bridges about the election campaign. 'Then Covid hit and all the problems were amplified. What were we going to do? Todd was a different figure, he was unknown.'

As he had with Collins, Bridges called Muller's bluff. He went public on a regular round of morning media slots. 'A couple of my colleagues want to challenge myself and Paula Bennett for the leadership and deputy leadership of the National Party,' he said. He declined to name the challengers, and added: 'The overwhelming majority of the caucus are behind me.'

A few days later a 1 News/Colmar Brunton poll solidified the slump, putting National on 29 and Labour on an unprecedented 59 per cent.

Muller called his friend of 30 years, political strategist Matthew Hooton. He wrote to party president Peter Goodfellow and Bridges, making formal his challenge. He also tried to call Bridges, who wouldn't answer. He asked whip Barbara Kuriger to call a formal vote. Then Muller emailed his colleagues. He shared the view of the majority of caucus: the party could not win the election under Bridges, he wrote. 'Our communities and our economy are at stake.' Publicly, he was saying the opposite. When asked about leadership ambitions a day earlier on talk radio station Newstalk ZB he gave an emphatic 'no'. Bridges was 'doing a bloody tough job well', he insisted.

By the end of the week, MPs assembled in Wellington for a special caucus meeting. Bridges drove down from Tauranga. 'Simon forced the issue. I don't know whether Muller would have gone through with it or not,' a senior MP says. Many MPs were uneasy about the vote, it being only a few months out from September's election. Alfred Ngaro, arriving at Parliament for the meeting, called the challenge 'dishonorable'. In frustration, East Coast MP Anne Tolley vented to her local newspaper. It was 'destructive' and 'nutty stuff', she said. 'It's a bit of panic from some of the newer MPs who have only been there since the halcyon days of John Key … They have no idea of what it's like when times get tough.'

Muller, speaking with notes as his rival waited outside the caucus room, passionately implored his colleagues to fall in behind him. And it was thanks to that speech that Muller won the vote, a senior MP believes. 'It was structured, it pointed out where we were at, and what we had to do.' The result was leaked from the caucus, reported by Newshub just a few moments later. After the secret ballot the new leader wandered to the back of the room and began chatting with MPs. Bridges and Bennett left immediately. 'As quick as that I was no longer leader,' Bridges later wrote. 'The bedwetters won.'

National was under new management.

9

INTO THE UNKNOWN

I<small>N ANTICIPATION OF HIS</small> win, Todd Muller had already installed his team in Wellington. Matthew Hooton — a silver-haired public relations consultant who writes biting political commentary for *The New Zealand Herald* and *Metro* magazine — flew down from Auckland. Muller and Hooton had long been friends, meeting as teenagers in the Young Nats, the party's youth wing, of which Muller had been the Waikato University branch chair.

In 1991, Hooton accepted a summer job speech-writing for Education Minister Lockwood Smith and then stuck around. Muller followed after the 1993 election, working as an executive assistant to Jim Bolger, who deeply approved of his Catholicism. Included in his tasks was pouring the prime minister's evening whisky.

As young men in their early twenties they bonded further over their addiction to politics. After long hours in the Beehive, they'd drink at The Shamrock, an Irish pub on Tinakori Road, or at 3.2 in the Beehive. At the time Muller was sharing a flat with young MP Gerry Brownlee, but the pair rarely saw each other. When they both left politics after the 1996 election, Muller joined Hooton backpacking through India. As a child, Muller had wanted to be US President and emulate Jimmy Carter. Ineligible as a New Zealand citizen, he would eventually shift his goal post to prime minister. That Hooton would follow him back to Parliament was inevitable. They had both always assumed that the strategist would be Muller's consigliere when the time came.

Hooton briefly returned to politics after 1999. He worked for dairy co-operative Fonterra before setting up Exceltium, a consultancy that specialised in connecting Auckland's business community with Wellington's politicians. Firmly on the free-market Right, he also had a spell consulting for David Seymour's ACT party. Notorious for political scheming over long boozy lunches, he was a bogeyman of the Left whom he loved baiting on Twitter. An acerbic writer, he parted ways with business paper *NBR* in acrimonious circumstances after Steven Joyce sued the publication over one of his columns. In 2020, now sober and writing for *The New Zealand Herald*, Hooton had recently returned from completing a philosophy Master's at King's College London. He'd also (temporarily) quit Twitter.

As MPs deposed Simon Bridges, Hooton was waiting a few miles away at the home of Nicola Willis, in the capital's Karori suburb. That morning the *Herald* had published his weekly column with the headline: *Simon Bridges v Todd Muller — why National had to choose Muller*. 'It makes me sad that things have reached this point,' he wrote of his 13-year friendships with both Bridges and Kaye. He went on to accuse Bridges of an 'unfortunate lack of judgement' and said his leadership was 'unsalvageable'. Labour strategists were 'drooling in anticipation of regular gaffes on the election trail', he added. With a somewhat lukewarm, if realistic, argument for his friend's promotion, he concluded: 'He can make a pitch that he and National's indispensable finance spokesman Paul Goldsmith are better than Ardern and Grant Robertson … It may not be the most brilliant or visionary pitch, but it might contrast well with a Labour front bench made up of former student presidents and prime ministerial staffers of which, ironically, Muller is also both.'

Hooton was joined by Tim Hurdle, who'd made the journey from his Tauranga home. One of the country's most experienced behind-the-scenes operatives, Hurdle was Gerry Brownlee's right-hand man for half a decade. During the Canterbury earthquakes, Brownlee had handed out a cellphone number to MPs and other community leaders so that they had a direct line to share problems with the government, no matter the time of day. The number was Hurdle's. After leaving Parliament, he worked for infrastructure giant Downer, and had recently established the New Zealand office of Crosby Textor, an Australian lobbying firm and political consultancy.

Hooton got to work on the speech Muller would give to a post-caucus media conference. Co-writing was Sean Topham. A former president of the Young Nats, Topham had founded Topham Guerin, alongside Ben Guerin, a digital advertising firm that was pivotal in the success of the pro-Brexit campaign and the re-election of Boris Johnson and Scott Morrison. Topham Guerin was renowned in political circles for their provocative memes. Topham was fresh from Britain's fraught general election, where Johnson had called a snap vote to get Brexit through Parliament. The UK prime minister called them his 'digi-Kiwis' after they created a campaign video parodying the much-loved film *Love Actually*. Simon Bridges had labelled them traitors after the pair deserted National under his tenure. For a time, they contributed to the government's coronavirus ad blitz.

Hooton slipped into the back of the press conference to watch his friend deliver the speech. Muller filed into the Legislative Council Chamber with his MPs. He was joined on stage by Nikki Kaye, Judith Collins, Gerry Brownlee, party president Peter Goodfellow, Chris Bishop, Shane Reti and Paul Goldsmith. Goldsmith would remain in finance and Kaye was his deputy; the only roles Muller would confirm. Willis sat in the audience, beside Muller's wife, Michelle. 'There is no Team Todd, there is no Team Nikki, or anyone else — there is only Team National,' Muller said.

Bridges stayed away. He was pictured in the corridor of National's offices being embraced by wife Natalie and toddler daughter Jemima. 'More time for the most important job I have,' he tweeted. Many of his team went to the pub expecting to lose their jobs. This included his chief of staff Jamie Gray and chief media advisor Rachel Morton. Only one press secretary, former *Dominion Post* journalist Michael Forbes, was left behind to deal with reporters' queries late into the night.

Muller's performance was passable if a little uninspiring. He tried to keep the focus on the government's economic mismanagement but was inevitably questioned about caucus unity. As his confidence grew, he removed his spectacles and talked about his faith, family and motivations. But there was a telltale blip. When asked if he could work with New Zealand First, a question that was easily anticipated, Muller stumbled. It was a matter for caucus, he said. (He was wrong. While caucus is consulted, the decision is ultimately one for the leader.) It underlined that Muller was untested and inexperienced.

*

Muller was born in 1968 in the Edwardian spa town of Te Aroha and raised on a kiwifruit orchard in Te Puna, near Tauranga. His rise to the top job marked a golden era for Tauranga Boys' College. At the time they could count among their alumni the current skippers of the Black Caps, the All Blacks and Team NZ — Kane Williamson, Sam Cane and Peter Burling, respectively — and now the National Party.

After his initial foray in politics, Muller had moved into the primary industry sector, working for Zespri, a co-operative of kiwifruit growers and the world's largest marketer of the fruit. By 2006, he was chief executive of Apata, the kiwi and avocado service supply company founded by his father, Mike, in 1983. Before entering Parliament in 2014 he was an executive at Fonterra. The path was carefully plotted: he had always intended on rising through National's ranks. Once the safe Bay of Plenty seat became vacant with the retirement of colourful former health minister Tony Ryall in 2014, Muller made the move back home from Auckland. He won easily, with a margin of more than 15,000.

While he had a relatively low profile as a backbench MP, he was always mentioned in speculation about future leaders. 'He always said he would be PM,' a friend says. 'In retrospect, he was enormously arrogant about it. It became an assumption that he would be "the one" [a future leader] and he used that to his advantage.' Muller's trajectory really took off in Opposition when he was handed first the climate change and then primary industries portfolios. The first is a poisoned chalice — some National supporters are yet to be convinced the problem even exists. The latter is a powerful one within National, connecting the political wing to its rural base, and one of the country's main economic drivers.

His background in horticulture gave Muller a running start. Before long, he was winning plaudits for his deft handling of the government's radical climate change proposals. Opening her 2017 election campaign, Jacinda Ardern had promised to transform New Zealand's approach to tackling global warming. 'This is my generation's nuclear-free moment, and I am determined that we will tackle it head on,' she said.

Under Green Party co-leader James Shaw, as minister for climate change, Ardern's government embarked on an ambitious suite of policies that would enshrine emissions reduction targets in law. To ensure the legislation would endure through changes of government, Ardern insisted that it be passed with cross-party consensus. That meant getting New Zealand First and National, both with firm roots in rural New Zealand, to swallow a plan to tax farmers on their emissions from 2025. Months of wrangling between Shaw and the two parties ensued. 'The ag sector really respected him [Muller],' a source close to the negotiations said. Muller proved to be a tough negotiator and went into bat for farmers. 'He drove a very hard bargain because he understood the sector well. My sense was that he is a person of great integrity; strong, values-based.'

Shaw and Muller struck a deal. An announcement was pencilled in for late 2018. Over the course of the talks, Shaw had intermittent contact with Winston Peters. But as the deadline drew near, New Zealand First began stalling, and over the summer break Peters went quiet. The source says Jon Johansson, a respected academic and Peters's chief of staff, 'decided to throw a spike in the whole thing. He tried to kill it.' The source says New Zealand First reneged on some of the previous agreements. A frenzied period of back-and-forth followed. Ardern had to bring in Helen Clark's former chief of staff Heather Simpson to mediate. Shaw 'couldn't be in the same room with Jon'. As the Greens tried to resolve the impasse, contact with Muller dropped away. 'But then we got over the line with [Winston], and we were way past our deadline at this point. Things moved very quickly.' Shaw rang Muller to break the news. The National Party had pushed for — and thought they had agreement on — a more generous methane target, and for the goal to be removed from the Bill and instead set by a commission. But New Zealand First would not support it, and won the day.

Muller, understandably, 'completely flipped out'. But, realising what was at stake, he calmed down and brought Shaw and Bridges together for talks. 'He used a tremendous amount of his political capital in the caucus to get them to go for it, because their attitude was "fuck those guys".' The bill passed with near-unanimous support in November 2019, despite threats from Judith Collins to cross the floor and vote against the legislation. ACT had intended to oppose the final reading, but its sole MP, leader David Seymour, was not in the House.

Muller proved much more combative when Bridges promoted him into the agriculture portfolio. In December 2019 he took on Te Papa, the country's beloved national museum, over an interactive display that highlighted the water-quality problems associated with intensive dairy farming. It featured fake water, dyed muddy brown, and an image of a cow defecating in a stream. 'I've just had a gutsful, bluntly,' he told a rural radio show.

Muller was assumed to be socially conservative. He had voted against the decriminalisation of abortion, the legalisation of euthanasia, and a law that would make medical marijuana widely available. On other issues he was moderate, the friend says, feeling this inconsistency to be telling. 'I think in the end, as it all played out, there was no purpose to his leadership, or his ambition. He has no ideology.'

At that first press conference as party leader, Muller promised his 'absolute focus' would be the country's economic recovery from the pandemic. 'We will save jobs, we will get the economy growing again, and we will do so by leveraging our country's great strengths; our people, our communities, our great natural resources, our values of hard work, tenacity, innovation and aspiration.' He added: 'I know the size of this task and I will bring my all to it.'

*

By 8pm on the night Muller took over the leadership he had retired to his Wellington flat for a meal of reheated chicken and coleslaw with Michelle. His team was incredulous. It was the most important day of his career, and he was knocking off comparatively early. 'The rest of us were told to stay put and put the transition in place,' one says. 'The whole thing was a shambles, and I should never have gone near it.' Amy Adams reversed her decision to retire, and she and Nikki Kaye took over. It was they, not Muller, who chose the shadow Cabinet. Paula Bennett was dumped as campaign chair and replaced with Gerry Brownlee. Adams took on the Covid-19 recovery portfolio.

The front-bench selections would be a problem that would come back to haunt Muller and Kaye. 'Because Amy is from the South Island, it was examined through a geographical lens, and it was certainly examined through a feminist lens. But it was not examined through an ethnicity lens,' an insider says. 'Nor did it take into account private commitments Todd had made to people.' That included Shane Reti, who believed he would be on the front bench, with the health portfolio. 'It didn't happen because he wasn't involved in his own reshuffle,' the insider says.

Bennett would later talk of her hurt, after 20 years of service to the party. Muller had called her early on the Sunday at 7am. 'He said to me: "I'm going to rank you really poorly. I don't see a role for you." That was incredibly tough.' Bennett felt Muller showed more respect to Bridges. 'And I'd done nothing. It's not like I did anything to cause me to lose that role. I was, kind of, the consequence of the caucus wanting a change from Simon.'

Within just a few hours the newly franked leader also almost lost his two most experienced advisors. Summoned to a meeting with Amy Adams, Hurdle and Hooton knocked on the door only to be sent away, without explanation. Already uneasy, they were ready to quit. They left through the rear door, walking through the Press Gallery corridor and onto Museum Street. As they paused at the traffic lights to cross to The Terrace, a breathless aide caught up with them. Both were persuaded to return.

As Muller sat at home, a Twitter firestorm was brewing. A photograph from a 2019 profile showing political souvenirs on display in his Bay of Plenty electorate office was repeatedly shared. It included one of Donald Trump's signature *Make America Great Again*, or MAGA, red caps. Muller had bought it while in the United States with Jami-Lee Ross during Trump's first presidential campaign. At first, Muller was unapologetic. 'I got one of those and I got a Hillary Clinton badge,' he told *Newshub Nation* the following morning. 'I've got them both in my office. But for some reason, the Hillary Clinton badge never gets looked at. Everyone sees the MAGA cap and somehow reaches a conclusion that perhaps [that] is where my sympathies lie.' Muller doubled down, telling 1 News he would display it at Parliament when he shifted into the leader's office. Oddly, he had already demonstrated he was alive to the hat's problematic symbolism: he'd refused to put it on for the profile's accompanying photograph, a year earlier.

Shane Te Pou, a former Labour Party activist and prominent commentator, advised Muller to burn the hat. 'MAGA caps are used by extreme racist right wing groups to recruit … It's the modern day equivalent of the confederate flag,' he wrote. Muslim groups said it was inappropriate. 'That hat represents the denial of the freedom of beliefs. That hat represents the denial of minority voices. That hat represents the vitriol that has been harming that nation and has been harming the world for the last four years,' Aliya Danzeisen of the Islamic Women's Council said. 'If he wants to be the Prime Minister of New Zealand it would be nice if he'd choose to display objects that represent the values of New Zealand.' For four days the controversy swirled, dominating his first days as leader. By Tuesday he was forced into a backdown. The hat was packed away.

But there would be more gaffes. Muller unveiled his predominantly white front-bench line-up. Ranked 13, of 14 places, Paula Bennett was the only Māori MP. No other ethnicity was represented. Muller and Kaye defended the appointments. When challenged over this glaring lack of diversity, Muller initially appeared to flounder, and Kaye stepped in. She pointed out that the shadow front bench included three women in the top four jobs — herself, Adams and Collins. Then she added: 'Paul Goldsmith obviously is of Ngāti Porou.' What followed was cringeworthy. Goldsmith, who was there as part of the new line-up, said awkwardly: 'No, I'm not. My great-great grandfather had European wives and Māori wives, and so I've got lots of relatives across Ngāti Porou. I don't claim to be Māori myself.'

Bennett could not contain her glee, which was caught by the cameras. Devastated by Muller's betrayal and her removal from the campaign, Bennett would announce her resignation at the election a few weeks later. Lawrence Yule says the transition was rushed, and it showed. Kaye's blunder was 'a complete own-goal'. Yule says not enough care was taken to get diversity in the top 20. 'Simon tried to put it [the leadership challenge] to bed, which meant that Todd's team had to get organised a lot quicker. They were a month ahead of where they needed to be.' Yule says Muller wasn't ready. 'There wasn't enough grunt in the people around him: a lot of the grunt was in Simon's team, and they weren't that keen about helping.'

Muller's first week was certainly chaotic. He was rattled, and on 27 May he had a panic attack as he was being driven from Auckland to Tauranga. 'It started with an intense prickling sensation in my head, followed by what I would describe as "waves" of anxiety. I had never experienced these sensations before despite having lived through some very high pressured moments at Fonterra dealing with global food safety scares.' He broke down in Michelle's arms. 'As Michelle did many times over the subsequent 50 days, she comforted me, soothed these feelings of wretchedness with unconditional love and positivity. I awoke the next morning tired, but excited for the day that lies ahead.'

Muller kept his staff and MPs in the dark about his deteriorating mental health. 'I feel ashamed about this,' one says. 'I should have picked it up earlier: that he was a man in the midst of a nervous breakdown.' Another says: 'Maybe if he'd been honest at the beginning it could have been dealt with.'

Over the long Queen's Birthday holiday weekend, National brought in Janet Wilson to do some media training. She spent much of the time encouraging the uncertain leader, propping up his confidence. Wilson was unimpressed but would eventually return to be his chief press secretary after a string of telephone pleas from Kaye.

Muller partially recovered, helming a couple of policy announcements aimed at supporting struggling small-business owners. But his psychological state continued to deteriorate. The panic attacks returned the following weekend, lasting 15 minutes. 'This time with even more ferocity. Night sweats, deep sensation of anxiety and nausea, shortness of breath and the ongoing prickly buzz and sense of tightening pressure in my head.' His sleep was disrupted, and he'd wake after only three hours. 'No matter what I tried — stretching, yoga or calming apps on my phone — nothing could stop the waves of anxiety and dread that would start the moment I woke up.' He sought help but not from his party. He was prescribed sleeping pills and anti-anxiety medication. 'At least this would get me through to maybe five hours sleep a night, maybe enough to function.'

Helpfully, the country's attention was elsewhere. On 8 June, Ardern eased Covid restrictions down to level one of the four-stage alert framework, although the borders would stay closed indefinitely. In mid-June, two women, recently arrived from Britain and infected with Covid-19, were allowed to leave quarantine without being tested. It gave Muller an issue to run with, and he repeatedly attacked the government on competency.

By now, his leadership had started to gain momentum. He made a homecoming trip to Te Puna, where he delivered a wide-ranging speech that revealed how his upbringing had shaped his values. He spoke of being one of the few Pākehā children at St Joseph's Convent. 'Even then, in an unformed childish way, I was aware of socio-economic disparity. I knew my family was very comfortably off, relatively speaking. I felt that rare experience for Pākehā in this country — the sense of being different and in a minority,' he said.

His was an old-fashioned, traditional family, he said. 'But as we grew older we were also taught to make our own decisions about what we accepted and did not. To me that is what drives social progress. That we learn from our parents but we challenge their ideas and develop our own. One thing that will never change is that, for me, what makes a family is love.' The speech was written by Hooton, who'd visited the Te Puna chapel with Muller 20 years earlier and understood what made him tick. Muller barely changed a word. 'That's me. You've got it,' he said on receiving the draft.

As well as a personal statement, the speech was significant because it made explicit criticism of past governments and policies, including National's punitive reforms of social welfare and labour relations in the 1990s under Ruth Richardson. 'For all their strengths, I do not believe that previous governments or the current government moved fast enough or boldly enough to address the social deficit or help the underclass or however you describe the deep-seated social problems we continue to see all around us,' he said. He even criticised Bolger. 'I think both Labour and National could have done those economic reforms more gently, more caringly and with a greater sense of love for our fellow Kiwis. If we look across the Tasman to our sibling rivals in Australia, it pains me to say that Bob Hawke, Paul Keating and John Howard managed the reform process better than David Lange, or my friend and mentor Jim Bolger.' The speed and sequencing of the economic reforms did terrible harm to the institutions of our communities and to too many families, he said.

Muller was sending the message that National would not respond to the looming economic crisis created by Covid-19 with the flinty free-market policies of National Parties in the past. He was trying to 'outkind' Labour, which had built a brand around Jacinda Ardern's compassion. And he was capitalising on the lingering sense that Labour could not translate Ardern's kind words into meaningful policies. 'In my lifetime, New Zealand prime ministers have tended to be kind, competent or bold. Some have managed to be two of those things. My background in business and politics and my grounding here in Te Puna mean I plan to be all three — kind, competent and bold.' He finished with a flourish that borrowed from Ardern's signature slogan. 'Someone else once said, "Let's do this". I say, sure — but you need a National Government to get it done.'

Muller also underscored National's commitment to Treaty relations, including tino rangatiratanga, or self-determination. 'Later in life I became very proud that it was my party — the National Party — that has done so much to honour our nation's founding document, the Treaty of Waitangi, and address the breaches of the past and the present.' In adulthood, Muller said he had come to see a relationship between the Treaty promise of tino rangatiratanga and the importance the National Party places on the values of self-determination for individuals, families and communities. 'As prime minister, I will seek to advance those values,' he said. This was significant because Muller was saying that under his leadership National believed more in tino rangatiratanga than Labour did — but it was for none of these things that the speech would be remembered.

Instead, the media highlighted two gaffes. The first was Muller's momentary slip when he began speaking: 'I joined the Labour Party.' He recovered to applause. The second was the Tino Rangatiratanga flag in the background, which also appeared in the party's memes. Media coverage of the speech was dominated by the fact that it was upside down. 'Today, he posed in front of an upside-down Tino Rangatiratanga flag and what he was saying was a bit backward too,' said Newshub in their evening bulletin. The *Herald* published a flurry of scathing tweets on the error. Three days after the delivery, The Spinoff ran a snide 700-word 'investigation'.

The mistake wasn't National's. The flag had been hung that way many years ago in the rugby club hall that National had hired. Club member Tommy Wilson said it was a cheap shot to blame Muller. 'The flag has been hanging that way for at least a year and no one has said anything until now. Even I didn't notice it was the wrong way up and I have been in that hall many times,' he said. Muller's staff were frustrated. 'It was portrayed as some sort of deliberate insult by the National Party to Māori,' one said. 'It does say something terrible about the media, frankly, that that became the story.' But Muller's advance team hadn't spotted the problem. Neale Jones, a former chief of staff to Ardern and Andrew Little, had seen Labour fall victim to similar gaffes during his time in Opposition. 'The problem with doing poorly in politics is each mistake compounds and makes new gaffes more likely,' he astutely observed. 'The MAGA hat makes no Māori on the front bench even worse. That in turn gives greater meaning to the upside down tino rangatiratanga flag. It's a downward spiral until you drown.'

For now, Muller had a life-raft. The first poll since his coronation revealed he had at least staunched the bleed of National's support. National was up nine points and Labour was down nine, albeit to a still healthy 50 per cent. Labour would still be able to govern alone. While Muller's preferred PM ratings were acceptable at 13 per cent, the public was clearly still making up its mind.

10

THE COUP THAT SHOULD NEVER HAVE HAPPENED

WITH 12 WEEKS TO run until the election, National's first hoardings went up. Featuring Todd Muller and Nikki Kaye, the slogan was *Strong Team. More Jobs. Better Economy.* Behind the scenes it was not a strong team. People were starting to hate their jobs. After their first few days, Matthew Hooton and Tim Hurdle were told to remain at home. Hooton's role as a political commentator was creating tensions.

As well as writing a Friday column in the *Herald*, Hooton would appear regularly on Radio New Zealand's *Nine to Noon* programme to talk about politics. In the days before the leadership spill, he'd also been a guest on its *Morning Report* and evening *Checkpoint* shows. 'Heaven knows how RNZ chose repeatedly to use lobbyist Matthew Hooton as a commentator,' wrote *BusinessDesk* editor Pattrick Smellie. 'Most journalists know that Hooton has been working on Muller's behalf to help achieve this outcome.' Hooton had been straight-up with the national broadcaster and had mentioned his role in Muller's leadership bid in his interviews. He also included disclaimers in his articles. However, Smellie's piece was republished by the *Herald* and gained traction among Left-leaning Twitter users. Hooton had no choice but to withdraw from commentary.

Before long he and Hurdle were back in Wellington. Hurdle was appointed campaign manager alongside his old boss Gerry Brownlee. But no one could decide on Hooton's job description, and this infuriated him. Megan Campbell, a former Saunders Unsworth lobbyist who had also worked for National's pollsters Curia, was appointed Muller's chief of staff.

At the top of this sat what became known as 'The Triangle'. If it was a triangle, it was inverted, with Muller constantly deferring to Kaye and Adams. Chris Bishop and Nicola Willis, arguably two of the caucus's brightest talents, were instantly sidelined. They were baffled and deeply hurt. Their role in the coup had damaged their standing with mistrustful Bridges supporters, and with others who wrongly assumed they were asserting influence. Behind her back, colleagues called the sharply dressed Willis 'The Devil Wears Prada'. She would later, rightly, point out that this was deeply sexist, although by then they had swapped the moniker to 'The Devil Wears ASOS'.

Staff, MPs and candidates soon became confused about a lack of direction on policy and a persistent indecisiveness. There were endless, circuitous meetings. Staff began calling Adams 'Whiteboard Amy', a nickname given by her Selwyn predecessor Ruth Richardson. The Triangle had decided to turn away from Nick Smith's policy discussion documents, a body of work diligently prepared by MPs over the previous two years. 'No one could understand it,' one MP says. It debilitated the team. 'We got nowhere, no one would ever agree,' an insider says. 'There were never any serious meetings.' The insider believes to a degree it was a matter of chickens coming home to roost: National had relied too heavily on the talents of Key, Joyce and English. 'They were so good they did everything, and the people who had been ministers had officials. The idea that [in Opposition] you have to do your own research, meet experts and type out your own policy paper was just beyond all of them.'

Staff felt Kaye and Adams had a strange relationship, described as 'a weird "frenenemy" thing'. A staffer remarks: 'They kept saying they are [friends] and they don't feel [like] friends.' Another exasperated staffer said the pair were out of their league. It was decided Adams would become 'the policy guru'. 'I think the whole thing was a power-play by Adams,' the staffer says. 'She wanted to be head of Covid. She wanted to control the policy. She wanted to be chief of staff as well. She suddenly became a policy wonk and she'd never done it before in her life.' This all led to months of dithering. 'There were hours of these meetings, such an inefficient use of time. They'd start after Question Time and go on until after it was dark.' That started a chain reaction with Kaye. 'Policy wasn't written. Nikki's reaction was to double down and just get more frenetic. Really, she should have just been the balm that was trying to soothe things.' There was no direction from the top and Muller couldn't make a call. 'We staggered into a series of crises.'

With the election looming, one senior MP was in despair. 'Todd just had trouble making decisions, big time. It was a nightmare, absolutely. The policy was a mess. Everything was a mess.' By then, the party's grassroots support was starting to grumble. 'We were bleeding from our base. They didn't like the second-guessing and the indecisiveness,' another MP says. 'Right from [Nikki's] first balls-up with Paul Goldsmith they didn't like that we were excusing the lack of ethnicity on the front bench. Our supporters could see that [Todd] didn't trust his gut and it went from bad to worse.'

Kaye argues the criticism is 'pretty unfair'. She also disputes the claims around policy. 'When we took over the leadership we found ourselves with very little policy. In part because of Covid. We had the discussion documents but [there was a] need to pretty quickly develop some policies. I think with any campaign team coming together there will be natural tensions, but that is in part due to being in a pretty short runway to the election with little policy and having to get some stuff down quickly.' Another staffer backs up her assertion on policy. 'There were some discussion documents that were pretty fucking lightweight. There were spelling mistakes. You just don't have spelling mistakes in the education policy document.'

Staff began to suspect that Kaye and Adams were controlling the flow of information to Muller. 'No one ever saw Todd,' one staffer said. High-energy and driven, Kaye has a reputation as a demanding employer. Staff and MPs were working long into the evening and late-night phone calls were common. Decisions — even on minor arrangements like travel — were often re-litigated. Staff began to dread the 7am campaign meetings. 'Nikki would whitter on, slurring about Auckland and what people were saying in Commercial Bay,' one said. 'It was meant to be a national campaign.'

A friend of Kaye's defends her, and cites the pressure she was under because of Muller's passivity. 'Nikki wasn't personally ambitious. Far from it. She has great skills, but she is a huge micro-manager. When she started as a minister she drove people batty, but over time relaxed and became a very effective minister, and her attitude to risk stopped probably a number of problems.'

Kaye second-guessed everyone. 'They got such a good team. Love him or loathe him, Hooton is absolutely good at what he does. Tim Hurdle, Megan Campbell. And if you have got good staff then you need to actually trust their judgement and lead from that. It was a pretty challenging period for everyone. It was just chaos.'

Nick Smith says the result was National 'looked messy': 'When you took Simon out we broke down the machine. Jamie Gray was a good operator. We got a whole lot of new people coming in, and Nikki Kaye didn't know anything.' Another MP recalls that Kaye was 'completely running everything' but second-guessing almost every decision. 'There were a number of occasions when people reported her phoning them at two or three in the morning to talk about something that she's just thought of. Afterwards she did feel like she was totally blamed. And I'm not critical of them [Kaye and Adams]. It is not entirely fair, because they were only allowed to do what Todd let her do. I think his headspace was completely stuffed a few minutes after he became the leader.'

One casualty of the dithering was Muller's first major speech on the economy. It was slated for early July with the Christchurch Employers' Chamber of Commerce as the audience. Hooton was tasked with writing the speech, which was meant to set out a five-point economic plan. Adams told the team that Muller wanted a series of economic policies and an estimate of how many jobs each would create. '[We told her] that's completely idiotic,' one staffer says. They weren't allowed to speak directly with Muller about their concerns. On a skiing trip with his family, Hooton spent two days writing the speech in the packed cafeteria at Mount Hutt. In the end, he was forced to write four different versions because the leadership team couldn't agree on what

Muller was meant to be saying. Another aide says 'the really bad days' came when there were policy announcements, with details being written right up until the last minute.

The launch, over lunch, was a car crash. 'He could barely read it out,' one exasperated aide said. Another says: 'He was given a lot of time to prepare for that. We did a lot of trial runs of the speech. I think it was the nature of what was going on in his head at that stage.' Muller praised the previous National Government's track record in the quake-stricken city. 'Our legacy isn't one of ruined buildings behind fences, awaiting insurance settlements, it's of a new vibrant city, from the beautiful riverside to the shiny new buildings.' he said. He pointed to the Christchurch Central Recovery Plan, put together in just 100 days. 'Our execution of that plan returned life to a devastated CBD.' Muller also praised Gerry Brownlee, a lightning rod for criticism who had to apologise after branding homeowners awaiting a fair insurance deal 'carpers and moaners'. 'We rebuilt — Gerry rebuilt — this city, along with you, the business community,' he said. This was news to the city's residents still battling insurance companies and waiting for large areas of their city centre to be restored.

It was slowly becoming apparent to National's staff and MPs, as well as to the wider public, that Muller was struggling. A party teleconference on the evening before he left for Christchurch left many unhappy. 'I really like Todd as a human being,' one advisor says, 'but he was not leadership material. He'd been told all his life that he was going to be prime minister one day, but he hadn't actually put in the hard mahi [work] to get the qualities that ensure that you do well.' He started to draw the inevitable comparisons with Key. 'John Key *had* worked. From Burnside High School it was a trajectory he devoted himself to and worked on all his life. That's the difference.' The advisor believes Muller was also blind to the upset he'd caused by rolling Bridges. 'He was a little naïve. He didn't realise the hornets' nest that had been created. He'd engaged with Simon — the greatest bloody get-down-drag-him-out fighter in the entire caucus.' And Muller wasn't going to be allowed to forget it. 'It's rule number one for a politician: know the consequences of your actions.'

Behind the scenes, Muller's panic attacks were more frequent. He tried to keep them at bay with deep breathing and 'self-actualising future moments of success'. He found himself talking out loud to try to get on top of it. 'I was increasingly fraught with the fight ... for me it had become a daily wrestle of my mind and it took an astounding amount of mental energy to get through each day,' he wrote in a Facebook post. His family bore the brunt when he returned home for a day on the weekends. 'I would have nothing left to give them.' He was unable to get out of bed and was mentally distant. 'Michelle kept trying to put up emotional scaffolding to stop me falling further in a most generous and patient way. But inside it felt like I was slipping down a slope and however hard I tried to grip the bank, I couldn't stop.'

Knowing none of this, the restless caucus was underwhelmed with his performance. They had begun leaking again. Among Bridges supporters there was a degree of *schadenfreude*. 'Simon and Paula behaved appallingly,' Nick Smith says. 'Of course they were hurting; but they didn't buckle down. The real test of character in politics is when you get your arse kicked, even unfairly, are you still able to put the party and the collective interests ahead of the individual? And Paula and Simon both failed that.' Smith says they were actively leaking. 'And if there was a *faux pas*, Simon would go on news or Paula would grin from ear to ear. My view is that Simon and Paula need to take some responsibility for the train wreck that was Todd Muller's leadership.' A staffer believes Muller should have offered his former rivals senior positions. 'It created two enemies when there could have only necessarily been one. Bring someone inside the tent, don't have them pissing outside the tent.'

Around the same time Collins was due to publish her memoir, *Pull No Punches*, which was seen as a fresh declaration of her leadership ambitions. Muller and Kaye decided to try to instill discipline with a stern warning to caucus. But it backfired. Muller was unable to deliver the message at the meeting and it was left to Kaye. MPs, particularly the seasoned ones, did not appreciate the lecture from Kaye. Nick Smith was angry and rebuked Collins. 'I said: "You shouldn't do it. To anybody who's got half a brain, it blares: I want to be leader."' Another former MP says the coup meant distrust lingered. 'The way it was done was dirty, and as a consequence of that they couldn't stand there in front of us and say you all need to be loyal and united. Because where had that been from them for 12 months?'

Not everyone felt that way. One MP, a Muller supporter, criticises 'revisionist history'. 'It's factual bullshit and needs to be called out for what it is. When the leadership changed from Simon to Todd, we were at 27 per cent the night before in those public polls.' That was down to Bridges's 'deep unpopularity'. 'This idea that we were in the forties, we were going to win — it is just belied by the actual facts.'

But one MP took the leaking too far — and it would bring down the entire House of Cards. In early July, first-term Clutha-Southland MP Hamish Walker had issued an unauthorised press release claiming that up to 11,000 travellers from 'India, Pakistan and Korea' could be placed in Covid-19 quarantine in Dunedin and Queenstown, without consultation with the community. This was 'disgraceful,' he claimed. At the time, New Zealand's borders were closed and only citizens or permanent residents were allowed to enter the government's managed isolation facilities.

Labour's Megan Woods attacked the statement as 'racist'. It was an accusation Walker refused to accept, even after he was publicly and privately reprimanded by Muller. To prove his point, Walker sent to four media outlets a spreadsheet containing the names and quarantine locations of 18 Covid patients. Both Wilson and Campbell had told him not to. Yule, who counts Walker as a friend, says he took Woods's attack personally. 'He was hugely offended. He's got a lovely Māori wife [Penny Tipu], and he just took it right to the heart. And he fought back, which he shouldn't have done.' The *Weekend Herald* revealed the leak of confidential patient details but did not disclose their source. Unaware of the leak's origins, Muller slammed the government for the breach. 'Is it a deliberate leak or is it accidental? It doesn't really matter at a level,' he told Radio New Zealand. 'It's loose, it's shabby and it's a reminder these guys can't manage important things well.' The party's health spokesman Michael Woodhouse also issued a press release titled 'This Government can't be trusted with anything', saying the leak was 'unconscionable and unacceptable'.

The government swung into action. State Services Commissioner Peter Hughes, the country's chief mandarin, appointed respected Queen's Counsel Michael Heron to investigate. At this point Walker went to see Muller and confessed what he'd done, but Muller said nothing for more than 24 hours. His hesitation was due to a letter from Walker's lawyers which argued that revealing his involvement would breach his privacy. Muller sought his own legal advice, and the following day Walker publicly came clean in a press statement. The leader followed with his own, announcing the Clutha-Southland MP had been stripped of his portfolios.

Within a few moments a third press release dropped into reporters' inboxes. Former National Party president Michelle Boag was resigning from her role as acting chief executive of the Auckland Rescue Helicopter Trust. It was she who had leaked the information to Walker, whose parents she was friendly with. It later emerged she had also sent the information to Woodhouse.

Boag also had to resign from Kaye's Auckland Central electorate and campaign committees. In hindsight, there were signs of her involvement. Earlier, when Muller had started publicly criticising the leak, the public relations consultant had emailed his office saying 'you're on the wrong side of this argument' but without disclosing the true situation. Staff decided to ignore her, and in doing so unwitttingly set Muller up for an own goal.

The day after Walker's confession, Muller came out swinging. He wanted the party board to strip Walker of his candidacy. But before the board could meet, Walker finally resigned. 'It was a clusterfuck of biblical proportions,' a staffer says.

Initial anger at Walker's actions was replaced by an unease at Muller's performance. It was the party's Southern regional chair Rachel Bird — not Muller or Kaye — who had to talk Walker into stepping down. Chris Finlayson says Muller dealt with the incident poorly. 'Hamish was feeling isolated after the first press release' but was offered no support, nor treated with compassion. 'Then Michelle Boag gave him advice. And never rely on anything she says. He should never have felt so isolated that he'd rely on Boag.' Walker would later tell Heron that his judgement was impaired due to 'the pressure and distress' of being labelled a racist. The barrister concluded: 'Their motivations were political. Their actions were not justified or reasonable.'

The political commentary was scathing. 'Clutha-Southland is a safe enough seat that even a last-minute substitution will probably not affect National's chances,' the *Dominion Post*'s editorial writers assessed. The article ran in six of the Stuff stable's papers. 'But damage has been done to the image and reputation of a party that has never completely recovered from the "dirty politics" scandals of 2014,' it continued. 'Walker is a young MP who went rogue, either because of poor management or blatant arrogance ... his unapproved leak left Muller and health spokesman Michael Woodhouse looking confused and uninformed for more than three days. Nothing unites a political party like winning, but nothing splits a political party like losing. Current polling suggests National is staring down the barrel of its worst election defeat since 2002.' The editorial said that while a sense of panic had driven the coup that installed Muller, a lack of discipline had permeated since Key left. On the same day, the *Herald* wrote: 'Boag's involvement points to an own goal of electorally disastrous proportions.'

The episode left Muller bruised and exhausted. His mental health was crumbling. 'We didn't see his absolute stress,' Yule says. 'Once I asked him how it was going. He said: "I go from white-hot fear to everything's brilliant. And everything in between." ' Muller was tipped into crisis the weekend following Walker's resignation. Those around Muller point to different events over those two days which ratcheted up the pressure.

'The thing that I think broke the camel's back was Rio Tinto and the smelter,' one staffer says. The Anglo-Australian mining giant was again threatening to close its aluminium smelter at Tiwai Point on the southern coast of the South Island, putting more than a thousand jobs in Bluff and Invercargill on the line. The smelter is also the biggest consumer of electricity, using roughly 13 per cent of the country's power. Rio Tinto had previously threatened to close operations, and it was widely viewed as a tactic in negotiating for a cut-price electricity deal in an election year. 'Nikki was convinced that it was real and that National should ride to the fucking rescue,' a staffer says. She wanted Muller to fly into Invercargill, meet the workers and promise they'd keep their jobs under a National government. Brownlee, as a former energy minister, Hurdle, and Hooton, who had previously held Rio Tinto as a client, advised against it. 'Hurdle had this line: don't get between the government and a problem. They all said that we should shut up and let the government explain why all these people lose their jobs.'

But Kaye was insistent. 'The woman just keeps going,' another staffer says. 'It's a double-edged sword. Where others would give up because it was hopeless, Nikki keeps going. And that became a problem. There were nine of us versus Nikki.' Muller said he must back his deputy. 'Normally it's the other way around,' the staffer sighs. Hurdle was sent home to come up with a speech and a policy. Hooton was ordered to start working on a speech on Chris Bishop's new transport infrastructure policy for Auckland, which was to be delivered on Monday. Muller also went north, to spend time with his in-laws in the east Auckland suburb Stonefields.

Insiders point to Kaye and Hooton's volatile relationship as the tipping point. 'They clashed like fuckery. It was incredible,' one aide says. Both rang Muller to complain, and both threatened to quit. The leader, already under extreme pressure, had to mollify and arbitrate between them both.

Others put the blame on Kaye's decision to front for a television interview to explain the Walker saga. It was Muller who was invited to appear on TVNZ's Sunday politics show *Q+A*. He declined, recognising there was no upside to another interrogation of what he knew about the Covid-19 patient leak.

His answers would be sliced and diced into soundbites, dragging the story out into the high-rating evening news bulletin. Kaye saw it differently. Ignoring advice from both advisors and Brownlee and a direct order from Muller, she fronted up to the show. The appearance was — as one MP coarsely put it — 'a shit show'.

Kaye was forced to deny that National had once again embroiled itself in 'dirty politics'. She faced questions about what she'd been told by Boag, and the links to her re-election campaign. Looking back, she defended her decision: 'Todd was having time with his family and that was the message I had. I had committed to it ... and I thought it was really important to talk through what had occurred, and that is the way I have always operated in my political career: to front up. I think that's the right thing to do.'

Muller could no longer cope. 'In the end the frequency and intensity of the panic attacks took me to a place where I had to step away from the fire, the anxiety and the pain.' As one staffer says: 'That weekend everything just melted down, for everybody.' Calls and emails to Muller went unanswered. The team suspected he was suffering a nervous breakdown and cancelled the policy launch, citing a stomach bug. Megan Campbell flew to Auckland on the Monday to see what she could do.

Brownlee was in Napier campaigning with Katie Nimon, a well-thought-of candidate who was challenging Labour's Stuart Nash. They spent the day touring local businesses in the heart of the art deco city. After a long day on the hustings Nimon and Brownlee joined former Hawke's Bay ministers Chris Tremain and Craig Foss, and local MP Lawrence Yule, for craft beers at the Westshore Beach Inn. At 4pm Brownlee's phone rang. It was Campbell calling to say Muller had suffered 'an incident' and would be relinquishing the leadership. Brownlee said, 'Aw, he's just tired,' and flew immediately to Auckland to try and talk him around. 'It was a pretty broken situation,' the staffer says.

Campbell, Brownlee and Wilson worked long into the night drafting a press release announcing Muller's resignation, effective from the following morning. 'It has become clear to me that I am not the best person to be Leader of the Opposition and Leader of the New Zealand National Party at this critical time for New Zealand,' it said. 'It is more important than ever that the New Zealand National Party has a leader who is comfortable in the role. The role has taken a heavy toll on me personally, and on my family, and this has become untenable from a health perspective.'

A conference call was held to inform a small inner circle, sometime after 9pm on Monday. Muller did not attend. The rest of the party was blindsided when the news was made public at 7.30am on Tuesday. Kaye and Adams followed him out the door, both resigning on Thursday. It drew a line under a chaotic 53 days within the Opposition Leader's office. But the party was again thrown into turmoil and the MPs were furious. 'I remember thinking: it is all over. Why don't we just concede right now?' a senior MP says. 'Todd will justify it in all sorts of ways, but he has got no concept of how much damage that did to so many people who were working so hard.' Another MP says it was a deeply stressful time for everyone. 'Todd didn't look like he was enjoying it. You have got to want the job, and he overworked himself or he let himself be overworked.' An MP loyal to Bridges rages: 'The problems for us started with Jami-Lee Ross. Then we had a coup that should never have happened.'

With just 67 days until polling closed, senior party figures and MPs began calling the person they believed to be their only viable alternative. A caucus meeting was hastily organised in

Wellington. At the eleventh hour Judith Collins was ready to take the job she had coveted for almost 20 years.

*

Collins had had a sleepless night 'full of possibility and adrenaline'. Senior party figures and MPs had begun calling as soon as the news began to leak out of Muller's upcoming resignation. Among those urging her to step up were Key, English, Brownlee, Chris Bishop and Matthew Hooton. 'I had a few phone calls,' she says. 'People ringing who I would never have thought. When I determined there was overwhelming support, I decided I would do it. It wasn't a sleepless night of worry, it was ooooh. I love being needed and I know I shine through in a crisis. I'm good at that.'

But she was not unopposed: Mark Mitchell attempted a challenge. 'She tries to create the impression she was anointed, but she wasn't. She had to stand,' an MP says. '[Mitchell] didn't believe in Judith's leadership, one iota. For a guy like [Mitchell], leadership *does* matter. He thought she was completely devoid of integrity and morals.' Mitchell, who wanted Taupō MP Louise Upston as his deputy, couldn't quite muster enough support to beat Collins. 'People were spooked and scared and thought she could lock in the base.'

For a few hours after Muller's dramatic resignation, Nikki Kaye was elevated to acting leader. Panicked MPs held a teleconference to discuss what to do, and decided on a caucus vote later that evening. MPs not already in Wellington rushed to the capital. Shuttered away in her Ponsonby home, Kaye paced, talking on her cellphone, until leaving for the airport just after midday. By coincidence Steven Joyce was on her flight south.

Neither Kaye, Collins or Bridges would say publicly that they wanted the job.

Around 7pm, MPs began filing into their caucus room. They could scarcely believe that just seven weeks after the last leadership vote they were being asked to choose again. Within a few minutes of the meeting starting, both Mitchell and Bridges ruled themselves out. It took two hours before a vote confirmed Collins as leader with a loud cheer, and a further 30 minutes to decide that Gerry Brownlee would again take on the deputy's responsibilities.

There was no time for an introductory campaign, another MP explains. 'People know [Collins] and she is unapologetic. Our base loves that.' A staffer said she was the nuclear option but the only choice. Nick Smith says the decision was about 'minimising the pain' at the election. 'Muller was a train wreck. And Judith had positioned herself beautifully. To go back to Simon was too big to swallow. Did we sit there and say: "Judith is going be a great prime minister?" No. It was about who could try and save the house.'

But Collins could not save the house — instead, she burned it down.

11

THE HOSPITAL PASS

'THIRD TIME LUCKY,' JUDITH Collins said, standing in front of her caucus, late on the evening of 14 July 2020. She was referring to her previous leadership bids. But none of her colleagues felt lucky. Six months earlier she had been an unpalatable choice, her support so thin that she ruled out running against Muller. Now, after years of fending off her ambition, the demoralised MPs had to finally accept her as a lifeline. They had misjudged her determination and her obstinance. 'I love it when people say I can't do something.'

At age 14 Collins would not be dissuaded from the idea of becoming a lawyer. She bet a classmate's father $5 that she would make it. 'He said: "Oh dear, you won't do that. You're such a nice girl, you'll get married and have children." I said: "I'll do both and I'll bet you."' A few years into her studies Collins doubled down on the bet. When she graduated, he paid out the $10. 'That vague ambition was made solid when someone made the mistake of telling me that I could not do it,' she later told fellow MPs.

When studying at Auckland University she met David Wong Tung, a police officer of Chinese-Samoan heritage. Her father disapproved. 'Nice bloke, shame he's black,' he told his daughter after their first meeting. Knowing he would never support the marriage, the couple eloped to Hong Kong after six years together.

Bill English had also tried to put the brakes on her ambition, giving her the low-profile associate health and internal affairs portfolios in her first term. She demanded the justice portfolio. 'I went and saw him, very grumpy.' English said it would do her good to tackle an area she knew nothing about. 'It was actually very good advice. It means I can range a whole lot of portfolios, if I am asked to do so.'

Since then, Collins had shoulder-barged her way through what was left of the glass ceiling in New Zealand politics. 'You cannot achieve to the level that we are expected to achieve worrying that you won't be one of the pack. I've never been someone who has been desperate to be one of the girls, or one of the boys, or anything else. You are one of the team, but at the end of the day, you've got to do your job very well.'

In June 2020, few MPs consoled themselves with the memory of Labour's last-minute substitution in the previous election campaign. None were deluded enough to believe Collins would deliver National a Jacindamania fairy-tale ending.

Support for Muller trickled through. 'No matter what side of parliament you're sitting on, politics is a difficult place,' Ardern said. She passed on her best wishes to Muller and his family. ACT's David Seymour graciously said politics was a competitive and bruising game. 'I just admire him for having the self-honesty and the honesty of others to see what was happening and make a decision — ironically the qualities required of a Prime Minister.' Winston Peters couldn't resist putting the boot in. 'Leading a divided and incompetent caucus would have tested even the best leader. Todd never had a chance given the fault lines of ambition, personality and ideology that run deep through the National Party caucus.'

There was little sympathy for Muller from his own colleagues. 'They got rid of Simon for nothing but personal ambition,' one MP said. 'They took us to the worst polling we've ever had, and now our campaign funds are being eaten up replacing billboards.' Another former MP said the caucus was angry that there was no apology or reflection. 'It was his ego and his team that put him in that position, and then he bailed out on us.' Kaye would later say: 'I don't at all, in any shape or form, have any animosity or think it's anyone else's responsibility but mine.'

Almost all of National's caucus — excluding Muller — followed Collins into her maiden press conference. With her signature bellicosity she declared: 'I am hoping that the National Party can crush the other lot when it comes to September 19. I can't wait. We're just going to have the most fun as we take back the country. The big thing for me is to see and to feel the strength of the team. This is a team game for us. You can't win it without the team.'

Collins also talked up her 'experience, toughness, and the ability to make decisions'. Within the week, she would have to call on those skills.

The following day, as Collins was getting her feet under the desk, the parents of a teenage girl approached the prime minister's office with a complaint. Andrew Falloon, the 36-year-old MP for Rangitata, had sent a picture of a naked woman to the 19-year-old university student on 30 June.

Although he was in his first term, Falloon had been a familiar face at Parliament for more than a decade. In the 2005 and

2008 elections he had stood as a candidate for ACT, and then went on to work as a researcher for ACT leader Rodney Hide. After a spell working for National's fisheries, energy and housing minister Phil Heatley, Falloon moved into Joyce's office. Falloon worked for Joyce for five years, most notably on Novopay, a school payroll crisis that left thousands of teachers out-of-pocket in 2012. There was a short spell as a lobbyist for banks before Falloon was parachuted into the safe blue seat of Rangitata. Technically, he was not a carpet-bagger: Falloon was born and raised in Ashburton in the heart of the electorate. Thanks to the patronage of one of the party's most powerful MPs, Falloon was set for life in politics. But he had his demons, and some of the caucus would later lament that Joyce did not draw attention to his personal problems.

The complaint didn't reach Ardern, who was in Invercargill, until Friday. She sought permission to forward the letter to Collins's office later that day. Police had investigated but determined the incident did not meet the threshold for prosecution. But Falloon would not escape punishment. Collins learned of the problem on Saturday. With Falloon at home in Timaru she decided to wait before confronting him. This was not a matter to be dealt with by emails or phone calls, she said. 'I look people in the eye when I make decisions like this.' Collins summoned him to Wellington.

One staffer was beginning the week in a positive frame of mind, and had stopped off at Copperfield's, Parliament's in-house café. Falloon was there, which was quite unusual for a backbencher on Monday. The staffer took his coffee up to the Leader's floor where Falloon was going in to see Collins. 'The chief of staff just shook her head. I thought: "Ah fuck, here we go." And it was like that just about every day. You'd think it can't get any worse. And then it did.'

At first Falloon was not upfront, telling Collins he'd left the phone unattended at a party and someone else had sent the explicit images. His story would change over the next few days. Chief whip Barbara Kuriger put Falloon on a plane to Christchurch. He was collected by Waimakariri MP Matt Doocey, also the party's mental health spokesman, who then drove Falloon to his parents' house in Ashburton. There were real fears he was a suicide risk. 'There were hints for years,' another staffer says. 'His drinking was out of control, and when they cleared his office out they found all these empty bottles stashed everywhere. Combined with this sexting, it was nuts stuff.'

As Collins made contact with the complainant to apologise, staff began working on Falloon's resignation statement. Like Falloon, it was not entirely truthful, something which Collins's advisors cautioned her against. It was likely the real story would eventually ooze out and only cause more damage. 'Today I spoke to National Party Leader Judith Collins to inform her I will not be contesting the upcoming election,' the statement said. 'As I noted in my maiden speech three years ago, when I was younger I lost three close friends to suicide. It was an extremely difficult period in my life. Unfortunately, recently, another friend took their own life which has brought back much unresolved grief.'

Falloon said he had made a number of mistakes, which he did not detail, and apologised to those affected. He said he had sought counselling. But he intended to stay on, collecting his salary until the end of the year. (MPs who resign, or lose their seat, are entitled to an additional three months' pay following a general election.) 'I want to thank Judith for her support during this time and I look forward to helping a new candidate in the Rangitata electorate in any way I can,' he said. 'I apologise for this disruption to my colleagues and to those I serve in Mid and South Canterbury.'

A sparse release followed from Collins four minutes later. 'Andrew Fallon has advised me that he will not be standing for re-election,' she said. 'The National Party was advised of an issue relating to Andrew late on Friday afternoon and we had dealt with it that morning,' she said. 'Andrew is suffering from significant mental health issues and his privacy and that of his family must be respected.' The mysterious hint of an issue was like blood in the water for journalists. Ardern gave little away at her 4pm weekly press conference. By 5pm Radio NZ was reporting that the complaint concerned pornographic images. The *Herald* website carried further details, including that the incident was 'alcohol-related'. Collins's hopes for a quick clean-up were diminishing. The following morning Stuff reported that a second woman had received explicit messages more than once.

MPs were furious and began demanding Falloon quit immediately. Collins agreed. As she went live to air on Newstalk ZB, Collins received an email, copied to Speaker Trevor Mallard, from Falloon. He has 'resigned from Parliament as of now', she told presenter Mike Hosking. With barely contained fury, Collins said she had lost all confidence in her MP. 'This has gone from clearly what was stated as a mistake to now being something quite different.' His version of events was 'clearly a lie'. Collins said she was no mental health expert. 'But I have to take someone at their word when they're sitting in my office telling me they have significant mental health issues and they have for some time and they're getting professional help and this is what is behind it.' She also raised Falloon's drinking, of which she claimed to have been unaware. 'It now appears that some people were aware that he abused alcohol.' The issue of heavy drinking among MPs would be raised at that morning's caucus meeting.

By the end of the week five women had come forward to say they had received unwanted images from the married MP. The nature of what he sent was unfathomably disturbing. Police re-opened their investigation but eventually decided not to press charges. Collins was furious. The saga had overshadowed her much-anticipated first parliamentary clash with Ardern, who she grilled over Labour's failure to deliver light rail in Auckland. It was a sore point for the prime minister, who had made it her first promise as Labour leader.

Once she dispatched Falloon, Collins turned her ire on Labour. 'Labour's got to learn. Go after one of ours, I'm going after one of theirs,' an MP says she told the caucus. One of theirs was workplace relations minister Iain Lees-Galloway. An MP since 2008, Lees-Galloway had enough of a reputation around Parliament to earn the nickname 'the notorious ILG'.

For a year the married father of three had had a consensual affair with a staffer in one of his agencies. Although it was over, he'd been the subject of whispers for months. Against the advice of her staff Collins used the information to her advantage. As she left her first Question Time as leader, Collins approached Ardern with the 'tip-off'. Ardern's chief of staff Raj Nahna followed up, and at 3pm Ardern's office received an email alleging that an inappropriate relationship had taken place. The fall-out was catastrophic for Lees-Galloway and his young family.

Just before 6pm, Ardern told Lees-Galloway his position was untenable. He would resign from his portfolios and decline to contest the upcoming election. The party would go public with the news on the following morning. Collins couldn't wait. 'She got all Machiavellian,' a staffer remembers. 'That's the way she operates, she couldn't help herself.' Collins gleefully told *The AM Show* she had passed on information about a Labour minister. 'I am not going to be indulging in any attacks on Labour on these things,' she said coyly. But just to make sure the media were titillated she then told Radio New Zealand the information related to 'fairly inappropriate behaviour'.

Ardern called a press conference. 'Over the course of the conversation with the Minister it became clear to me that his position as a Minister was untenable. I advised him of that at the time,' she said. 'The Minister has shown a lack of judgment over a period of 12 months. In undertaking this relationship he has opened himself up to accusations of improperly using his office.' Lees-Galloway had not modelled the behaviour she expected of a minister in charge of setting a standard and culture in workplaces. 'His actions have led me to lose my confidence in him as a Minister.'

Lees-Galloway did not make a public appearance but issued a statement. 'I accept the Prime Minister's decision and apologise absolutely,' he said. 'I have acted completely inappropriately in my position and cannot continue as a Minister.' He begged for his family's privacy to be respected. 'I have apologised to my family for letting them down ... I also apologise to anyone who has been hurt by my actions.'

*

Collins left Muller's remaining shadow Cabinet and staff largely untouched. One notable change was stripping Michael Woodhouse of his health role, passing it to Shane Reti, a Whangārei doctor. Louise Upston received a hasty promotion after staff pointed out that Collins had no women in her top

10. Little-known MP Harete Hipango, a Whanganui lawyer, was moved up 21 places and appointed shadow attorney-general. Collins and Hooton would part ways after a few weeks. Brownlee and Hurdle took over control of the campaign.

The campaign was, by any standards, in total disarray. Depending on which faction is doing the talking, there are different views on how much preparation had been done. 'They made it very clear to me within 48 hours that they weren't interested in the work I'd done and the prep I'd done for the campaign, it was all just completely thrown out the window,' Bennett would later say of her dismissal as campaign chair. 'I had a study at home and I literally called it the war room.' Those loyal to Bridges and Bennett say her work, including a treasure trove of data, was tossed out. Under Muller, little progress had been made on either the campaign or the policy. '[Simon's team] didn't have a campaign plan,' an insider from the Muller camp says. 'Or if there was, they never gave it to us.'

Under the previous leaderships, Crosby Textor turned down a contract for polling. Talks with Isaac Levido — a Lynton Crosby protégé behind Scott Morrison's unexpected 2019 win in Australia and the British Tories' successful re-election — went nowhere. Levido's name was famously chanted to the tune of The White Stripes' 'Seven Nation Army' in Conservative HQ in London on election night. Insiders say there was a difference of opinion on whether National's campaign should revolve around big-picture ideas or the finer details. 'Levido's all about the details,' an insider says. 'It's all about making sure everything's tidy. And, I mean, what would he know? And Topham Guerin didn't want to get involved because Paula is very dictatorial.'

An ex-Crosby Textor strategist had compiled some polling and analysis, but Collins's team discovered it was geared to an aggressive style of politics generally disliked by Kiwis. 'The material was really Australian. It was exactly what an Australian would tell you to do: aggressively attack Jacinda Ardern. Why would you attack the most popular politician in the world? It was stupid advice,' the insider says. Brownlee also baulked at the bill for the advice.

Certainly, there was less money in the war chest. National is used to fighting elections with a huge budget. In 2020 it received $2.8 million in donations. While it was double what Labour pulled, it was much lower than the 2017 haul. 'The money followed Key, and, to an extent, it followed English,' a former party board member says. Fundraising was substantially diminished. 'I'd say we raised a quarter or a third of what we would have raised at previous elections. And a lot of that money came from party members.' The party operates a Victory Fund. As well as levies to the party, each electorate is expected to contribute a lump sum to the fund. The blue-ribbon seats often come up with $30,000. 'This was a million-dollar-plus fund that came from the grassroots of the party,' the member says. 'It was very disciplined. I understand that all went to bits, with some regions and some electorates that failed to pay.'

A campaign insider says initially money was tight. '[Party president Peter] Goodfellow said that was because of the lockdown. It put a lot of pressure on Todd because he was running around trying to pull in money.' The insider cut back campaign expenditure. 'I wasn't spending where I could have because it wasn't very transparent what the budget was.' The leadership changes had also chewed through funds. The party had filmed an ad, with Japanese company Dentsu, featuring Bridges with the caucus on a beach. It had to be scrapped. 'I've worked on other campaigns when you knew the money was flowing because they were hiring; you'd take flights everywhere,' another campaign staffer says. '[This time] they were really watching what they could spend their money on. That showed itself in the number of cars we could hire, down to basics like that.'

Collins and her team made the best of it. A 'policy wheel' — modelled on the Trivial Pursuit boardgame — which had been developed by Hurdle under Muller, was now sharpened up. Policies would sit under five key priorities, or 'wedges'. Collins would announce each policy as part of an overall plan. 'Unfortunately, Labour also came up with a five-point plan,' a staffer says. 'It was basically the same.' Some in the team suspected loose-lipped MPs.

In her first days, Collins made a pledge that one of her first acts in office would be to reform the *Resource Management Act*, replacing it with environmental standards legislation and an urban planning Act. The cumbersome 30-year-old law had long been a bugbear for Collins: she believed an overhaul was key to fixing the country's housing woes. The new policy reflected ideas she laid out in her memoirs. A few weeks later a group of advisors, appointed by the government to review the legislation, would recommend broadly similar proposals.

In her first weekend, Collins also dutifully launched the $31 billion transport policy that Muller had been due to announce. An ambitious plan, it included an expressway linking Whangārei, Auckland, Hamilton and Tauranga. A $1.1 billion policy for roads north of Wellington followed. Collins also scored an early hit by pledging to give unemployed workers access to their KiwiSaver retirement fund to start a business. 'She started off all right,' a staffer says. 'She was also actually reasonably influenceable in terms of message and what to talk about.' That would change, dramatically, over the course of the following weeks.

The first opinion poll was not kind, with National's vote plummeting to 25.1 per cent. (Labour was on an unrealistic 60.9 per cent, and Brownlee dismissed it as rogue, questioning the methodology.) By the end of the week another poll showed support for National had rallied to 32 per cent, with 20 per cent favouring Collins as PM, someway behind Ardern's 54. Interestingly ACT's vote was on the rise, up to 5 per cent. Labour was also on 53 per cent and on those results could govern alone. Collins consoled herself with internal polling, which put National's support higher, but she was also keenly aware that a dissatisfied party had rolled Bridges when polling hit 30 per cent under him. She was also haunted by her own words just two years earlier. In running for the leadership then, she had insisted she would quit if support dropped below 35 per cent. 'Once things start getting under 35 per cent, people start saying, "Can we win?" And I know I am putting a mark up there which at some stage in the future, if I am successful this time, that people will say, "Well, you set that mark,"' she said. 'Yep, let me set that mark.'

Parliament dissolved in early August, and a few days later Ardern launched Labour's re-election campaign with the war cry: *This is a Covid election.* To a sea of red packed into Auckland's town hall, she said: 'If you had told me then that our launch in 2020 would be in the midst of a global pandemic with our borders closed I would have found that very hard to fathom. If you'd told me that Clarke [Gayford] and I would have a toddler I wouldn't have believed we would have been so lucky. And if you'd told me that we would have just completed a term in government with both New Zealand First and the Greens, I'd assume you'd been watching excessive amounts of *Stranger Things* on Netflix. And yet here we are.'

The launch was accompanied by a $300 million package to get the unemployed back into work. The Flexi-wage, a subsidy to help employers hire those on a benefit, was largely an expansion of a National Government policy introduced in 2012. It was also safe and centrist and a clear pointer to Labour's approach to the campaign. The launch was exuberant, with just the right amount of Ardern's stardust. Kicking off with country and soul singer Tami Neilson, the MC was actor and comedian Oscar Kightley. Ardern's television host partner Gayford also warmed up the crowd.

Ardern was forced to delay election day until 17 October after National complained the public health restrictions gave Labour an advantage. The public health emergency gave Ardern a public platform, with daily press conferences, denied to the other parties who had to suspend campaigning. Parliament resumed until early September, but most MPs remained in their electorates. Over those few weeks, Collins proposed a raft of policies. There was a plan to establish a National Infrastructure Bank, to organise funding for big projects. Another proposal would see car insurance details displayed on vehicles. She also revived the party's 'war on P' — the street name for pure methamphetamine in a crystallised form. Tackling meth abuse was a hallmark of the Key administration. An inquiry into the Whakaari/White Island disaster was also promised. However, as the country grappled with the return of Covid, National found it difficult to gain traction. It was reduced to attacking the government's broadly successful response.

Once the campaign resumed, Labour threw everything at it. A battery of policy launches kicked off with the populist proposal to create a new public holiday to celebrate Matariki, the Māori New Year. The following day they announced a new tax policy, hiking the tax rates on incomes over $180,000. This was tipping the hat at fairness but in reality affected just 2 per cent of Kiwis. At the end of the week came an energy policy geared towards making all of New Zealand's electricity generation from renewable sources by 2030.

The following day, Collins travelled to Auckland to launch a policy around electric vehicles, developed by rising star Erica Stanford. At a dealership in the beachside suburb of Takapuna, Collins promised to have 80,000 EVs on the road by 2023. The policy sat under the 'smarter, greener future' wedge. But Collins appeared reluctant. 'In modern politics, you have to say stuff about the environment,' a staffer says. 'Judith didn't like that green stuff. She's quite funny about climate change. She's got a real hard-on for farmers.' She returned from Auckland in a fury after receiving a slew of emails from angry supporters. 'People were telling her she'd gone woke and they were going to vote ACT.' What followed became known to staffers as 'the Monday Night Massacre'.

A meeting was called for early evening. Reti, Brownlee and Todd McClay were among the 40 or so people in the caucus room. Over the weekend, Collins had ordered the campaign team to come up with new slogans. The entire network of billboards was to be replaced at a cost of about $50 per hoarding. 'She tore strips off us,' the staffer says. 'Told us what was going wrong.' Collins told the team she didn't want to wear another high-vis jacket — a hallmark of campaign factory visits — or drink another cup of tea. 'She does this mad stare. It was quite uncomfortable.' Collins decreed she was taking charge of the campaign. She ripped up the campaign diaries that were carefully plotted on a grid. There would be relentless demands for new policy, provoking a split among the campaign team. 'The wheels started coming off when she decided to change the entire campaign at the eleventh hour,' another staffer says. 'She invited us in to upbraid us. From that time onwards, she increasingly didn't seek out counsel or advice. It was like a great dénouement.' Collins chose a new slogan and the meeting wrapped up. The change-up was 'squarely Judith's decision', Janet Wilson later confirmed. 'It was very much a captain's call. She decided that she didn't like the campaign, that she wanted to throw everything out.'

The original billboard design featuring Collins and Brownlee and the slogan *Strong Team. More Jobs. Better Economy* was replaced with just Collins and the message: *Your economy, Your future.* In some electorates, the leadership team disappeared altogether from advertising. The central campaign was a disaster, an MP says. 'Candidates were getting collateral [advertising material] very late. We saw collateral go out there with wrong spelling, graphics had our numbers wrong.'

Collins also had a new demand, the staffer says. She wanted a fiscal plan to emulate one waved by Ardern during a Newshub debate in the 2017 campaign. 'She thought that was great.' The team cautioned that alternative budgets almost always go badly wrong. 'Why would you go there? You don't have the resources to get something like that right: normally the entire Treasury does a Budget.' The staffer says the task was given to Goldsmith, as finance spokesman, who then entrusted it to a young researcher. Economics agency NZIER was paid to review the figures.

On 18 September, Collins and Goldsmith unveiled the alternative Budget. Journalists were treated to a Friday morning breakfast at Wellington's InterContinental hotel and given an hour to scrutinise the documents.

The big selling point was a 16-month temporary tax cut that put an extra $50 a week in the pocket of an average earner,

Collins claimed from a podium in the hotel's grand ballroom. The package was worth about $4.7 billion, to be paid for by raiding a Covid-19 response fund. Goldsmith's plan was a better way, Collins boasted. 'Responsible economic management has been a hallmark of successive National Governments. The government I lead will continue that tradition,' she said. Commentators were enthusiastic: finally the campaign delivered a bone to chew over. Ten days earlier Labour's Grant Robertson had announced he would bring back the top 39 per cent income tax rate. There was now a real choice between what the two main parties were offering: a dose of fiscal stimulus sugar set against Labour's wage subsidy and infrastructure spending.

The fast-paced drama of an election campaign means politicians are expected to deliver an instantaneous, snappy reaction. Robertson had his soundbite ready: National's policies were 'desperate and reckless' he concluded, two hours after the plan was made public. It was standard election mud-slinging and Collins shrugged it off, returning to her Auckland home. She took the following day off public events to rehearse and prepare for her party's official campaign launch to be held at Avalon Studios in the Hutt Valley.

But something was niggling at Robertson. Returning from Palmerston North in a heavy rainstorm, he began to look through the supporting documents released with National's policy. National had used the wrong numbers in calculating how much it would save from halting NZ Super Fund contributions. It had relied on Budget numbers from May, but the numbers had changed in the Pre-Election Fiscal Update (PREFU) a week earlier. From the back of his Crown limo, Robertson placed a call to his economics advisor Craig Renney. At his desk in Robertson's ministerial offices, Renney got to work, meticulously poring over the fiscal policy. Renney, a Geordie whose chirpy demeanour belies a razor-sharp mind, was part of Robertson's team that were blindsided in 2017 by Steven Joyce's accusations of an $11 billion fiscal hole in Labour's Budget. Bitter experience taught the former Treasury analyst to scour the spreadsheets. Renney checked and re-checked the calculations. The boss was correct — National's numbers were out by at least $4 billion.

Ardern had spent the day campaigning in the Wairarapa, squeezed with a camera crew from the Augusto creative agency into the soon-to-be-infamous red ute of local MP Kieran McAnulty. They were making a Facebook video, *It's not every day you get the PM in your ute*, later celebrated for folksy interactions between Ardern and her MP. Robertson and Ardern met that evening in Greytown's picturesque White Swan Hotel. The finance minister and his aide excitedly relayed to Ardern what they'd learned. 'Sit on it,' said Robertson.

That Sunday, National had planned their launch. Originally to take place in South Auckland in late August, it was delayed when an outbreak of Covid-19 forced the city into another lockdown. The launch was to focus on the party's track record in economic management. There was no choice but to make it virtual, with Covid restrictions dictating that only 100 people could attend in person. MPs contributed via livestream, with the event hosted by outgoing MP Maggie Barry.

Three hours before it was due to start, Robertson dropped a press release pointing to the mistake and delivering a blistering critique of National's competence. He then held a press conference on the steps of Parliament. 'If National can't even do the basics required on their own policy costings, they cannot be trusted to run the country,' he said. 'Making mistakes like this have real-world consequences that New Zealand does not need in this challenging time in our history.' Rubbing salt into the wound he went on: 'There is no John Key or Bill English there anymore. No one who knows how to run a Budget would have made a basic mistake like this.' He would repeatedly return to the theme throughout the campaign. He said National would oversee massive cuts to public services. 'National's policy is desperate, irresponsible and unaffordable ... This is a time for stability and certainty, not policy made up on the fly that does not add up.'

The launch script remained unchanged, but the $4 billion mistake dominated Collins's post-speech press conference. At first she tried bluster, claiming 'nothing Grant Robertson says worries me' and that the error was 'entirely inconsequential'. Eventually she conceded the error. 'It was owned up ... if everybody went through life thinking they could never ever make an error, no one would get out of bed in the morning.' The numbers were simply forecasts, she said. 'Goldie is feeling very bad on it,' she added, shafting home the blame.

It was satisfying political theatre for Robertson, who'd been irritated by Joyce's tactics in 2017. It also served to underline what Labour's internal poll had been telling the party since at least the beginning of the year: voters trusted Ardern and her team on the economy over National for the first time in perhaps a generation. 'The mistake that was made with National's fiscal plan could have been forgiven if people trusted them on the issue,' Labour campaign chair Megan Woods said. 'It became so big for National because people were having doubts about their ability to lead New Zealand out [of the Covid-19 pandemic].'

The leadership team had given candidates little notice of the economic plan, which included the pitch to cut taxes, despite Collins having ruled that out in early August. 'Policy was a disaster zone,' one incredulous MP said. 'All we saw at the start was big spending — whether it was Bishop [on infrastructure], [Nicola] Willis on education, or [Shane] Reti on health. They were coming up with big numbers, and that was a massive mistake because it made us indistinguishable from Labour.'

The tax cuts confused voters, the MP believes. 'Grant Robertson made the best point of the entire campaign: we'd fallen into some sort of economic Bermuda triangle. We were going to spend everything, but we were also going to be better on debt and provide tax relief.' The MP believes tax relief was the right policy: just at the wrong time. 'If we had done it at the very start of the Judith Collins time and relentlessly pushed that, while giving a very serious nod to health and education, that would have been a very effective campaign.' Goldsmith's blunder had torpedoed what was left of National's best weapon — economic credibility. The campaign was floundering.

Collins sidelined many of the campaign team and some of her inner circle, including Goldsmith and agriculture spokesman David Bennett. She turned her attention to debate preparation, with Nicola Willis again standing in for Ardern. The first of four planned head-to-heads took place at TVNZ's studios in Auckland. Covid restrictions meant there was no live audience. Collins opted to have two loyal staff members — press secretary Julie Johnston, who had worked for her in government, and policy head Paul Melville — at her side. Chief press secretary Janet Wilson was frozen out and had to watch the broadcast with journalists in the green room.

The tone was set by a new poll that saw Labour drop five points to 48 per cent. It was still enough to govern alone and National had also dropped a point to 31 per cent, but Collins was energised. Over 90 minutes she lambasted Ardern over failures at the border that saw Covid seep in, the 20,000-long wait-list for state housing and increasing rates of child poverty. Commentators largely declared Collins the winner. A super-fan revealed his tattoo of Collins holding a pistol and posing like a Bond girl. Underneath was inked: *Crusher Collins*.

But Collins's decision to take charge soon came unstuck. In early October, she was scheduled to cast her advance vote at the hall attached to the old stone St Thomas's Church in the Auckland suburb of Kohimarama. She went off-script. Collins was greeted by priest Father Bob Driver, who invited her to pray. To the horror of her staff, she agreed and took along the cameras, being captured on camera kneeling in the tiny chapel. The symbolism of the 'come to Jesus moment' was unfortunate, and Collins was later accused of politicising her faith. The stunt also played badly with the party base. 'The moment you have to resort to kneeling down and praying in a church in the middle of an election campaign: oh fuck,' says long-serving former MP Maurice Williamson. 'That looks so desperate. It was about as bad as Don Brash trying to walk the bloody plank.' (A picture of Collins's mentor balancing on a piece of wood between a wharf and a boat became the defining image of the 2005 election.) Winston Peters mocked her in quoting a biblical verse, Matthew 6:5–6. 'And when you pray, do not be like the hypocrites for they love to pray standing in the synagogues and on the street corners to be seen by others ... But when you pray go into your room, close the door and pray to your Father, who is unseen.'

Collins then decided to launch a new plan to review Auckland Council. The idea had come from Hurdle, who'd noticed the anniversary of the supercity was approaching. The existing policy was to have an audit function. 'That's about as exciting as a cold cup of tea,' a staffer says. The team decided to make some last-minute changes. 'It was quite a good issue: one of the few organisations that is more hated than the National Party is Auckland Transport and Auckland Council.' Appearing on Newstalk ZB's *Leaders Breakfasts* series, Collins announced she would hold an inquiry within 100 days of taking office. 'I have a particular beef with Auckland Transport. I just think it's destroyed the central city,' she said, railing against plans 'to make everything about cycling and walking'.

Paul Melville was tasked with informing Denise Lee, a first-term MP and the party's spokeswoman on Auckland Council. The message didn't get through, and Lee, the daughter of Graeme Lee, a National MP who had broken away to found the Christian Democrat Party, was incandescent. Neither Hurdle nor Brownlee was able to soothe her. In a fury, she fired off a strong email, copying in the entire caucus. Lee panned the idea as 'highly problematic' and said it would be 'a nightmare'. Bypassing her was 'incredibly poor form and displays a shockingly bad example of poor culture', she wrote. As well as around 50 MPs, the missive also went to about 100 of their staff. 'The minute I saw it I thought: ah fuck, here we go,' a staffer said. 'We started debating whether it would make the 10 or 11 o'clock news.' The email was duly leaked, and Collins was confronted by reporters as she tried to launch a rent-to-buy state housing policy. She was forced to deny making up policy on the hoof, saying the policy was developed over several weeks. Lee publicly apologised, but the damage was done.

Labour pounced, issuing a press release from Robertson. 'National are still the chaotic shambles they have been all year and are not fit to govern,' he said. He challenged Collins to release evidence that the policy had been worked on for weeks. 'If she can't then it raises serious questions around the accuracy of her statement. They are now a divided party who pose a real threat to our economic recovery if they were elected.' The staffer laments that two good policies were ruined by leaks. 'By the end of the day the story ended up being about disunity in the National Party and in the campaign.'

Collins was also facing allegations that she was refusing to show internal polling to the caucus, which was disaffected by a lack of communication. Later, Collins would write: 'The destabilisation from this leak was a body blow to the National Party that we never recovered from.' She believes Lee's leaked email cost the party five points in opinion polling.

Rattled, Collins headed to Christchurch for *The Press* Leaders Debate. It was a feisty match but the crowd were undeniably friendly to Ardern. It was shaping up to be the week from hell for Collins. Back in Auckland, staff had planned for Collins to do a 'walkabout' in Commercial Bay, a slick new shopping precinct in the heart of the city. 'We had to do something public, otherwise we look like we are hiding,' the staffer says. The team judged the mall would be a safe venue, full of lunching office workers. But Collins refused, saying she was embarrassed by canvassing people while they ate. 'She just was very absolute.' The advance team scrambled. The Auckland Central electorate visit was already going to be problematic. After Kaye's shock resignation, the selection process to find a new candidate was messy and bungled. The party had broken their own rules by not shortlisting enough people. Emma Mellow, a 30-year-old bank communications manager, was eventually chosen. Hamish Price, an eccentric activist known for his incendiary social media posts, was involved in planning.

Collins was to walk up Ponsonby Road, an affluent stretch of road populated with cafés and boutiques. She was greeted by well-wishers, but the interactions were blatantly staged by Mellow and Price. It went from bad to worse: an optometrist turned her away, saying, 'We don't want you here.' And in a café she sat next to a poll, counted out in M&Ms, which put Labour well ahead.

As Collins campaigned, Matthew Hooton jumped to her defence. Muller's former right-hand man tweeted: 'When Nats' deputy leadership changed in May there was no policy, no benchmark polling, no campaign themes, no campaign grid and the Curia track polls were worse than any public poll this year. However the election turns out, Judith has done better than what would have happened.' Paula Bennett, the former campaign chair, bit back: 'Bullshit. It just wasn't shared with you.' Grant Robertson couldn't help himself, sharing the exchange with a simple: 'Strong. Team'. In a post-walkabout media conference, Collins was left to explain away the internal divisions. She was heard to exclaim 'Dear God' as she walked to her waiting car.

The debacle was contrasted on the tea-time news bulletins with Ardern being rapturously greeted first in Lyttelton and then later at Otago University. Wilson, who shared duties with another press secretary that day, later described it as 'one of those moments that you knew was going to go completely pear-shaped. I knew that there was going to be people who would go and meet her but not people who lined up like soldiers down Ponsonby Road. In the pantheon of bad, that wasn't the pinnacle of bad. There were other moments that were equally as bad.'

In a bid to salvage the last few days of the campaign there were more demands for policy. Collins was advised by Todd McClay, who believed the party should announce something every day. 'And so she kept wanting to have something fresh to say,' a staffer says. Her advisors wanted her to stay on-message. 'She starts wandering off. The Gallery started working out that they could bait her and drag her off-topic.' A viticulture plan was rushed through in time for a last-minute visit to Blenheim. 'It got so silly that in the last week we [were told] we need five announcements,' the staffer says. Another adds: 'Who was driving the campaign car? It was by and large Judith, and Judith didn't know anything about running a campaign.'

MPs began to dread the call that she was coming to their electorate. Leader visits are a mainstay of modern political campaigns focused on increasing the party vote. In 2014, such was David Cunliffe's unpopularity that candidates were desperate to avoid a constituency visit from the Labour leader. One Labour MP talks of feigning illness to stave off a tour. 'If I had [Collins] in my electorate, it was actually a net negative for me,' one MP confided. 'I'm capable of locking in our National supporters myself. But I need to appeal to the Centre voters to get our party vote up, and Judith doesn't appeal to the Centre. She's our Cunliffe.'

One such electorate visit was cancelled at the last minute. Three days out from polling day, she was due in Tauranga. It was a strategic blunder, an awkward reminder of the party's recent internal struggles. The city is home to Muller and the man he rolled, Simon Bridges. No one told Bridges. He learned of the planned visit when his former parliamentary staffer Michael Fox, now working for kiwifruit co-operative Zespri, called to firm up plans. The Collins caravan diverted to Hamilton. One MP says the gaffe was symptomatic of the 'complete disarray' that enveloped National's campaign. 'It was probably the right decision and better to be in Hamilton. But in the end we lost both those seats, too,' another MP said.

Six days out from polling day, Collins tacked further right. She announced 'Stop the Wealth Tax' day, railing against a Green Party policy that targeted anyone with a net wealth of over

$1 million. Joining a 'human hoarding' event — where volunteers wave placards, usually at busy intersections — Collins grabbed a bullhorn. 'Do we want a wealth tax?' she demanded of supporters wearing windbreakers in party colours. 'What does a wealth tax mean? Labour and Greens.' A press release followed. 'National out to stop the Wealth Tax,' it said. 'The burden of the tax will be particularly felt by the elderly and those who have saved for their retirement,' Collins said. 'Labour have already promised to raise income taxes but the wealth tax will be a point of pride for a Labour/Green government desperate to raise revenues to pay off its spending.' The tactic was problematic. Labour had repeatedly ruled out introducing the tax no matter their post-election arrangements with the Greens. In response the Greens downgraded the policy from a 'bottom-line' in coalition talks, signalling they were prepared to walk away if it meant a role in government.

Collins was asking voters to believe her assertion over that of Ardern, one of the world's most trusted leaders. It reeked of desperation. Ardern dismissed the claims as 'the last roll of the misinformation dice'.

Ignoring the flawed logic and the advice of her team, Collins ploughed on. She hammered the issue throughout the following day on a campaign stop in Christchurch. 'I don't believe for a moment that these guys aren't going to come after everyone's money that's been hard worked for and they want to take it off them,' she said. The party came under fire for a Facebook advertising campaign that claimed retirees would pay an extra $140 a week because of the tax. She dismissed the inflated figures as a 'digital error', but the Advertising Standards Authority ruled it misleading. (It would be the third complaint upheld that year, with earlier decisions on ads about car emissions and welfare).

Later, MPs and supporters would blame Collins's wealth campaign for a cratering of support in provincial electorates. It was assumed rural voters, also anxious about freshwater reforms, voted Labour to keep the Greens out of government. David Clark, Mid Canterbury president of advocacy group Federated Farmers, said: 'I think potentially plenty of farmers have voted Labour so they can govern alone rather than having a Labour–Greens government — there's been a lot of chat around about that.' Speaking post-election, Collins also backed the theory. 'We've certainly heard from some media who have asked and some parts of the farming communities that they voted Labour because they wanted to stop the Greens. I think the main thing is that nobody wanted the Greens in government.' However, the New Zealand Election Survey later concluded the idea was 'a little far-fetched'.

In the final straights both Labour and National focused their attention on marginal seats. Ardern went to Hutt South where National's Chris Bishop held one of the smallest margins in the country. Rather than fighting his corner, Bishop was diverted to the neighbouring, tightly contested Ōhāriu seat to join candidate Brett Hudson and Collins. She went all in on the wealth tax. Over three days, the campaign spent thousands of dollars on a social media advertising blitz. But Collins was quickly dragged off-topic when bored reporters asked about earlier comments on obesity. In a radio interview she'd said: 'People need to start taking some personal responsibility for their weight.' Experts widely condemned her remarks. (One in three New Zealanders are obese, with the problem more prevalent in areas of socio-economic deprivation.) 'Do you know what is heartless? Is actually thinking someone else can cure these issues. We can all take personal responsibility and we all have to own up to our little weaknesses on these matters,' she told reporters gathered in the Grenada Community Hall. 'Do not blame systems for personal choices.'

The outburst sparked days of debate, opinion pieces and headlines. Brownlee defended her, saying he believed his size was his responsibility. MP and former defence minister Mark Mitchell broke ranks with Collins, saying the issue 'was a lot more complex than that'. Collins's public appearances developed an absurdity familiar to viewers of *The Thick of It*, a satirical comedy set in the world of British politics. Nick Smith calls them 'her weird brain farts'. Many in the caucus believed Collins was still in regular contact with Cameron Slater, and with his apprentice in attack politics Jordan Williams, director of pressure group Taxpayers' Union. 'It is partly down to the people that you put around you,' Smith says. 'If I look at some of the people that Judith put around her, and the people that she takes counsel from, it scares the shit out of me.'

At one point Collins was attacked for weaponising her husband's Samoan ethnicity. Answering a question in a debate she started off by saying, 'My husband is Samoan, so: talofa.' It sparked a spin-off line of merchandise, including a mug featuring her face and the greeting. As well as the digression into fat-shaming, she accused Ardern of lying, goaded the Labour leader to sue her, and then accused her rival of name-calling. There were attacks on the media and an incautious explanation of how, as a tax lawyer, she used to help people avoid inheritance tax. 'What typified the whole campaign for me was we had [Brownlee], our deputy leader and campaign manager, in the media explaining that he is responsible for his own obesity,' one MP said. 'How mad is that? How off-topic is that?' Another said senior MPs weren't talking to each other. 'Judith would say what she wanted at the media stand-ups because there wasn't anyone else giving her clear direction, certainly in the last two weeks.'

Some insiders backed Collins. A campaign staffer says she had 'a real dignity' about her in the dying days of the campaign. 'Judith was given the hospital pass,' another rueful MP said. 'I don't think anyone can criticise her. She took the bull by the horns, got up every morning and fronted; she was herself. If anyone could have pulled a rabbit it was Judith Collins, but it was just too much of a tall ask.'

As voting day loomed, a poll sent by Labour's polling company UMR to its corporate clients was eerily prescient, putting National on 27 per cent. By the final day Collins had dumped the wealth tax issue. In the last 1 News/Colmar Brunton poll of the campaign the Greens gained two points and National was down a point to 31 per cent. In the fourth and final television debate, Ardern shut her down on the wealth tax. 'I have to call you out on this,' Ardern said. 'I am putting an end to it. It's just wrong. I would never stand here and blatantly call someone a liar. And that is what Judith is doing. It's a desperate tactic and, frankly, it's sad.'

Collins looked defeated. Less than 48 hours from the close of polling booths, she conceded: 'There's a lot worse things than to be sitting on the Opposition benches.'

12

CRUSHED

THE DAMNING VERDICT OF the postmortem was: 'The genesis of the many issues faced by the Party in the last term stem fundamentally from poor leadership and resulting bad culture and actions by bad actors which were often not called out early.' National's crushing election defeat triggered an internal review. The party had lost 23 seats, dropping from 56 to 33. Around 20 MPs lost their jobs, including former ministers Alfred Ngaro and Tim Macindoe, party stalwart Jonathan Young and Lawrence Yule.

A red tide swept National from heartland seats, including Rangitata, the country's most conservative electorate. Nelson and Christchurch's Ilam, held since 1996 by Nick Smith and Gerry Brownlee respectively, were lost. The party vote was decimated. On 50 per cent, Labour had enough support to govern alone, the first time this had happened under MMP. Te Pāti Māori returned to Parliament, with Rawiri Waititi taking Waiariki from Labour, bringing in with him co-leader Debbie Ngarewa-Packer. The Green's Chlöe Swarbrick secured Auckland Central, the party's first electorate win since 2002.

ACT's goofy leader David Seymour defied the polls and rode a wave of success from 0.5 per cent in 2017 to 8 per cent on election night. For six years he was a lonely figure at Parliament, the party's sole representative. Now he would return to Wellington with nine new MPs. Despite travelling 12,000 kilometres over six weeks on his campaign bus, Winston Peters could not hold onto his 41-year political career. New Zealand First secured just 2.7 per cent of the vote. National sat on a miserable 25.6 per cent. Epsom — which Seymour held — was the only electorate where it won the party vote. They had lost over 400,000 votes. The review said the results should be 'both a sobering and awakening moment for the Party'.

After 70 gruelling days and a stuttering campaign, Collins watched the final counts come in from a hotel room on the twenty-first floor of Auckland's SkyCity Grand hotel. Her electoral chances were so crushed that she was forced to partly rework her speech. 'We expected it, but just not so bad,' one departing MP revealed. Collins telephoned Ardern to offer congratulations on her 'outstanding result'. Around 10pm Collins, with husband David Wong Tung, made the short trip to the Royal New Zealand Yacht Squadron on Westhaven Marina to deliver her concession speech. The wrap party was a maudlin affair. Auckland-based MPs Paul Goldsmith, Melissa Lee, Chris Penk and Simeon Brown joined around 100 supporters. Glass bowls of sad-looking blue and white streamers were dotted around the room, with a handful of balloons the only other decoration. Guests consoled themselves with sushi and limp sandwiches. There was no bar tab.

Despite the result, Collins was given a hero's welcome, with the crowd chanting her name as she made her way to the stage. A drunken woman yelled 'Talofa, bitches!' 'Anyone would have thought we won,' Collins said, reaching the stage. 'Boy, did we know this was going to be tough,' she said. 'Even though tonight has been a very tough night for us all … three years will be gone in the blink of an eye and I say to everybody, "We will be back."'

True to form, Collins gave no signal that she would be resigning. The party would reflect, review and change, she promised: 'National will emerge from this loss a stronger, disciplined and more connected party.' With that, Collins retired upstairs for her first drink in weeks, a glass of red wine.

Consigned to the political wilderness for another three years, the recriminations began. In the live election coverage, Bridges told 1 News: 'It's grim. I can't think of a worse night except for possibly 2002.' The party didn't have a plan or a strategy, he said. Candidates 'weren't really sure what they should be saying on the issues'. The party would have to do 'some real soul-searching'. Bridges held onto his Tauranga seat.

Other MPs were livid with the leadership. 'Gerry and Judith both share fault in this. It's galling to see them portraying themselves as reluctant heroes who it was thrust upon,' one said. 'Judith crawled over broken glass for a decade to get this job; she isn't some Joan of Arc figure. Sadly, when she got there, there was nothing. She didn't even have an A4 of a plan.'

Another predicted her demise. 'She has had her day. She is from a bygone era. She's brittle, I don't believe she is the face of National, and she definitely won't be the leader going into '23.'

Brownlee said he would not seek re-election as Collins's deputy. 'It's my strong view that Judith campaigned extremely well in what was an unprecedented election,' he said in a statement. Brownlee was proud to have stepped up, but he added: 'I've always believed that influence is more important than position when it comes to politics … I want Judith to have the strongest and most complementary support beside her as leader.'

Collins hung on. There was no appetite to get rid of her, and no one else wanted the job. Mark Mitchell, the only realistic contender, ruled himself out almost immediately. There was half-hearted speculation about Christopher Luxon, but as he had been a MP for mere days it was unrealistic. Shane Reti was appointed deputy leader. When the gentle doctor was elected to Whangārei in 2014, he was the first Māori MP for the region.

In late November the party drafted a panel to review the defeat. It was led by Botany electorate chair Mark Darrow, and included former president Judy Kirk. Former minister Kate Wilkinson was enlisted, but her name does not appear on the final report. Their conclusions made ugly reading. Of the Key administration, they wrote: '[It] was characterised as a strong team with tight management of caucus but relied on a smaller group of key people. The Key/English/Joyce/Eagleson team encouraged back-benchers to concentrate on learning their trade and focusing on their own electorates, while the Board focused effectively on fundraising.' But that created an 'underlying frustration and growing unrest' from newer MPs who were not involved in government proceedings. The panel formed a strong view that the National caucus never accepted the 2017 election loss. 'Resentment pervaded their approach to opposition,' they concluded. Being the largest Opposition since the introduction of MMP was a double-edged sword. 'Managing a large team is even more difficult, particularly with a large intake of new MPs.'

They described the 2018 leadership contest between Simon Bridges, Mark Mitchell, Steven Joyce and Judith Collins as 'divisive'. It thrust MPs, and in particular the 2017 intake, into 'a position where they were quickly very important'. Twice more, after the ascension and resignation of Todd Muller, less experienced MPs were placed into areas of great responsibility and profile. 'Accounts of chat-groups, factions, undermining and resulting poor behaviour were prolific.' In a blistering verdict, the panel said: 'The abhorrent acts of bad actor individuals with disunity, undermining and ongoing information leaks plagued the 2017–2020 term.'

English and Bridges both came in for criticism. Both leaders had offered each of the National MPs a spokesperson role. That led to 'entitled and emboldened individuals, resulting in selfish and divisive factions, rather than a cohesive team'. The Muller coup 'caused a disconnection point' and a loss of strategy, planning, momentum and continuity. What resulted was 'a party operating within an out of date and opaque policy paradigm'. The panel found 'a toxic culture of bullying, mistrust, disunity and undermining within caucus'. MPs had acted 'in self-interest showing poor behaviour'. It was coupled with 'ineffective governance from a Board too involved in operational matters'.

Covid-19 and the government's response undoubtedly had a significant effect on the election result, the panel conceded. But it was also damning of MPs' reactions. The party 'neither responded well … nor conducted themselves in a way to gain the public's confidence'. The pandemic was a tipping point that set off a chain of events, one of which was the disastrous campaign. 'The analysis shows that the National Party did not connect with large parts of society and struggled for relevancy within an old policy paradigm.' The reviewers pointed to many mistakes in policy and strategy, which created 'poor messaging, a lack of clarity and a perverse outcome of tactical voting'.

Its conclusions on the campaign were brutal. Rather unfairly, the panel did not interview Hurdle and only spent a brief amount of time with Brownlee. It found 'a lack of professionalism of campaign team leadership' and the discontinuation of policy formation. The panel pointed to 'poor choices' on campaign policy. The review specifically singled out the positions on obesity and wealth tax. There were also 'weaknesses and errors' in talent identification, candidate selection and list-ranking processes, and in 'governance and basic processes'. All of this contributed to 'a complete loss of continuity and momentum in 2020'.

Only the party's nine-member board were given copies of the report. Instead, MPs had to file into a caucus meeting and read the documents, which they were not allowed to take away. Collins was worried the report would leak. 'We do not give our opponents extra ammunition to attack us on every day,' she said.

Rebounding from the defeat was always going to be a difficult task. The voters had comprehensively rejected Collins and her brand of politics. Her leadership was blighted by the perception that she was only ever a placeholder until a more viable challenger emerged. Her first set-piece speech of the year identified the party's priorities: housing and infrastructure, the pandemic response, economic recovery, hardship and safety, technology, and post-Covid opportunities. Climate change and environmental issues were conspicuous by their absence. Speaking to the Rotary Club of Auckland at Ellerslie Racecourse, she called for emergency legislation to make it easier to build houses. Under her leadership the party would be 'relentlessly focused on the things that are important to making New Zealanders' lives better', she said. MPs would push the government to focus on the causes, not just the symptoms, of the country's problems. 'National will be kind but not at the expense of getting things done,' she said.

It didn't take long for that relentless focus to be knocked off course.

'Nothing changed,' a senior MP says. 'She created a very poor culture immediately.' Staff morale was low. Hooton, Hurdle,

Wilson and Campbell left soon after the election. 'We couldn't hire people. She's a bully. She threatens. And she was never ever going to be someone that could unify a caucus because she'd spent her whole career undermining every leader that she served under.'

Collins decided to return to her old stomping ground: law and order. She saw mileage in attacking the government over the resurgent motorcycle gang scene. Australia's policy of returning people with criminal convictions — who became known as 501s after the relevant clause in legislation — was blamed for a rise in gang-related violence. Collins had demoted Bridges after the election, but the former criminal prosecutor held the justice portfolio. Bridges launched several attacks on new police commissioner Andrew Coster, calling him a wokester who was more interested in being nice than catching criminals.

The spat culminated in a fiery exchange during a sitting of Parliament's justice select committee. Bridges opened with: 'Do the police still arrest people in this country?' He went on to suggest Coster was tougher on MPs than gang members. Coster gave as good as he got. Over a week the row generated plenty of headlines. Not all of them were positive. Collins, a former police minister and still popular with rank-and-file officers, felt bound to defend the force. She publicly and privately reprimanded Bridges. He was not the police spokesman and this was not the party's position, she said. She also disapproved of the term 'wokester'. 'I've always made it very clear we don't attack the commissioners, it's the ministers who set the agenda,' she said. 'I've made it clear that the focus needs to be on the government and the ministers.'

But Bridges defied her. He appeared on *The AM Show* and continued the attacks. 'I respect Judith, she's doing a good job.

There's only one person that reprimands me, and that's Natalie Bridges,' he said. The whole episode only served to remind the public that National's internal divisions were not behind them. Polling was barely shifting from the election result, although Ardern's personal popularity was now beginning to slide.

By April 2021 a fresh batch of leadership speculation was brewing. The *Herald*'s political editor, Claire Trevett, used her regular Saturday column to reveal the party was considering reinstating Bridges, with Christopher Luxon as his deputy and finance spokesman. 'This plan is still in its infancy,' she wrote. Some believed Bridges could make a comeback as Ardern's Covid honeymoon waned, she wrote. 'The theory is that if Bridges cannot pull it off, Luxon would at least be ready to go.' The discord had its roots in yet another leak from a caucus meeting. MPs had voted down plans by Collins and Reti to oppose the government's plans to centralise the control of water fluoridation. Even to hold a vote was a rare move.

The dispute was aired by Newshub. Collins was once again forced into defending her leadership, claiming it was mischief-making. 'Actually everyone is on-side and I have the 100 per cent support of my caucus,' she said. She claimed the story was 'highly wrong' and pointed to her consistent support for removing control from councils. Bridges fronted up to a radio station to deny he was plotting. He dismissed the 'rumour' as 'crazy silly talk'.

Nonetheless, the scuttlebutt made the commentariat take a closer look at Luxon. Christchurch-born and Auckland-raised, Luxon spent the first 18 years of his corporate career working around the world for Unilever, growing sales of men's deodorants and soap, and then taking charge of Unilever Canada. In 2011, he returned home to work for Air New Zealand. Within a year he was chief executive of the national carrier. By 2018, he was earning more than $4 million a year, making him one of the country's highest-earning executives.

By 2016, the airline was earning record profits, helped by weak fuel prices and booming tourism. He had big plans. The airline signed new code-share agreements and alliance deals and opened new international routes. With New Zealand's tourism sector booming, there were record profits and Air New Zealand placed orders for the latest aircraft. 'He shat all over [former CEO] Rob Fyfe in one interview when he said that when he took over it was basically a disaster,' a former colleague says. 'It wasn't. Rob Fyfe did a fantastic job to get it to where it was.' Luxon benefited from a worldwide tourism boom, the source says. 'When you are making x many million dollars a year that covers up many sins, including probably opening up too many routes, buying too many aircraft, and Greg Foran [Luxon's successor] hinted at that quite recently in public.'

The colleague points to Luxon's impeccable timing. 'He has been pretty tinny in getting in on the good times and leaving before the bad. Very John Key-esque.' Although the tourism boom waned in 2016/17, Air New Zealand made an 'enormous purchase' of aircraft in 2019. 'Everything was geared towards growth, growth, growth and didn't understand that the music stops eventually.' By 2019, even before the arrival of Covid-19, cuts had to be made. 'To be slightly unkind, maybe part of that was he didn't want a story of decline so he kept the music running a bit too long. And then got out,' the colleague says.

John Key's first post-parliamentary job was on Air New Zealand's board, and he was quickly impressed by Luxon. It was during this period that speculation first began about Luxon's ambitions. Luxon was focused on progressive policies, such as tackling climate change, the colleague says. 'It was good for the brand as well. How much of that was done with half an eye on his future in mind, because he was a big planner? He was making sure the back story at Air New Zealand was as good as it could be.'

In 2018, Luxon's stock rose further when he was appointed chairman of Ardern's Business Advisory Council, tasked with supercharging the economy. Senior execs, used to his patterns of short-term, intense focus, believed the job would hold Luxon's interest for six months before he became bored and frustrated with how government actually works. 'That's kind of how it panned out,' the source says. 'He had a hundred thousand ideas, and then met MBIE where ideas go to die. He got more and more frustrated. And then ended it in quite a shitty mood.'

Luxon had other quirks. The colleague says he suffers from a 'it's so bloody easy' disease, with a naïvety about the realities of governing. 'He used to say — which you hear a lot among senior corporates in Auckland, and it is kind of boring — how governing is so easy.' The colleague says his political analysis is shallow. 'He's got this quite superficial view of how the world works and is quite prone to the latest McKinsey idea.' (McKinsey & Company is an American management consultancy that espouses technocratic solutions.)

He also displayed another unfortunate habit. The colleague claimed he sometimes had a tendency to bag other business leaders: 'If you are doing that in Canada, fine. But in New Zealand it got around. A little bit clumsy.'

In 2019, Luxon resigned from the airline. 'Politics is something I am interested in,' he confirmed. Key immediately began championing him, calling him 'a world-class candidate'. The colleague says Luxon is 'obsessed' with the former prime minister. 'He has got a chip on the shoulder about Key being wealthier than him. But he'll work day and night. For his own ego, he cannot lose.'

Luxon began signalling that he was interested in Botany, a vacancy triggered by Jami-Lee Ross's resignation from the party. A television interview before he was selected irritated MPs, but he was chosen and easily won the safe seat. From mid-2019 he began appearing in preferred prime minister rankings. Within months of arriving at Parliament he found himself having to throw cold water on speculation about his ambitions. 'My focus is to continue to learn about my electorate and my portfolios. There is a lot to learn,' he told *The Timaru Herald* on a visit to the South Canterbury town where his father and grandparents were born. 'I'm not here pushing for the leadership. I'm here to do my job. Judith has been a great leader.'

Feeling under pressure, Collins reached for that last resort of the desperate: racial separatism. It was an echo of her mentor Don Brash's divisive 'one law for all' campaign in 2004. In a speech to the Ōrewa Rotary club, he raised fears of a 'dangerous drift' towards racial separatism and a divided nation. National shot up 17 points in the polls and a polarising and damaging national debate on race relations followed.

Collins saw an opportunity now in the government's proposal to create a Māori Health Authority as part of an overhaul of the country's bloated and inefficient health bureaucracy. 'There is nothing in being Māori that intrinsically makes anyone more in need in the health system,' she said, wilfully ignoring the bleak statistics that showed the current system was failing Māori. 'We're not going to go down that path, any more than the National Party will ever agree to racist separation in education or in the justice sector.' In early May she expanded on the theme in a speech to a regional party conference in Auckland. She accused the government of secretly attempting to set up separate systems for Māori at all levels, including at Parliament.

Her claims were based on *He Puapua*, a 123-page document commissioned by Te Puni Kōkiri, the Ministry of Māori Development. The previous National Government had signed up to the UN Declaration concerning the Rights of Indigenous Peoples in 2010. The report was a first step in realising these commitments; it was not government policy. Collins was undeterred. She went on to launch a 'Demand the Debate' campaign. She was in touch with Brash, but supporters and the caucus were increasingly nervous about using race as a political tool.

Writing in *The Dominion Post*, former staffer Ben Thomas said that in the Opposition Leader's office 'there must be a small see-through cabinet labelled "racial separatism" with a sign saying "in case of low polling, break glass"'. He went on to remind readers: 'we could speculate about whether Collins is motivated by the high-risk gamble of a temporary Orewa-like sugar hit, or what Freud called the "death drive", because the most salient feature of Brash's strategy is that he never became prime minister'.

MPs were baffled. It seemed counterintuitive to focus on trivial identity issues when the country was still preoccupied with the pandemic and a slow roll-out of vaccines. The government was also faltering in the face of a range of problems, including inflation, soaring house prices, labour shortages and looming industrial action from nurses. National was failing to capitalise on any of this, while Collins was trying to stoke a culture war similar to a battle of values being fought in the United States.

The tactic was not paying off. She was chasing issues that ACT's David Seymour was already prosecuting and with greater finesse. Humiliatingly, in early August, Seymour overtook Collins in the preferred prime minister stakes. The Newshub-Reid Research poll posed the question: 'Who do you think is a better leader, David Seymour or Judith Collins?' Seymour scored 41.7 per cent over Collins's 25.9 per cent. Labour was slipping — down 9.7 points, it could no longer govern alone on those numbers — but National was not picking up the support, languishing on 28.7 per cent. Conversely, ACT's vote lifted 4.2 points to 11.1 per cent. Within days of the poll, Collins was demanding a referendum on whether government departments should be able to use 'Aotearoa', the Māori name for New Zealand.

The party went into its annual conference deeply dissatisfied. Earlier in the week Collins had performed an astonishing U-turn, withdrawing her support for a ban on the abhorrent practice of gay conversion therapy. The practice, often undertaken by religious groups, attempts to repress or 'cure' people of their sexuality or identity. The bill introduced two criminal offences: one for performing a conversion practice that causes serious harm, and one for doing it on someone who is under 18 or lacking decision-making capacity. In a tense caucus meeting, MPs in the liberal wing failed to secure a conscience vote on the issue and were whipped to vote against it at first reading. Collins's objection to the new law stemmed from the belief that parents could face charges for preventing their children from taking hormone blockers. The medication is used to delay physical changes that don't match gender identity.

Collins didn't speak during the parliamentary debate. Instead, it was Bridges who argued there must be an exemption for parents. 'This Bill lacks common sense. It's an ideological overreach … We are opposing this Bill until [Justice Minister] Kris Faafoi does the right thing.' National stood alone, and there were tense scenes in the chamber, with Labour MPs denying the proposed legislation did what National was claiming.

Nick Smith believes Collins was manipulated by Bridges into reversing her position. 'They are as cunning as each other. My view was Simon deliberately took a provocative conservative position to bait Judith to try and build support, because he knows the numbers very well.' There are a number of morally conservative MPs in the caucus, but Collins's instincts are more liberal, he says. 'Judith put the white flag up to keep the leadership.' Smith says it was in the best interests of the party to support the bill to select committee, where changes could be made. 'National's policy position was being compromised by these interior scrappings,' he says. Bridges rejects this theory, insisting he genuinely believed the law is problematic. He consistently voted against it in the latter parliamentary stages. John Mitchell, Collins's chief press secretary, believes Collins was responding to the reaction of supporters, who were writing to her with their concerns. 'We thought it was a sensible question to ask. I never had any palpable sense of a revolt over it. I'm sure they had vigorous discussion over it, as all caucus rooms do.'

The Young Nats, the party's youth wing, were appalled. Over the three-day conference at the vast Vodafone Events Centre in Auckland's Manukau, the bloc handed out rainbow ribbons. They were sported by MPs Nicola Willis, Erica Stanford, Nicola Grigg, Matt Doocey, Joseph Mooney, Mark Mitchell and Chris Bishop. In a closed-door speech to grassroots activists, Young Nats president Stephanie-Anne Ross voiced their 'deep disappointment'. She reportedly received a standing ovation. In a statement Ross said: 'Conversion therapy does not work, yet it causes irreparable harm within our rainbow communities.' Rainbow youth are more likely to experience depression, deliberately self-harm and attempt suicide, particularly when faced with parental rejection, she argued. The unease in caucus was underlined when a Wellington lawyer made public a private exchange in which Chris Bishop confirmed he 'hated' the vote. Collins publicly supported Bishop, saying he was only re-affirming the party's position.

Retribution came within weeks: Bishop was stripped of the Shadow Leader of the House portfolio. It was a calculated blow, as Bishop was a skilled parliamentarian. A champion teenage debater, he'd learned the ropes under his former boss Brownlee. He took pride in his knowledge of Standing Orders, Parliament's complex set of rules. In an emailed statement, Collins said the change enabled Bishop to 'focus solely on his critical role as National's spokesperson for the Covid-19 Response'. But the message was clear. Willis was removed from the finance and expenditure committee, with her associate economic development role scrapped.

It was a pattern of behaviour that was beginning to worry the caucus. The reshuffle that demoted Bishop came about because Collins had to deal with the retirement of two other MPs, Nick Smith and Todd Muller.

Smith had a temper that was legendary around Parliament. 'Nick Smith is like a fancy Italian sports car,' one MP says. 'When it goes, it is unbelievable. But when it breaks down, the costs and the complications are appalling.' In July 2020, shortly after Muller's resignation as leader, Smith was involved in an altercation with his executive assistant (EA). Smith admits swearing at the younger man. A female staff member, passing by the office, overheard and made a complaint to Parliamentary Service, which provides administrative support to MPs and employs staff. Smith made a counter-complaint about the man's work.

In an anonymous account to Stuff, the EA described an 'onslaught' in which Smith was 'slamming his fists on my desk, standing over me'. He claimed Smith repeatedly said, 'I am the MP and you are just the fucking secretary'. The investigation into the complaint dragged on for months. The agency and Parliament were already at the centre of multiple allegations of bullying and harassment. More than 35 staff had left over a period of months in 2019. An investigation by consultant Debbie Francis concluded it was a toxic workplace where MPs were 'treated like gods' in a 'master-servant relationship'.

The EA was moved out of Smith's office but lost his job at the election. More than a year later he was still in dispute with Parliamentary Service. In September 2020, Smith's lawyers became aware that the female staffer had made a recording of the argument. The agency hadn't disclosed its existence and the woman had refused to hand it over, worried it was illegal. This further complicated the investigation. Because of an insistence on secrecy by Parliamentary Service, the exact sequence of events is unclear. However, the agency almost certainly briefed Collins's then-chief of staff Megan Campbell and chief whip Barbara Kuriger. Collins has admitted she learned of the investigation 'late' in 2020. Smith says Collins made repeated inquiries to him about progress in the investigation. 'Judith's office was getting frustrated. I was a little bit suspicious.'

Because of her place on the party's list, Harete Hipango, a friend and ally of Collins's, would return to Parliament if an MP was to resign. Smith says he'd had a conversation with a board member warning him 'that Harete had said in February [2021] that Judith had given her assurance that she'd be back in the caucus by May'. During a caucus meeting in May, Collins warned MPs about a scandal that was about to break. 'I need to tell you the media have got something on one of you that's going to turn very ugly,' Smith says she told the meeting. About a month later, on a Friday afternoon, Smith says Collins called to warn that Newshub were planning to confront him about the story in the upcoming week, and told him his position was indefensible. Smith was sceptical; it would be highly unusual for an outlet to sit on a story for that long, let alone warn the party before 'doorstepping' an MP. 'I reflected over the weekend. Is Judith stitching me up?' He came to the conclusion that she couldn't be that Machiavellian. 'I took seriously what she said was correct.'

Smith decided he had no choice but to call time on a 30-year career. That Monday he released a forthright statement: 'I have decided to retire for personal and professional reasons, including a current Parliamentary Service inquiry into an employment issue ... I have come to realise that the role as a List MP is just not me. I had decided to retire earlier this year and the only question was when.' He revealed the confidential inquiry into the verbal altercation, and said it was not yet concluded. 'I was advised on Friday that the inquiry and its details have been leaked to the media for release tomorrow. It is inappropriate for employment disputes to be litigated in public.' Smith said that he regretted the incident, had apologised at the time and reiterated that apology. 'I have decided the best course of action for the parties involved, the National Party, my family and myself is to retire now.' Collins followed with a press release thanking Smith for his service and listing his many achievements, including holding 14 ministerial portfolios. She said it would be inappropriate to comment further on the ongoing employment dispute.

Smith's exit is regarded by many as a costly loss of experience. 'He is a great bloke; he would do you a good turn before a bad turn. He made people understand their own portfolios and policy development better than anyone else I know,' a senior MP says.

The full story never emerged as Collins had predicted, although dribs and drabs eventually leaked out. She denies she engineered the saga to allow Hipango to return. The senior MP defends her. 'That's absolutely not true. Nick has a long history of issues with staff. He is very short-tempered. And he has this expectation that he can blow his top and next time smile at someone.' Another MP says: 'I like Nick. He does have a temper. And I bore the brunt of that on a couple of occasions. But he is a loss to the caucus. Everyone says Judith got him sacked, but I'd be surprised if that's actually true.' But one of her former staff is unconvinced. 'Basically, she was back to her tricks of 2014. Getting rid of Nick Smith in her underhand, nasty way so that her friend Harete could get in next on the list.' The demotion of Bishop was 'completely petty, because she could see that he was starting to do well and she didn't want him to succeed when she wasn't. And the late-night star chamber with Todd Muller — outrageous.'

Muller was the next to go. There was a great deal of trepidation about Hipango's return. In her previous three-year stint she'd made an impact only in her final months. The anti-abortion former lawyer made a false claim about Ardern's support for legislation that decriminalised abortion. (Her Facebook post was supported by fellow MP Simon O'Connor, who'd trained to be a priest.) It caused a minor public outcry, to which Ardern responded by making a plea for 'views based on fact'. Hipango took no heed and followed up with another post, a meme wrongly quoting Ardern as saying 'dairy farming is a world of the past'. She added the caption: 'This is what the PM really thinks of our dairy farmers. She said it!' Matt King, National's Northland MP who was also unseated at the election, circulated the meme as well. It was later labelled 'false information' by Facebook's fact-checkers. Hipango was unrepentant. She argued it was not a false quote but 'a construction of key words aligned with Jacinda Ardern'. Despite widespread concerns about the dissemination of misinformation in the election campaign, Collins defended both Hipango and King.

Later, former MP Jo Luxton would reveal how Hipango's behaviour, including correcting people's pronunciation, led to her being isolated. 'She would say to people, "This is how you pronounce this in te reo",' Hayes told the *Herald*. 'It's very much a pecking order ... The first-timers usually keep their mouth shut.' Worried about her return and her closeness to Collins, 'several' MPs spoke anonymously to Newsroom. One of them was Muller. Oddly, he did so in a telephone conversation in front of Kuriger, as they drove around his electorate. As a fellow senior MP recounts it: 'He gets the call and suddenly switches from being Todd Muller MP for Bay of Plenty to Todd Muller future leader of the National Party at some point. And in front of a senior whip starts talking about a colleague. What is she meant to do?' The MP says Kuriger was placed in a dreadful position. 'She had to go — quite rightly — to Judith. It's not on.'

Collins and Reti confronted Muller. They wanted to know if there were any other instances of gossiping to journalists. 'He just blurted it all out and justified it by saying that he had long-term relationships with journalists who trusted him,' the senior MP says. Muller claimed he was acting only in the best interests of the party. 'Who hit him on the head with this crazy idea?' The MP says Muller wasn't interested in apologising, nor promising there would be no repeat. 'He would not come to a reasonable position.'

Collins called a late-night meeting of the caucus. 'In the ordinary course of events, a journalist being talked to — off the record or accidentally or whatever — would not be the cause of a late-night meeting,' another MP says. But there was a lot of residual, unresolved anger at Muller. It spilled out during the meeting. The senior MP says Muller's explanation to his colleagues was 'just extraordinary'. Muller told Hipango: 'I'm very sorry, I just said what I think.' It settled his fate. 'Everyone immediately thought: Well, fuck, what's he said about me? So, he was done for.' Muller wasn't expelled but was asked not to attend caucus. The following morning he announced that he would resign at the next election. He said he wanted to prioritise his health and family. Muller then took five weeks' leave in order to care for his wife, Michelle, who was recovering from surgery. Collins would say little about the meeting or Muller. 'I think it shouldn't come as much of a surprise to people,' she told reporters. The senior MP says she 'treated him pretty fairly. Remember that the caucus voted him out, nothing that she did.'

Shortly after the party conference, Simon Bridges published his new memoir. Politicians really only write books for two reasons: they have retired or they are plotting their way to the top. Since his defenestration, Bridges's image had undergone something of a renaissance. He'd gone from a 'serious dryballs' (his words) to a man who cavorted with yaks in a popular online video. 'Social media has destroyed me and then built me up again,' he wrote. It was a funny and self-effacing book. Bridges made surprisingly frank revelations about his feelings of inadequacy as a father, his struggle with his Māori identity, and his hurt at public mockery of his distinctive Kiwi accent. Naturally it prompted a fresh round of speculation about his leadership ambitions. 'My cute answer is: this isn't the book you write if you want to be the leader,' he said. 'I mean, I put a lot of stuff in there. If that was what I wanted when I wrote it, I would have done it differently.' It was entirely unconvincing.

Collins gritted her teeth. There were soon more important things to worry about: New Zealand was plunged into another lockdown in mid-August 2021 when the contagious Delta variant was detected in the community. At that time only 18 per cent of the country were fully vaccinated. Auckland would endure 107 days of restrictions. Despite growing frustration with the glacial pace of inoculating the country and other missteps in the government's Covid response, Collins did not rise to the occasion. National and ACT had refused to support a virtual Parliament, and Collins had flown from her Auckland home to Wellington despite the restrictions. Questioned about the decision by TVNZ *Breakfast* programme's Indira Stewart, Collins flew off the handle. 'Why is this all about me today?' she exclaimed. 'This is ridiculous.' In the fiery interview she claimed the media were not asking Ardern the right questions. Later she accused the presenter of being underprepared and having a 'political agenda'.

A few days later Collins was drawn into an unedifying row about high-profile microbiologist Siouxsie Wiles. Wiles, herself a polarising figure, had made a name for herself tirelessly giving advice about the pandemic. During the current lockdown she was filmed at a beach with another woman about 5 kilometres from her Auckland home. The pair were unmasked, and her friend had gone for a quick swim in the ocean, stretching restrictions. The footage was shopped around various media outlets and was eventually published on a website run by Cameron Slater. Collins (wrongly) insinuated that Wiles had broken the rules. 'I think she's a big, fat hypocrite actually. I'm sick and tired of listening to her telling everyone else what to do.' She was immediately accused of fat-shaming, although later said her comments were nothing to do with Wiles's appearance. It also drew further attention to her association with Slater. 'Judith's a friend, we communicate with each other on a regular basis,' he later confirmed.

A war of words with her former press secretary Janet Wilson followed. Wilson, in a podcast interview, accused her former boss of 'paranoid storms'. Wilson said that, a year on from the election, the party had learned nothing. She predicted it would become irrelevant. 'Fear is a very big operative word here,' she said. 'There is a real sense of fear within that caucus … the enemy is within, it's not outside.' Collins accused Wilson of being disgruntled and unprofessional. Wilson's attack came on the back of 'The National Party death spiral', a biting essay by Matthew Hooton for *Metro* magazine. 'In the place of mainstream New Zealanders, National has been infiltrated by radical Christian evangelicals, mainly from the top half of the North Island,' he wrote. 'The current leader, president and MPs must pander to that group, dubbed "the Taliban" by the party's remaining centrists … there's no obvious way out of this vicious cycle that is turning National into a Trump-like cult.'

All of this was bookended by two dreadful polls. Curia, National's former pollster, put the party on 21.3 per cent, hovering just above its worst-ever election result. ACT had climbed to 14.9 and Labour was sitting comfortably on 45.8. A leaked UMR poll put National slightly higher, at 26 per cent. The caucus had had enough. With John Key urging Luxon to bide his time, Bridges seemed the only viable alternative, but restless MPs were hamstrung. Although the phones and online chat groups were ringing hot, Covid-19 restrictions prevented Auckland MPs from getting to Wellington for a no-confidence vote. ACT's support continued to climb throughout October, but Collins was safe — for now.

In the end, she pulled the pin on her own leadership. As the government removed the last remnants of the Auckland lockdown,

Collins knew her days were numbered. MPs were planning to remove her — it was just a question of whether that would happen before or after the Christmas break. Late on the evening of 24 November, Parliament was unusually busy. MPs were in the House debating legislation that would set up a new 'traffic light system' to replace the country's Covid four-tier alert-level restrictions. The laws, which included mandating vaccinations for some workforces, were being pushed through under urgency. That means a bill can be introduced and passed through all its stages quickly, without undergoing expert and public scrutiny in a select committee. National, ACT and Te Pāti Māori were all opposed, and there were rowdy scenes in the debating chamber. Just before 9.30pm a startling email dropped into the inboxes of journalists and National MPs. It blindsided everyone.

Several weeks earlier, Waitaki MP Jacqui Dean was attending meetings related to the Parliament's ongoing work to implement the recommendations of the Francis review on bullying. Updating Collins, Dean disclosed an incident that occurred in early 2016. During an all-day caucus meeting at Premier House, National MPs were relaxing in the grounds. Chatting with Jami-Lee Ross and Todd McClay, Bridges called out to Dean and made a crass comment. 'We discussed our wives, our children; I can remember talking about the fact I had two boys and I wanted a girl, and I engaged in some old wives' tales about that and how to have a girl,' Bridges would later reveal. Dean took offence and made a complaint, and Bridges apologised after being reprimanded by Bill English. Bridges considered the matter closed, encouraged in this belief by the fact that since then Dean had twice supported him in leadership contests.

Collins sat on the information until later in November, before disclosing it to John Mitchell. Then she waited another week. A poll on 22 November put Bridges's public support at 40.7 per cent, well ahead of Collins on 23.2 per cent. Confronted by media about the poll results, he refused to rule out a leadership challenge. 'That's very flattering. I hope at the end of the day I'm a bit older and maybe possibly a bit wiser than I was when I was leader of the Opposition.' At that point, Bridges wasn't 'doing the numbers'. 'But at that point it was pretty clear it was either going to be Bridges–Luxon, or Luxon–Bridges,' an insider reveals. In the afternoon Bridges was called in to see the deputy leader, Reti. Whatever the two men discussed, Dean's allegations were never formally, or fully, put to Bridges.

The following day Bridges made an appearance at a central Wellington bookstore, signing copies of his memoirs. He then posted a series of photos documenting the event on Facebook, showing queues of people spilling into the street and television cameras. Sources say this was the final straw for Collins. She launched a pre-emptive strike. Collins called a meeting with Reti, her chief of staff Megan Wallace, deputy chief of staff Julie Johnston and chief press secretary John Mitchell. Collins explained the situation, and what her planned response was, and why. 'She said she found it very offensive, totally inappropriate. She reiterated that Jacqui was still very upset about it.' Mitchell says she was emotional. 'She actually got a little bit teary about what women have to put up with.'

Bridges was ordered back to see Collins and Reti. His camp assumed it to be a showdown about the leadership. But then Collins tried to raise the accusations. 'There was no way [Bridges] was going to be Muller or Nick Smith,' a friend says. 'It wasn't his first rodeo, and he hadn't been through all that stuff just to get shot at the ranch.' Bridges called her bluff and left without hearing the full extent of the accusations. He told Collins to put it in writing.

Bridges retired to Huxley's, a popular new bar in an office complex to the rear of Parliament, spending the dinner break with Mark Mitchell. Collins was desperately trying to reach him to get him back to her office. While Bridges and Mitchell dined, Collins made a flurry of calls to the party's board, which unanimously agreed to a tentative investigation. Its members did not discuss any sanctions, but Collins didn't hesitate. She had John Mitchell fire off a press release. 'This evening, with unanimous support of the board of the National Party, Simon Bridges, Member for Tauranga, has been demoted and relieved of his portfolio responsibilities,' it read. Collins accused Bridges of 'serious misconduct relating to [his] interaction with a caucus colleague', which required a 'swift and decisive' response. In failing to detail the incident, the media release was potentially deeply damaging to Bridges. Collins also scheduled a press conference for the following morning, at 10am.

With most MPs still in the House debating the later stages of the bill, an immediate ripple went around Parliament as MPs opened the email. 'We were head down, taking calls, trying to delay [the legislation], trying to cause malarkey,' an MP says. 'I got it and was like: holy fucking shit. It wasn't good and it just flowed out from there.' And because Parliament was sitting, there were plenty of journalists still in the precinct. It didn't take long before they eked out the details.

Brownlee, when shown the email by another MP, initially thought it was spam. Once again, he stepped in to try to broker peace. Bridges demanded a 10pm caucus meeting that night, but Collins wanted MPs to gather after her press conference the following morning. 'He doesn't call caucus meetings, I do,' she told colleagues. Sometime after midnight, it was agreed to hold the meeting at 9am. A memo from senior whip Matt Doocey went out just before 12.30am.

The caucus was boiling with anger. 'There were moves afoot to change,' a senior MP says. 'Most of the caucus wanted it. The debate was about whether we did it before or after Christmas.' Collins, aware she was on shaky ground, 'tried to take Simon out'. The MP found her reasoning offensive. 'It was outrageous. Classic Judith. She was trying to use the Me Too movement as a vehicle for her own political agenda.' It incensed the caucus, he said. 'She signed her own death warrant.'

Bridges arrived at Parliament early. 'What we saw yesterday was truly desperate stuff from Judith Collins,' he told waiting reporters. 'I think it shows that she'll go to any length to hold onto her leadership of the National Party.' A few minutes later, Simon O'Connor, Bridges's brother-in-law, spoke to Radio New Zealand, resigning his portfolios and saying he could no longer work with Collins. 'You cannot have a party where a leader is acting this way against party members,' he said.

The caucus meeting lasted three hours, with an eventual vote of no confidence in Collins. 'It's a bit unfair to compare her to Jami-Lee,' an insider says. 'But it does show [we need to be thinking] about the psychology of people and how they cope with what's an incredibly stressful job.' Collins can be warm, generous and kind but also possesses a darker side. 'I don't think she had many senior [people] in caucus that she could trust or was personally close to. Having said that, it doesn't justify the way she took out Smith and Todd and Bish [Chris Bishop] and Nicola. Bridges only escaped because he didn't fall into her trap of a kangaroo court.' There was also anger at Dean, whose story had shifted.

Reti was now the party's interim leader, the fifth since Key's exit, with MPs agreeing to vote on Collins's successor in the following week. The scene was set for a showdown between

Bridges and Luxon. Collins confirmed the news in a tweet and left the building for the pub with John Mitchell and list MP Melissa Lee.

Mitchell resigned the following day. An experienced PR operative who'd worked for Terry Serepisos, the star of the Kiwi version of *The Apprentice*, Mitchell believes Collins was genuinely outraged by the allegations against Bridges. 'There was something more than simply political to it. She was legitimately angry. It wasn't just about knifing Simon.' But he acknowledges: 'There was a degree of a political masterstroke to it. She knew what Simon was doing in terms of white-anting. It's typical Judith. It was written afterwards that it was the most Judith Collins exit ever.'

13

THE TEA PARTY

In the winter of 2005, two young ACT activists sat forlornly in an office in the affluent inner-city Auckland suburb of Remuera. The air was thick with smoke from their Peter Stuyvesant cigarettes. They were at a loss. Their party was in the doldrums.

Former MP Donna Awatere Huata was awaiting sentence for stealing from a state-funded trust set up to help under-privileged children. Some of the money had been used to pay for her stomach-stapling surgery as well as for school fees. She was later jailed for two years, nine months. ACT had expelled her but that had led to a protracted legal fight. It was finally resolved when the Supreme Court decided the party could use the so-called party-hopping legislation to remove her. The whole fiasco meant that ACT was now tainted by two things it had campaigned against: a misuse of taxpayer dollars, and utilising the 'waka-jumping' law.

With polling hovering between 1 and 2 per cent, the party was in a death spiral. A year earlier, the party's leader and most effective campaigner, Richard Prebble, had quit, setting off a bitter internal struggle to find his successor. Four out of the party's eight MPs had contested the leadership. The party's founder, Sir Roger Douglas, had supported Wellington lawyer Stephen Franks. But Rodney Hide — Prebble's apprentice, who'd won himself a reputation for exposing scandal — had pipped Franks by just one vote. There was disquiet that the former economist was not committed to the party's purist economic reform ideals. 'There was a huge amount of competition and conflict in caucus,' former MP and president John Boscawen says. Hide had developed a reputation as a 'perkbuster', attacking the fringe benefits that came with being an MP. 'There were people in our party who considered that very populist.'

Hide was a colourful character who took to carrying a plain manila folder, with the hint its contents contained details of a yet-to-be exposed scandal. He also collected ornamental rhinoceroses, a nod to his supposedly thick skin. But for all that, he could not lift the party's support. As the election approached, the Right-wing vote was draining back to National in the wake of Brash's Ōrewa speech. 'Brash's leadership made ACT redundant,' Hide would later say.

With support well below the 5 per cent threshold needed to get into Parliament, ACT had to win an electorate seat. The Epsom campaign became central to the party's survival. Hide had come within 2000 votes of seizing the electorate in 1999, but in 2002 he had been hamstrung by the party's strategy for all MPs to target the party vote. To now beat Epsom's sitting MP, National's Richard Worth, would be a huge task. ACT had not won a seat since 1996, when Prebble had picked up Wellington Central. And, further, the 2005 electorate campaign was disorganised and under-resourced.

It was late in the evening, after the sun had set behind nearby One Tree Hill, when the two activists were brainstorming in Hide's electorate office. One was Willie Seabrook, a sharp IT consultant, recently hired by Hide. The other was president of Auckland University's ACT on Campus, David Seymour. Within the next 15 years, Seymour would become the party's most — and least — successful leader. But for now, he was knocking on doors.

'The party was in very bad shape,' Seymour says. As they fretted and chain-smoked, in strode Boscawen. Almost 20 years earlier, he'd lost everything in the sharemarket crash of the late 1980s. He'd bounced back, making a fortune in commercial property, retiring at 36 and travelling the world. Joining ACT in the mid-1990s, he was now the party's chief fundraiser. In the previous election, the party had spent $1.6 million, more than both Labour and National combined.

Fanning away the fug — Boscawen deeply dislikes cigarette smoke — he set to work with a pencil, pen and exercise books. 'Right, here's what we're gonna do,' he told them. 'We're going to take over this campaign, we're going to win Epsom. And then I'm going to buy a new cellphone.'

Boscawen duly secured a campaign headquarters — an enormous building in Newmarket, which is now the sprawling Nuffield Street shopping complex. In it, he installed a call centre, staffed with 20 employees of wealthy Christchurch property developer Dave Henderson. 'John is a man of serious action,' Seymour recalls. 'And Willie a genius, computer-wise.' They used predictive dialling to call 'everyone in Epsom'. Henderson's team was an added bonus. 'I remember the day that they walked in. These were very high-EQ, glamorous saleswomen. And you can imagine what that did to lift a political campaign.'

Boscawen also established a large-scale direct-mail campaign. 'Bosco had more printers per square metre than in any other area on Earth at the time,' Seymour says. 'We could have given the *Herald* a run at that point.' They worked all night, printing and photocopying direct mail-outs. 'It was one of the great grassroots campaigns in history.' This was also helped by the size of the electorate: at just 23 square kilometres it was the smallest. It covered the wealthy suburbs of Parnell, Remuera, Epsom and Mount Eden.

The message was simple: Hide was telling National-leaning voters that an electorate vote for him would not mean the loss of Richard Worth, who would remain in Parliament by virtue of his high placing on the party list. Essentially, the electorate would get two MPs and ensure ACT remained in Parliament as a potential support party. But the party was even divided on that strategy, with some MPs believing it would institutionalise Hide as leader and hand him too much power. 'All of his parliamentary colleagues would be there because of him,' Boscawen says. 'And then people like Roger Douglas thought unless we can get 5 per cent we don't deserve to exist anyway.'

But while ACT clearly needed National, the larger party couldn't see the mutual benefit in the 'Epsom strategy'. In 1996, National had given a nod and wink to Prebble — until near the election when it was feared he was syphoning off too many party votes. Labour had also struck a deal in 1999 when the Greens were struggling to reach 5 per cent, by helping co-leader Jeanette Fitzsimons win the Coromandel seat. Voters were already familiar with strategic voting and electorate accommodation. Add to this, Brash and Hide and their Singaporean-born wives were friends and their young sons played together. And ACT was willing to withdraw its candidate in Tauranga to boost the chances of National's Bob Clarkson beating Winston Peters.

But if Brash was amenable, his party, and more particularly Worth, wasn't. Party president Judy Kirk sent a letter to all voters in Epsom urging them to put 'two ticks' for National. Nevertheless, the message was not pushed. 'Don Brash showed some political acumen and didn't publicly repeat the message,' Seymour says.

Worth, a former naval officer and a lawyer, also accused Hide of dirty tricks. In a newsletter he claimed ACT's phone canvassers were asking voters who they would vote for if Worth died. National's campaign strategists were also frustrated when Hide awkwardly gatecrashed a walkabout by Brash in central Wellington. Seymour says the National Party's apparatus 'was doing everything it could to ensure' Worth's victory.

Ten days out from the election, Brash sent his signal — and it wasn't in Hide's favour. He staged a publicity stunt with far-from-home Ōhāriu MP and United Future leader Peter Dunne, sharing a cuppa (actually a cappuccino and a herbal tea) outside a café in Auckland's Mount Eden. The 'cup of tea' deal settled in political legend, a potent symbol that voters should consider strategic voting to help a mainstream party with minor party support. But in choosing to publicly raise a cup with Dunne, Brash effectively ruled out any seat-saving deals to help ACT or New Zealand First. Even so, Hide defied the polls — winning Epsom by a majority of over 3000 votes and bringing a second MP, Heather Roy, in on his coattails. His gritty effervescence could not save the overall party vote, though, as it slumped from 7 per cent to 1.52 per cent, thereby reducing their caucus from seven to two MPs. That was not the only loss ACT suffered: Seymour, an engineering student, failed two papers and had to return to university the following year. Boscawen bought his new cellphone.

Hide was frustrated at National's 'first-past-the-post' strategy, a reference to New Zealand's previous electoral system where the candidate with the most votes wins. 'They've cost Don Brash the opportunity of being Prime Minister,' he said. John Key would not make the same mistake.

By the next election, in 2008, National's move to the centre under Key opened up more opportunities for ACT to win votes. Hide healed his rift with Roger Douglas, who had quit over the perkbuster campaign, saying the party should not become a front for the Serious Fraud Office. Douglas agreed to stand as a candidate in Hunua, and the party was making all the right noises to reclaim its old support base.

Worth was again selected as National's candidate in Epsom, and his reselection was interpreted as a tacit nod that the party was content for Hide to keep Epsom. Hide campaigned by claiming to be National's backbone. 'We are going to support the next National-led government, whether they want us or not,' he said. He was instantly recognisable in a canary-yellow blazer and 'Noddy car' — a Mercedes Smart car. Although Worth continued to insist there was no deal, Key arranged to drink coffee with Hide in front of the cameras. As they sipped their drinks, both dressed in stripes, Key said he was happy to work with ACT. Hide would make a fantastic minister, he said. But Douglas would get no such offer. ACT used a photograph of the meeting in newspaper advertising in the final days of the campaign, with the slogan *Strengthen the Coalition*. A framed copy now hangs in Boscawen's home. From that point on, National's and ACT's fortunes were tied together, and both needed each other.

Promised a seat at the Cabinet table, Brash's former afternoon-tea buddy Dunne also aligned himself with National. With Key refusing to have anything to do with Winston Peters, that left Te

Pāti Māori as the only other option to get a National-led coalition across the line. In the last week of the campaign, Te Pāti Māori co-leader Pita Sharples said it would be difficult to cut a deal with National, but his co-leader Tariana Turia said he was speaking out of turn. Turia's dart was aimed at least as much against Labour as for National. Labour and Te Pāti Māori also had a tense relationship — former Labour minister Turia especially: she had resigned from government over the 2004 foreshore and seabed controversy; a year later Helen Clark refused to deal with her new party. By 2008, Te Pāti Māori were really only left with National.

National voters did their duty to ensure they had a coalition partner: Hide re-captured Epsom, with a 12,000-vote majority, once again ensuring ACT's survival. However, the evidence of electoral-seat rat-swallowing was clear, with fewer than 2000 people giving ACT the party vote in Epsom, and 10 times that support going to Key's party. Nevertheless, with 3.7 per cent of the vote, and returning to Parliament with five MPs, ACT was about to have a real influence on government policy for the first time in its 14-year history.

ACT, which bases its philosophy on individual freedom and personal responsibility, had campaigned on crime and taxation: harsher on one and laxer on the other. On election night Prime Minister-elect Key telephoned Hide, now his local MP, to ask ACT to help him form a government. With 58 seats, Key was just shy of the 62 needed to govern. He met with Hide and Dunne two days later in Wellington. Dunne would be no problem — he would be happy continuing as Revenue Minister. ACT had three policy demands: a 'three strikes' law to see any violent offender convicted of three offences imprisoned for life, the repeal of the emissions trading scheme (ETS), and cuts to government spending. It wanted to push National back from the centre, where Key knew the votes lay.

But, surprising everyone, Key also invited Sharples and Turia to the table in the hope of reaching a confidence and supply deal. Gaining Te Pāti Māori support gave him 69 seats, and meant National would not be beholden to ACT and could trade the parties off against each other on legislation. Offering his minor-party allies ministerial positions, but outside of Cabinet, would also allow them a safety valve to criticise the government. This was especially attractive to Sharples and Turia, who were facing push-back from their members over aligning with the Tories.

Within eight days, the deals were done (by contrast, Clark had taken 32 days in 2005). Key worked fast, conscious of the looming financial crisis and keen to make a crucial Asia-Pacific Economic Cooperation summit in Lima, Peru. Hide was made local government and associate commerce minister and got a new regulatory reform portfolio. Heather Roy was consumer affairs and associate defence and education minister. National agreed to much of ACT's agenda: promising to introduce a three strikes bill, establish a special select committee to review the ETS, and review spending.

Sharples took on Māori affairs as well as associate education and corrections. Turia was the new community and voluntary sector minister, with associate portfolios in health and social development. National pledged not to abolish the Māori seats without consent, and agreed to review the contentious *Foreshore and Seabed Act*. This last was close to Turia's heart, the 2004 legislation having triggered her to resign from Labour and establish her new party, a key part of whose kaupapa was foreshore law reform. The 2004 law enshrined the right of access to beaches for all New Zealanders, and in so doing some Māori believe it removed their customary rights. Key envisioned a compromise. Dunne kept revenue and gained associate health. He won concessions on public–private partnerships (known as PPPs) to build major roads, such as the proposed Transmission Gully project, north of Wellington. National also agreed to bring in a bill allowing income-splitting for couples for tax purposes.

The relationships with support partners were carefully managed by Key, English and chief of staff Wayne Eagleson. Boscawen says the monthly meetings between Hide, his deputy Heather Roy and Key were cordial. But within a year, friction developed within the party. There was disquiet that ACT was doing little to pressure National into sweeping economic reforms. Roger Douglas was especially frustrated. Hide's leadership was also under question: he'd publicly criticised Key at a business breakfast, and made use of taxpayer-funded travel perks, something he'd vigorously campaigned against. Reports emerged that Douglas and Roy attempted to depose him. Key stepped in and told Roy their confidence and supply deal would be cancelled if Hide was dumped. At the time Te Pāti Māori were also struggling to deal with a rogue MP, Hone Harawira, who would later be expelled for criticism of the party's relationship with National. It was claimed Key briefly considered a snap election to obtain an outright majority for National.

Hide saw off the challenge, but he conceded ACT was in 'the death zone'. It is a position most smaller parties in government find themselves in. They struggle with the compromise required to get core policies on the Cabinet agenda, while retaining ownership of successful policies which the major party often brands as its own.

By late February, the schism between the party's ideological purists and political pragmatists was on public display. Roy gave an extraordinary speech to their national conference, at Wellington College. It was a barely disguised attack on Hide's leadership and the party's direction. In August, she paid the price for attempting to unseat him. At a caucus meeting, the party stripped her of her deputy role and forced her to resign her ministerial positions. Boscawen took her place, and was sworn in as consumer affairs minister and associate commerce minister. For a time, it put National on shaky ground. If Douglas and Roy abandoned ACT and withdrew their support for the government, Key would have to rely on his other support parties to pass legislation, handing more power to Dunne and Te Pāti Māori.

Roy and Douglas stayed, but the party's president Michael Crozier quit. The fallout was toxic, and the party appeared riven with petty vendettas. Commentators began questioning if ACT would survive the next election. Hide's leadership went from bad to worse. It was revealed he'd kept secret law and order spokesman David Garrett's conviction for stealing a dead infant's identity. And he was also accused of hypocrisy after taking his partner on taxpayer-funded overseas jaunts, despite railing against MPs' perks.

Faced with declining support and funding, board members secretly approached Don Brash, asking him to return to Parliament as deputy or co-leader. Brash refused: it was leader or nothing. Securing the support of John Banks, a former National Party police minister and Auckland mayor, he ousted Hide and forced a takeover of the party. The duo were quickly nicknamed the 'codgerati': Brash was 71 and Banks approaching 65, and both had served in senior positions in the National Party. It was an extraordinary comeback — if it can be called that, as Brash was yet to even join ACT, being still a member of the National Party. He was also unelected but became leader outside Parliament.

For the remaining six months of the parliamentary term, at the monthly evening get-togethers, Key sat opposite the man he had toppled in 2006. 'Those meetings continued to be very cordial,' Boscawen says.

When the 2011 election campaign kicked off, National was vague about endorsing the ailing ACT party. ACT had agreed not to stand in marginal electorates Waimakariri, West Coast–Tasman and New Plymouth. But National's Paul Goldsmith was still running against John Banks in Epsom. Aligning with such a damaged and weakened party could harm National. But by not doing so, Key could face a backlash from voters who did not want to see one party hold a majority.

Midway through the campaign, Key agreed to a symbolic cuppa with Banks at Newmarket's Urban cafe. The pair made polite small talk, before the media was hustled outside. In the scrum, freelance camera operator Bradley Ambrose left a small black bag containing a microphone on the table. It captured the entire conversation. Ambrose was working for *The New Zealand Herald*, who sought permission from Banks and Key to publish a transcript. Key's office refused, so the *Herald on Sunday* published a story of the existence of the recording. What followed was a 'brew-ha-ha' that dominated the final two weeks of the campaign. National's campaign manager Steven Joyce accused the paper of carrying out a 'deliberate *News of the World*-type covert operation'. Key laid a complaint with the police, and officers subsequently searched media outlets.

National insisted there was nothing embarrassing in the tape, but Winston Peters saw an opportunity, leaking what he claimed were excerpts. Key told Banks that Peters's elderly constituents were dying off as they discussed New Zealand First's chances of returning to Parliament. Key later apologised for any offence caused to older voters. The extra profile and publicity gave his support a leg-up, and New Zealand First were returned to Parliament after a three-year hiatus. ACT just scraped into office: Banks held Epsom, but the party vote share was 1.07 per cent. Brash quit on election night. National increased its vote — up to 48 from 45 per cent — and, with Dunne also re-elected, National stitched together a government. Although Key did not need Te Pāti Māori, he again struck a deal. Internally, National was beginning to question whether keeping ACT on life support was too harmful to their brand.

Banks and Boscawen met with Key in his Beehive office. Boscawen had quit as campaign manager six weeks before election day; the infighting and internal conflict had left him physically and mentally exhausted. The men had one bottom line: the establishment of charter schools. These would be operated by private businesses or organisations but receive state funding along with private donations. The schools would have the same freedoms as private schools in setting the curriculum, the length of the school year and teachers' pay. Teaching staff would also not have to be registered or even formally trained. Former ACT president Catherine Isaac drafted the agreement, and the finer details were negotiated between English and Boscawen. Banks served as minister of regulatory reform, minister for small business, as well as holding associate commerce and education portfolios.

By 2013, Key had lost two of his support party ministers. Dunne resigned his portfolios after refusing to provide emails to an inquiry into the leaking of a report into illegal spying by New Zealand's security agencies. Banks quit after a judge ordered him to stand trial over allegedly knowingly filing a false electoral return. A private prosecution was brought over donations worth

$65,000 made to his 2010 bid for the Auckland mayoralty by casino operator SkyCity and Kim Dotcom, an internet mogul fighting extradition to the United States. (Banks was convicted and then later acquitted.)

ACT chose little-known academic and writer Jamie Whyte to lead the party into the 2014 election. At the same meeting, 30-year-old David Seymour, then working as a policy analyst for Banks, was selected as the Epsom candidate. The party's support immediately slumped to zero. Boscawen, fearing the new appointments were too great a gamble, quit the party. Whyte promised to be 'pure ACT', moving the party back to principled neoliberal and social libertarian policies. He recruited Richard Prebble to run the campaign strategy. But his bid to revive the party's fortunes got off to a bad start. After dropping a clanger in an interview about the state intervening in cases of incest when it involves consenting adults, he chewed up value media time at his first party conference trying to explain his views. The campaign lurched from bad to worse. Once again, Epsom was ACT's only lifeline.

Whyte's troubles epitomised the minor-party scene. The rise of radical fringe parties like the Conservative Party, founded by millionaire oddball Colin Craig, and Internet Mana, bankrolled by Kim Dotcom, had seen support shift back to the larger parties. In order to attract the votes it needed to gain more MPs, ACT would have to set itself apart from National, in a way that put it in competition with Key's party. If ACT's policies were too radical, they risked upsetting National's more moderate supporters. Their relationship required a fine balance. And although ACT was a safe bet as a coalition partner, Key and his ministers weren't keen to see a resurgent party with increased representation in Parliament.

After the 'teapot tapes' debacle of 2011, National felt a symbolic cuppa with Seymour was unwise. Seymour was also opposed. Key did make it clear he would prefer to work with current support partners, and refused to do an electorate deal with the emergent Conservative Party in the East Coast Bays seat. Seymour worked hard to retain the electorate, even sustaining a tissue-damage injury to his hand after knocking on more than 30,000 doors. A campaign video in which he introduced himself no less than six times with a cheerful 'hi' went viral. With a feeble 0.7 per cent of the party vote, Whyte failed to secure a seat and quit. Seymour, ACT's sole MP, was now the party's fifth leader in four years. He promised a more positive tone from the often 'grumpy' party.

Key again sewed up a deal with the three support parties but this time offered no policy concessions. Seymour, as a rookie, asked that he be given no ministerial portfolios. A voluntary euthanasia proponent, Seymour wanted to spearhead a member's bill that would legalise medical aid in dying; a ministerial role would make that almost impossible. Seymour flirted with handing over the bill to newly elected National MP Chris Bishop but ultimately rejected Key's offer. To help Seymour with the administrative workload, Key made him a parliamentary undersecretary. That came with a bigger salary and staff but would not expose him to the same level of scrutiny as a minister. National looked after him in other ways: Chris Finlayson regularly took him to dinner, and Wayne Eagleson made sure he was taking time off.

But the major party also took advantage of their inexperienced coalition partner. Seymour inked the deal with Key in National's caucus room — he only twigged to the symbolism later. 'I was there as a de facto National MP. And I had no idea that was their caucus room,' he says. Seymour was focused on progressing the roll-out of charter schools. But he found National's Education Minister Hekia Parata intractable, and often had to call on Bill English to intervene.

Seymour's youthful awkwardness and self-deprecating humour began to endear him to the public. He was also a deft politician. Just a year into the job, he rode to the rescue of beer- and rugby-loving Kiwis by drafting a bill enabling licensed premises to open for the England-hosted World Cup screenings in the early morning. Seymour also championed the popular 'Red Peak' design in the country's referendum to change the national flag. It led to another viral video when he tried to explain why the silver fern logo needn't feature on the ensign. 'The French, for instance, love the coq,' he said before bursting into gales of laughter on Parliament's steps. He also negotiated more paid parental leave for families with premature, disabled babies and multiple births. Seymour was trying to shape his party into populist libertarians, but ACT's brand was still too badly damaged.

In 2017, the minor parties again took a battering, starved of oxygen by Jacindamania. New Zealand First and the Greens lost seats, and United Future and Te Pāti Māori were both obliterated. Te Ururoa Flavell's tears at losing Waiariki was one of the lasting images from election night. It was a heartbreaking end to nine years in government that saw the *Foreshore and Seabed Act* repealed, the controversial legislation to which the party could trace its origins. Over 50 Treaty settlements were concluded, a negotiation between the Crown and iwi to agree redress for historical claims of breaches of the Treaty of Waitangi. Whānau Ora, a family health initiative, became a cornerstone of the party's alliance with National. The party also pressed National into signing the Universal Declaration on the Rights of Indigenous People. Te Pāti Māori had never held the balance of power, and National hadn't needed their support, so its leadership were rightly proud of what they had achieved. But critics argued the party had become tainted by its relationship with Key's government. On their watch, Māori unemployment rose, home ownership rates dropped, obesity rates and other poor health measures continued to climb, suicide rates were higher, and over half the prison population were Māori even though they made up fewer than 15 per cent of the general population. The policy gains and concessions weren't enough for voters, who grew increasingly uncomfortable with the partnership with National.

ACT hung on; with 0.5 per cent share of the vote, it again owed its place in Parliament to Epsom. It was the worst result in the party's history. Seymour had been desperate to win a signal from English. The prime minister agreed to be guest of honour at a fundraising dinner at Parnell's Antoine's restaurant. Guests paid $10,000 to dine with English. In the end, it made little difference to Seymour's support. 'The relationship had started to distance by that point, become less relevant to us,' Seymour says. After National lost office, the parties moved into a new phase, in opposition together.

Winston Peters was present in the moment at which it all started to go wrong for New Zealand First. Seymour wasn't, but he reaped the rewards of what was one of the worst tactical errors of Peters's 41-year career in politics. It took place in the Cabinet room on the tenth floor of the Beehive, under a linen canvas painted with the steep, wooded valleys and pale blue of the Marlborough Sounds. The artist, Michael Moore, had painted *Pelorus Diptych* on a journey on the mail boat with his dog, Waldo. His work centres around the environment and New Zealand landscapes. Underneath his piece, ministers were debating an issue that would divide rural New Zealand and strike at the heart of what many saw as an important part of the countryside's cultural identity: gun ownership.

The nation was struggling to come to terms with the Christchurch terror attack of March 2019, during which a white supremacist used five guns — two semi-automatic rifles, two shotguns and a lever-action firearm — to shoot dead 51 people and injure 49 others. Jacinda Ardern's government moved swiftly, within weeks of the attack proposing reforms that would ban most semi-automatic firearms, many pump-action shotguns and large magazines. A nationwide buyback scheme would collect the newly illegal guns. Cabinet was meeting to rubber-stamp the reforms. The Greens were invited — a rare occasion — so ministers-outside-Cabinet James Shaw and Eugenie Sage were seated around the donut-shaped table. Police officers were also in the room, to brief the ministers and demonstrate rifles.

A minister who was present described how Defence Minister and New Zealand First MP Ron Mark put up a reasonably spirited argument, playing devil's advocate. But the public momentum was too great, and despite Peters having traditionally supported the rights of firearms owners, New Zealand First agreed to support the amnesty.

'It was the *coup de grâce* for New Zealand First. Their vote was always suffering but that just killed it,' the minister says. The buyback scheme launched in late July 2019. The week coincided with a 1 News/Colmar Brunton poll that saw New Zealand First's support slump to 3.3 per cent, below the threshold required to return without an electorate MP. By October, 100 protestors showed up at the party's annual conference, angry at a second tranche of proposed reforms, including establishing a gun register.

Instead, the mainly rural vote flocked to Seymour, the only MP to oppose gun control. Farmers were also attracted to his stance on climate change: he'd planned to be the sole dissenter on new zero-carbon legislation but missed the vote. His strident criticism of the government's handling of the Covid-19 pandemic starkly contrasted National's inconsistent positions, and offered a home to those who were opposed to the lockdowns.

Seymour had slowly been building his profile, twerking his way to prime-time exposure on *Dancing with the Stars*. The party brand had a facelift, dumping Hide's canary yellow for a palette of mustard, pink and blue. Seymour was gradually upending the public perception of ACT as the party where retired politicians went to die only to be kept on life support by National. By May, public polls were showing the party on 1.5 per cent. But the fact remained that, in April 2020, 87 per cent of people weren't keen on giving their party vote to ACT.

For the 2020 election campaign, Seymour drafted in campaign manager Nick Wright, who worked from Australia after Covid-19 forced the closure of international borders. An 'old-fashioned British liberal' who tends to back lefty causes, Wright worked for Tony Blair ('before the Labour Party went mad'), Facebook, Malala Yousafzai's fund for education in Pakistan, Australian elections guru Lynton Crosby, US strategist and Republican pollster Frank Luntz (a consultant on TV drama *The West Wing*) and Democratic political strategist Joe Trippi.

Trippi's 2005 book *The Revolution Will Not Be Televised: Democracy, the internet, and the overthrow of everything* was the inspiration for ACT's 2020 campaign. Trippi came up with the technology that Obama used to out-fundraise the Republicans, Wright explains. At that point funds were so depleted that ACT couldn't afford television advertising anyway. In 2020, only four supporters gave donations over $30,000, totalling $385,000. That amount wouldn't even cover the extra month of the elongated election campaign. It would be digitally driven and run on the smell of an oily rag.

The starting point was identifying who might be persuaded to vote ACT. 'We'd probably exhausted the rich, white prick vote,' Wright explains. Initial qualitative data research gave some clues about who to target: the 'potentials' were more ethnically diverse than average (Māori, Chinese, Indian), younger, better educated and entrepreneurial. A third was drawn from National, but 10 per cent was from Labour. The tight budget meant it was necessary to target social media advertising. ACT would typically spend $100 to $200 per Facebook ad, compared with thousands per post by National or Labour. By the final weeks, the major parties were outstripping ACT: in the last week Seymour's party spent about $25,000 to Judith Collins's $150,000. One splurge was on a Facebook video targeting rural voters and farmers, the natural home of New Zealand First.

Wright judged their campaign would have to be high-octane and draw media attention. They threw Seymour out of a plane. (It was a skydive stunt to highlight the plight of struggling tourism operators. He survived.) A national tour was planned by Mark Rigby, a man Seymour met on a plane. His Cheeky Kiwi tourism business was down 88 per cent, so ACT hired him and pasted pictures of its candidates on his bus. Seymour's neighbour Guy Quartermain, a cinematographer who had worked on TV shows like *Grand Designs* and *Seven Days*, filmed campaign videos. Seymour stayed away from traditional ACT preoccupations (one nation, monetary policy, bureaucratic red tape) and instead talked about climate change, housing affordability and cancel culture. He positioned ACT as a constructive party within a broken political system.

As National and New Zealand First's polling plummeted, Seymour's began edging up. Peters was delivered a body blow when the Serious Fraud Office filed charges against two unnamed defendants in an electoral funding case involving the New Zealand First Foundation, a mysterious organisation bankrolling his party. It served to remind voters of a past New Zealand First donations scandal that had dominated the 2008 election campaign. In the end, the final vote was an echo of that result, with MMP's kingmaker dethroned, perhaps for the very last time.

ACT's loveable nerd took the party to 8 per cent on election night. Jubilant, he arrived at the victory party on Auckland's waterfront in a speedboat. With National humiliated, Seymour and his nine new MPs set about transforming ACT into the main party of opposition. He retained senior staffer Andrew Ketels as chief of staff, and sharp lobbyist Brooke van Velden, once Seymour's policy advisor, was now an MP and deputy leader. Rachel Morton, National's former chief press secretary, joined the team as a media manager. The party's communications strategy was much bolder and more agile than their rivals in opposition. Under Judith Collins, National began shifting to the far-Right margins and away from issues of mainstream politics. But her positions on cancel culture and Māori separatism were a pale intimation of Seymour. Seymour relished the scraps.

Nine months on from the election, Seymour overtook Collins as preferred prime minister, on 12 per cent over her 10. But, being unlikely ever to be in the position of leading the country, Seymour had the luxury of saying more outlandish and populist things. While bruising for National's MPs, they knew National had only itself to blame for a failure to pick up in the polls. And although things looked desperate for a time, no one took seriously the contention offered by some pundits that ACT would eventually eclipse National to become the main party of opposition. As both parties focused on their own fortunes, the relationship between the two parties all but fizzled out; in late 2021 Seymour struggled to even name Collins's chief of staff. He likens it to winning a war over another nation: 'Who do you talk to in the country you've just beaten? You get to Tokyo in 1945; who the hell is in charge?'

ACT's rise was predicated on one thing: its growth was always at the expense of National's support. As the larger party recovered, ACT could only lose ground. National would continue to take ACT's support as a given. But if Seymour has permanently vanquished New Zealand First, National has a problem. Its future almost certainly hinges on its ability to build a multi-party coalition.

Either ACT must do better, increasing their vote without National's help and building a brand that is compatible but distinct — or National needs to find an alternative dance partner. A New Zealand First comeback is always within the realms of possibility, but presently Winston Peters's party does appear to be a spent force. Where there is persistent popular support for a Teal Deal, the Green Party is an improbable option. Its more radical left-wing faction has grown, and the party membership is already chafing against the leadership, which it believes has jettisoned core values in its co-operation with Labour. Even if National offered the Greens policy concessions — such as increased spending for environmental initiatives — the two parties' worldviews on economic and social policy would never align. It would be a volatile relationship, particularly if ACT was part of the make-up. The party's rank and file would never accept the alliance, and the internal damage would almost certainly tear the Greens apart.

Te Pāti Māori's current leadership — Rawiri Waititi and Debbie Ngarewa-Packer — are a new generation, acutely aware that voters fell out of love with the party because of its relationship with National. Ngarewa-Packer, a seabed mining campaigner and former deputy mayor of South Taranaki, is comfortable in both Māori and Pākehā worlds. Waititi is a tohunga, an expert in church law, of the Ringatū religious movement.

The party has positioned itself to the Left, and been an unapologetic voice for Māori, pushing for increased funding for Māori organisations and honouring te ao Māori (Māori worldview). Ahead of the 2020 election, under Muller's leadership, Ngarewa-Packer said working with National would be untenable. But the party seems to be without allies. Waititi — once a Labour Party candidate — has stressed the party is independent of any mainstream Pākehā party. Labour no longer suits his values and principles, and he has accused the current government of being 'abusive towards Māori'. On the other hand, trust must be restored after Judith Collins pursued race issues. Te Pāti Māori is also wary of National's recent opposition to Māori representation on local authorities and to co-governance (negotiated decision-making arrangements between Māori and central government).

If the 2023 election delivers another hung Parliament, both National and Labour may end up wrestling over Te Pāti Māori. But in a troubling sign, Seymour said in early 2022 that he was not prepared to enter an alliance that included Te Pāti Māori. As with 2017, failure to build a pragmatic coalition could cost National another term in opposition.

14

THIS IS YOUR CAPTAIN SPEAKING

In the six tumultuous days after Judith Collins's leadership imploded in November 2021, Simon Bridges wrestled with a dilemma. The National leadership contest came down to a choice between himself and ambitious former airline chief Christopher Luxon. A poll just before Collins was jettisoned had registered both men in the preferred PM rankings, neck-and-neck on 2.5 per cent.

Bridges had worked hard to restore his public image in the months since he'd been rolled as leader. He was wiser and more resilient. Writing his memoirs was a form of political rehab, but it had also allowed him to reflect on solutions for the widening wealth gap and inequity in the education system. It was his personal manifesto. He would also be taking back the reins in an entirely different climate. The country's mood had shifted, more fractious after nearly two years of the pandemic and less enamoured with Jacinda Ardern's leadership.

As Key had, Bridges drew inspiration from former Australian Prime Minister John Howard, who led his Liberal Party to defeat in 1987 before being ousted by his deputy Andrew Peacock. Howard rose to the top again, and went on to win four elections. In July 2018, Bridges and his wife, Natalie, had dined with Howard, who offered his advice and support. The Aussie political Lazarus had opened National's annual conference that year, urging MPs to get in behind Bridges, their new leader. 'Proud as you may be of your former leaders, every new leader is entitled to make his own impression,' Howard said. In 2021, Bridges was ready for another crack.

He had support but fell short of the 16 votes needed to triumph. Collins and her acolytes made it clear they would throw their lot in behind Luxon. The party's small band of liberals, led by Nicola Willis and Chris Bishop, also wanted a clean break. But there was still hesitancy. Luxon and Mark Mitchell had put their names forward during the marathon meeting that ended Collins's leadership. The caucus asked for more time to deliberate. Luxon was untested: he had been an MP less than 400 days, much of which was spent in lockdown in Auckland. Bridges kept his powder dry, although he publicly hinted he was considering a tilt. Mitchell offered to withdraw if Bridges stood.

Over the weekend, there was a furious round of lobbying and organising. The party wanted to avoid a vote. Senior party figures, including John Key, implored Bridges and his supporters to strike a deal with Luxon to restore harmony to the fractured caucus. Bridges weighed up his options. In taking a deal similar to that offered to Bill English in 2006, he saw a chance to influence and shape policy in the same way Key's deputy had.

On the morning of 30 November, Bridges contacted his rival. With mere hours to go until the caucus cast a vote, they agreed to meet in Wellington. Their advisors were oblivious, scrambling to book two venues for the post-decision media conference. Bridges wanted the grand Legislative Council Chamber, where he'd first addressed journalists as leader in 2018. Luxon wanted the curved marble walls of the Beehive's Banquet Hall, usually reserved for government announcements. Bridges accepted Luxon's offer: he would take the shadow finance portfolio, ranked Luxon's number three. They would keep the news under wraps.

'We are the reset,' Luxon told reporters on emerging from the caucus meeting. He noted his track record in reversing the fortunes of under-performing companies. Nicola Willis was chosen by the caucus to be his new deputy. The party's top three were all Key protégés. Willis owed her list MP place in Parliament to the departures of Bill English and Steven Joyce in April 2018. But unlike Luxon, she was not new to politics; she had pedigree. Her great-great-grandfather Archibald Willis was a Liberal Party MP for Whanganui and voted yes to women getting the vote in 1893. Almost a century later, her mother, Shona, was a political journalist in the Press Gallery while pregnant with Willis.

Willis arrived at Parliament in 2003 as a researcher for English, going on to work for Brash and then Key. Luxon had come to know Willis in the country's cliquish corporate scene. She had worked in senior management roles for Fonterra. (Luxon was tipped to head the multinational dairy co-operative in 2018.) Willis's husband, Duncan Small, had worked for Luxon, as Air New Zealand's head of government affairs. The mother of four powered through the party rankings, from 45 to 13 under Collins. She made a name for herself grilling Housing Minister Megan Woods, with a particular emphasis on how a shortage of homes was affecting low-income families. Willis, aged 41, was appointed for her political nous and experience. But with a no-nonsense, head-girl manner, it was also anticipated she wouldn't shy away from instilling discipline.

Her elevation to deputy leader was partly down to optics. The caucus liked the contrast of Willis's social liberalism, particularly on abortion rights, gay marriage and euthanasia, with Luxon's social conservatism. His worship at the Upper Room, a Christian fundamentalist church, made waves ever since his entry into politics. The church's American-born pastor had expressed alt-Right views on social media, which Luxon later decried. Shortly after Luxon's selection as the party's candidate for Botany, the Newmarket church stripped its website of some of the more controversial sermons. Once chosen, Luxon laid out his views, saying he was personally against decriminalising abortion or euthanasia. At the time the country was a year out from twin referendums on the issues. 'My faith is a very personal thing … it gives me mission and purpose,' he said. Luxon wore his social conservatism on his sleeve. On his first day as a candidate, he went further than National Party policy in supporting the withdrawal of single-parent support benefits from parents who don't vaccinate their children. Luxon later revealed he had recently turned down a job running a California-based cannabis company. He believed the risk to the mental health of young users was too great.

Luxon's faith continued to be a curiosity. New Zealand is a largely secular society, and both Prime Ministers Helen Clark and John Key were agnostic. Jacinda Ardern was raised a Mormon but renounced her faith in her twenties to support gay rights. For the past few years, there was concern that the balance in the National caucus tipped towards social conservatism, and one of its many fractures was along religious lines. The observant MPs were known as 'The Taliban'. Among their number were Bridges, an Anglican whose father was a Baptist minister, Simon O'Connor, Simeon Brown, Harete Hipango and Maureen Pugh. Alfred Ngaro, who holds a theological degree, Agnes Loheni and

Paulo Garcia, a devout Catholic, had not returned to Parliament after the 2020 election.

Media interviewers continued to bait Luxon on his beliefs. He confronted the issue head-on in his maiden speech, arguing that just because he held a Christian faith did not mean he had extreme views. It anchored him and gave his life purpose, he said, and he argued a person should not be elected nor rejected because of their beliefs. 'My faith is personal to me. It is not in itself a political agenda.' Luxon appeared to be trying to have a bob each way, placating those nervous of 'The Taliban' while appealing to the Christian Right. Willis was a ballast, but Luxon went further: ruling out changing abortion laws if elected prime minister, and changing his vote in order to support safe zones outside abortion clinics, when he had previously opposed legislation to create them. The 52-year-old also claimed he had stopped attending church five years earlier. Among the conservative elements in caucus, the apparent dilution of his principles was quietly noted. 'The media have got him wrong, thinking he's a Christian fundy conservative,' a senior party figure says. 'He is more comfortable with the ideas of Barack Obama than [former Canadian Prime Minister] Stephen Harper or Boris Johnson. He's not particularly different from Ardern. Economically, maybe.'

*

The equilibrium is important, both to National's roots, but also its future success. It was born out of a merger of two conservative parties: Reform and United (formerly the Liberal Party). The Reform Party was created by William Massey, a farmer-turned-politician, and focused on rural policies. United were aligned with the business community, particularly in Auckland. Pragmatism brought the two forces together. Aware they were splitting the vote between conservative factions, they campaigned together in the 1935 election to curb the rise of Michael Joseph Savage's Labour Party. They lost, disastrously. But the alliance was nevertheless formalised at a conference in May 1936.

It would be another 13 years before they took office, under Sidney Holland. There are some similarities between Holland and Luxon. Charismatic, a dogged champion of private enterprise, Holland was elected leader partly because he was a relatively fresh face in Parliament. More comfortable with the urban wing, he bought a Canterbury sheep station to win over farmers.

In its early years, National struggled to move beyond simply being the 'anti-Labour party'. Holland was fundamental in carving out its ideology. 'Passwords to Progress' was a 1943 pamphlet, later a speech, in which he argued a National government would deliver economic prosperity, individual freedom and a minimum of bureaucratic red tape. Until Labour's landslide victory in 2020, Holland's was the last government to be elected by a majority of voters, during the 1951 waterfront strike. Holland had called a snap election, seeking a mandate to deal with the industrial confrontation.

For close to four decades, National was the dominant party, holding office for all but the three years between 1949 and 1972. Holland's successor, Keith Holyoake, underlined the party's principles in 1959, when he said the party believes in a property-owning democracy, the maximum degree of personal freedom and individual choice, the least interference necessary with individual rights, and the least possible degree of state intervention. In the 1960s, the party enjoyed membership of a quarter of a million, and it was established as the natural party of government.

Despite this, National never succeeded in throwing off the proposition that it existed simply as a reaction to Labour.

Throughout the twentieth century, although it barely held the Treasury benches, it was Labour's interventionist ideology on health, education, welfare and housing that dominated. Like in Britain, New Zealand politics was characterised by a post-war consensus, a belief in Keynesian economics and maintaining a mixed economy guided mainly by the private sector but partly operated by the government.

Remaining in power came at the expense of advancing National's core ideals. Holland was a pragmatist who embraced the centre by preserving Labour's social security safety-net. He and Holyoake intended to liberalise the economy, but successive governments achieved little, apart from in trade with Australia. Grassroots members wanted compulsory unionism abolished, but Holyoake was no agent of change. Stability and consensus were the watchwords of his governance. He was National's most successful prime minister, winning four consecutive elections and serving for 11 years. For the latter half of the century, National was characterised by liberal individualism with a social conscience.

A wave of economic crises (in oil supply, rising inflation, increasing unemployment) hit the country between 1973 and 1984. New Zealand lost its guaranteed export market when Britain joined the European Economic Community. Welfare costs had doubled. To keep the economy afloat, Prime Minister Robert Muldoon imposed an extreme level of intervention, including restrictions on wages, foreign currency, import tariffs, farmer subsidies and large-scale infrastructure investments. His policies failed to stabilise the economy, and his party and voters began to resent the size of the state and its role in their lives.

National lost a snap election called by Muldoon in 1984. Divisions in the party, a split vote caused by the formation of the free-enterprise New Zealand Party, and the rise of charismatic

Labour leader David Lange saw their vote sink to 36 per cent. In office, this was a very different Labour Party. It followed a neoliberal revolution, led by Margaret Thatcher and Ronald Reagan. Under Finance Minister Roger Douglas, Labour adopted policies that favoured competition, investors, free trade and the privatising of state assets. The Kiwi dollar was floated. This economic deregulation — which came to be known as Rogernomics — disrupted farming, manufacturing and the public sector. It was an ideological shock to both Labour supporters and National, the latter conceding they were 'outflanked on the Right'.

Once again, the charge was led by Labour. National continued the reforms through the 1990s, overhauling the labour market with the controversial *Employment Contracts Act 1991*, reshaping social policy and developing an enterprise culture (known as Ruthanasia after finance minister Ruth Richardson). But the free-market liberalism also unsettled the party's Muldoonist conservatives. The party's ranks thinned and the caucus factionalised. National failed to adapt as quickly as Labour to the new mixed-member proportional (MMP) voting system, which presented alternatives to supporters in the form of ACT, United Future and New Zealand First.

With a clear move to the Right, Don Brash reclaimed the voters who had drifted away. Under Key the party repositioned to the centre; no more than a managed retreat from Clark's progressive policies. In the Holyoake tradition, Key divested the party's political beliefs in favour of getting a majority of people behind the things his government did. As it was in the 1950s and 1960s, the liberal–conservative tension was restored. Key chose not to overturn Working for Families tax credits nor paid parental leave, both central achievements of Helen Clark's government that he had opposed. Key, English and Joyce moved

National away from hard-core neoliberal deregulation. In the 2015 Budget, the government increased benefits by $25 a week for families with children. It was the first benefit increase since 1977. Under English, National settled a landmark pay-equity agreement for state-funded care workers and straddled the middle ground by boosting low to middle incomes. Partly because of the series of natural and economic disasters (among them the global financial crisis, the Canterbury and Kaikōura earthquakes, and the Covid-19 pandemic) that have befallen New Zealand in the past decade and a half, voters now expect a lot from the state.

National evolved into a party with a laissez-faire approach: responsibly managing the economy (intervening only in times of crisis) and maintaining stability. It returned to a pragmatic broad-church party that was a historically successful model. Shunning ideological commitment may also be one of the reasons it avoided the authoritarian populism that recently gripped right-wing movements in other Western democracies.

Luxon is very much in the mould of Key — and indeed the two talk regularly. Wayne Eagleson is also mentoring Luxon. And Cameron Burrows, chief policy advisor to Key and English, was appointed his chief of staff. Key was a candidate straight from central casting: a state-house kid to international banker, media-savvy and fluent in business and the economy. Luxon, too, was born in Christchurch, although in more comfortable circumstances. His father, Graham, was a sales executive for Johnson & Johnson. Kathleen, his mother, is a psychotherapist and counsellor. Luxon was the eldest of three boys, and the family relocated to Howick, in Auckland, when he was seven. Aged 15, he returned to Canterbury, and completed his schooling at Christchurch Boys' High. There is a consensus that mainstream party leaders should demonstrate a connection to Auckland, where most voters live. Luxon's South Island roots are also attractive to its heartland support.

Luxon's first job was at a McDonald's drive-through. He attended the University of Canterbury, studying for a Master's in Commerce, majoring in business administration, where he was recruited into Unilever's management trainee program. His first role in management was as brand manager of their local detergent business, at the Petone plant, then five years with sales and marketing in Sydney. He moved to the London head office as a global director of deodorants and grooming, and then to leadership roles in North America. He joined Air New Zealand in May 2011, managing international routes. Like Key, he is an internationalist, and they share similar conservative economic views, with a desire for strong trade links to the rest of the world.

Key believes Luxon will be an 'outstanding' leader. On the surface, Luxon's leadership style appears similar to that of his mentor: managerial and cautious. His priority is to restore faith in National's ability to manage the economy. To that end, Luxon has burnished his business credentials to such a degree that it has become a joke among pundits: didn't he used to run an airline? He set KPIs and annual performance reviews for his shadow Cabinet, and talks about parliamentary terms in business quarters. There are some parallels in parliamentary politics and running a business: setting a culture, solving problems, maintaining a ruthless message discipline and improving performance. Certainly, Luxon's business experience in branding will help enormously in politics, where brand is everything. But Key did not succeed because of his financial acumen: he was a weathervane who could accurately read the public mood.

There are also differences. Key has a gregarious personality and an everyman touch. Luxon lacks his charisma. Instead he has excelled in projecting a bland, corporate image. His only known idiosyncrasies are a love of country music and a habit of writing emails in a blue Comic Sans font. His motive might be divined from a book he likes to recommend: *Good to Great* by business guru Jim Collins. It shaped the thinking of a generation of business leaders, topping readership charts and selling 4 million copies, and was Amazon's number-one bestseller in 2004 and 2005. The book is typical of the brightly covered, jargon-ridden management books on sale in airport bookstores. Luxon's shelves in his Air New Zealand office were piled with such paperbacks, a former colleague reports. In researching his book, Jim Collins had analysed more than 1400 Fortune 500 companies over five years. One of his main conclusions is that 'rockstar' chief executives, whose deepest ambitions are for themselves, are harmful to success.

Early into his political career, Luxon is a policy and ideological clean slate. Like Key, he seems focused on outcomes, not ideology, and appears to adhere broadly to the same trickle-down economic policies. He has also expressed concerns about rapid growth in public debt and low productivity. In his maiden statement and in his first speech as National leader he espoused traditional National values, including rewarding hard work and initiative. 'I believe in a New Zealand that backs Kiwis to work hard, to convert opportunities, and to create prosperity,' he said in his maiden statement. An almost identical line appears in his inaugural speech as leader.

In line with Key–English doctrine, he expressed a belief that governments must make 'powerful and targeted interventions' on behalf of those with complex and challenged lives. He has indicated he supports English's data-driven social investment approach but has made a number of attacks on welfare dependency. His first major policy announcement was to promise tax reductions, unwinding increases imposed by Labour.

Luxon also appears conscious of addressing growing inequality, homelessness and deprivation but is yet to expand on how to do so. His attacks on the government have focused on the rising costs of living and inflation. On Māori affairs, he has said little so far, beyond saying that he respected the central role of the Treaty of Waitangi in national life. National Party sources also point to an increasing focus on climate change mitigation.

One of the most frequent criticisms of the Fifth National Government is that its leadership devoted their immense political talents to obtaining, and then retaining, power, at the expense of achieving a lasting legacy or making the country a better place. Because success was its north star, the caucus could not navigate the disruptive change brought about by loss and opposition.

For National to win in 2023, Labour needs to fail. The maxim is that oppositions don't win elections, governments lose. Governments eventually become shop-soiled as the incidence of misjudgements and cock-ups accrue. The gap between the Left (Labour and the Greens) and Right (National and ACT) blocs has narrowed as the public has grown tired of over two years of pandemic restrictions and become increasingly concerned about a surge in the cost of living, stagnant wages and a runaway housing market.

The 400,000-plus voters who deserted National in 2020 must come to see something they like in Luxon's party. Labour took 15 seats from National, including in several traditional safe seats like Rangitata, Ilam and Nelson. Women, provincial New Zealanders and ethnic Kiwis drifted away from the party — and Luxon needs to reconnect with them. The task is to both rattle voters' confidence in Labour and convince the electorate National better reflects their values and aspirations. Luxon is out of step with the average New Zealander: a millionaire and property owner who protested a $40 a week minimum wage rise. He must convince the electorate that he understands their domestic financial challenges, and that his 'confident, aspirational and prosperous future' does not mean a return to slashing and burning government expenditure on core public services or transferring wealth from working people to the owners of capital.

Upon taking the reins in November 2021, Luxon and Willis immediately went to work: revitalising the front bench, cementing discipline and unifying the party, and focusing on combating the Ardern Government in the House. The changes had a positive effect almost instantly. In late January 2022, Ardern's personal support slumped to its lowest level since 2017, although she still led by a significant margin. Polling also indicated growing pessimism about the economic outlook. By March, Luxon's National had overtaken Labour, up seven per centage points to 39, with Labour on 37 per cent.

Luxon developed a code of conduct to reign in bad behaviour within his caucus. Poor governance and an ability to fundraise were identified as key factors in the heavy loss in 2020. President Peter Goodfellow has loyal supporters who treasure his fund-raising abilities and, as part of a dairy and fishing dynasty, his connections to the country's wealthiest citizens. But there are an increasingly large cohort of members who believe that after more than a decade — and two election defeats — his influence over the party's affairs should come to an end.

Chief among their concerns are a series of unsuitable candidate selections that saw the party mired in scandal, including Todd Barclay, his replacement in Clutha-Southland Hamish Walker, and Andrew Falloon. The one that rankles most is former Upper Harbour hopeful Jake Bezzant, who held onto his candidacy after questions surfaced about his business experience and CV. Nearly a year after the 2020 election Bezzant left the party when a former girlfriend complained to police about his behaviour in the wake of a break-up. He was not charged with any crimes.

Senior party figures, past and present, were uneasy about Goodfellow's close involvement in selections, including a habit of turning up to meetings. In August 2021, former minister David Carter unsuccessfully challenged Goodfellow for the presidency, believing he had the support of Judith Collins. Carter resigned abruptly, saying he had no confidence in Goodfellow's leadership. He left a hole, with no strong rural voice on the board.

Within the ranks, there is an expectation Goodfellow's tenure will soon end, voluntarily or otherwise. In late January 2022, when Luxon failed to invite Goodfellow or the board's members to his first caucus retreat, it was taken as an explicit signal that he too expects change.

Key's influence has been central to Luxon's rise and his growing success. His patronage has given the party a sense that 'Daddy's home', with some relief and new energy among the ranks. It seems not to matter that National has lost its soul: Luxon achieved a significant support bump even before he had a chance to set out his stall. Key's sole legacy is as a responsible steward of the economy, and if he is confident Luxon can run things, then the party, and voters, seem willing to take a chance on him.

This partly explains why Luxon is yet to step out of Key's shadow and shape his own narrative and image: it works for National if the electorate see him as Key 2.0. His first state of the nation — delayed when the Omicron Covid-19 variant took hold — was supposed to focus on education. When it was delivered, he chose the comfortable turf of tax. It was an address that could have been delivered by Key, English or Joyce.

*

But this direction — or lack of one — did not sit well with one key National figure. Simon Bridges was soul-searching, and he was questioning if National could recapture its purpose, beyond simply governing.

For two years, since the caucus overthrew his leadership, he'd considered his future in politics, restlessly going back and forward. There was the lure of a bigger salary in the private sphere, and since he was only in his mid-forties, the promise of a third career. In penning his memoirs, he'd discovered a new pleasure in writing and stretching his intellect in exploring new ideas.

The matter was considered settled when he accepted the role as shadow finance minister at the end of 2021. He masterminded the party's strategy in attacking the government over the rise in living costs. Then in March 2022 he abruptly quit. The resignation sent shockwaves through Wellington. To pundits it seemed unfathomable: in just over a year's time there was a very real chance he would have been the country's next finance minister.

But, in reality, Bridges's internal conflict had persisted. Just as Luxon had been preparing to reveal his appointment to the finance role, Bridges's eight-year-old son, Harry, was hit by a swing in the school playground. The collision almost destroyed the boy's liver. Overnight, the family's priorities shifted. Luxon made the announcement of the finance role without Bridges present. 'It did change everything because life had to stop,' Bridges later told the *Women's Weekly*. If National was to win in 2023, Bridges was looking at potentially another decade in political life: he'd be duty bound to do at least two terms as finance minister. He chose family.

But there was another motivation: the tensions within the party hadn't been swept away with Luxon's new broom. Now they lay not within a restive caucus but among the upper echelons. And instead of quarrels centred on ambition, ego and jealousies, these were fundamentally much deeper divisions: they went to the very heart of what the party stood for.

'Luxon, Willis, Chris Bishop and Cam Burrows are peas in a pod,' a source says. Bridges felt isolated, and under pressure to safeguard the party's more conservative identity. 'In an interview, Luxon categorically said there would be no spending cuts,' the source continues. 'I sit there as a fiscal conservative and think: are you joking? What's the fucking point of being in Government? Is National going to come in again and just manage everything Labour's done?'

Luxon and Bridges disagreed on the party's first policy announcement of 2022. Luxon pushed tax cuts. Bridges didn't want to look reckless, pushing cuts during the Covid recovery, and preferred to stick with indexation that would adjust tax bands for inflation. He wanted to win the election, and he saw Opposition as a chance to pursue a bold, centre-right agenda. Luxon's approach appeared more passive: he was content to allow Labour to lose. The ideological incongruity didn't chase Bridges out, but it gave him comfort in his decision to leave while National was on the up.

The party's revival is tied both to worsening economic conditions and to a sense that Luxon can put things right. As one seasoned MP cynically puts it: 'A good chunk of New Zealand just wants a white businessman, who is successful, to manage the show.' Success breeds success — often a reversal of fortunes in opinion polling creates a self-perpetuating dynamic. And the political media, by now bored of Ardern's popularity, have enthusiastically seized on a fresh narrative. If the upward trend continues, Luxon and Willis will have to worry less and less about the ill-discipline and infighting that has debilitated the party in recent years.

Conversely, new faces enjoy a political honeymoon, and Luxon is yet to experience the harsh realities of the worst job in Parliament, where every mistake is unforgivingly picked over. Collins's implosion saw him take the helm much earlier than his supporters wished. As a first-term MP he is singularly inexperienced and thus more prone to slip-ups. Party sources say he relies heavily on Key's advice and is yet to learn how to instinctively set the agenda. He behaves very much like a CEO, delegating speech writing and research to staff.

A change in leadership has wiped clean the blood from the floor. But National's deep-seated issues remain just below the surface. It could not survive the crisis of losing office in 2017 without internal warfare. These conflicts torpedoed the leaderships of English, Bridges, Muller and Collins. Experienced politicians — among them Steven Joyce, Paula Bennett, Nikki Kaye and Amy Adams — left the party in its darkest hour. Valuable years in Opposition, which could have been spent reworking and improving policy, were wasted as they battled each other. Supporters drifted away, weary of the squabbling, and now trust will have to be rebuilt. And while Luxon has vowed to leave the baggage in the past, friction over ideology, values, direction and even governance are still unresolved.

Pragmatism and a desire to win may paper over the cracks. But if Luxon's momentum falters, an impatient caucus will soon look around for another silver bullet. And they will not need to search too far: waiting in the wings is another Key disciple in Nicola Willis. 'Willis is there thinking about her future,' a senior MP says. 'She is deeply tactical.'

ACKNOWLEDGEMENTS

As a journalist, born of an island of storytellers, I was powerless to resist commissioning editor Holly Hunter when she approached me with an idea to write this book.

It would not have been possible without her enthusiasm, calmness, wisdom — and love of a good yarn. Likewise, I have greatly valued the skill and sharp eyes of senior editor Madeleine James in Sydney. Thank you also to editor Kate Stone. It seems strange, but indicative of these times, that I've never met them 'in real life'. You have all taught me so much and my work will be better for it.

Largely, this book was written at the Southland farm of my parents-in-law, Murray and Lynda Halstead. Thank you so much for your hospitality, patience and regular supply of gin and fun. It was a wonderful summer — thank you to the whole clan: Prue, Sean, Ben, Tess, Grace, Henry, Louis, Max, Charlie, and of course the dogs Ruby, Mahe and Moss. Murray, I'm sorry if you hate the book!

There are colleagues at Stuff who I could not have done this without. My boss, Bernadette Courtney, editor in chief newsrooms, who said yes without hesitation, and whose support (as usual) was limitless. I will be forever grateful to her for giving me the best job in the world, and for putting up with me. And to Tracy Watkins, once my political editor and now editor of the *Sunday Star-Times*. She has forgotten more than I will ever know about politics and is an inexhaustive supply of advice and knowledge. Both amazing journalists, these women have kept me out of trouble more times than I care to think about. Some of this book is based on my reporting for them. And then there is photographer Iain McGregor, my partner in crime and adventures, who always has my back. Didn't I promise you'd make it into the book?

For a large proportion of the events described, I reported alongside dear friends Stacey Kirk and Katie Bradford. We are survivors of that crazy 2017 campaign. Stacey, you have been an unfailing support and a dear friend — going above and beyond to proofread, make sensible suggestions and prop up my confidence when it failed. Katie, where would I be without our long chats? Yes, we talk about life and other things, but it always drifts back to politics. I'm pretty sure we'll be swapping gossip into our dotage.

To David Torrance and Douglas Wight — both prodigious Scottish authors — thank you for your help and advice. And to my dear friend Clio Francis, and my swim squad and spin buddies. You all keep me sane.

I owe a huge debt of gratitude to many in the National Party. Good people in politics gave up their time for this book — busy and important people, who had much better things to be getting on with. They were prepared to speak frankly about a remarkable period of political history.

The account is largely based on dozens of interviews with politicians and staffers, past and present. I have profound gratitude for all who are named as sources, and privately salute those who couldn't be. I enjoyed all of our conversations very much. I am especially grateful to those who were willing to recount experiences that were traumatic and bewildering. In all the drama and excitement of campaigns and leadership spills, it is easy to overlook the devastation of those who work in politics, and their families, and who often make great sacrifices for their cause. A special mention to the Dilinger's boys, who know the bits I had to leave out.

I have cited the work of other journalists wherever possible and owe a debt to the Press Gallery and others for their tireless, and often thankless, work.

I thank my parents, Hugh and Claire, and my sister, Laura, for their love and support. I miss you all. My father, himself a journalist, dutifully read this book in draft for which I will be forever grateful. It was beyond the call! My mother is the kindest person on the planet, and I hope I have inherited even a smidge of her empathy. Laura, you always reduce me to giggles — you're the improved version.

This book is dedicated to my incredible husband, Sam, and our darling Dubh. You make everything possible and life joyful.

ENDNOTES

1: LOST KEY

In a testy Parliamentary debate ... *Hansard*, 10 November 2015, vol. 710, p. 7787.

Only weeks after the 2014 general election ... David Lomas, 'National MP Mike Sabin in police assault inquiry', *Sunday Star-Times*, 21 December 2014.

Finance Minister Bill English risked appearing ... *Hansard*, 16 June 2016, vol.715.

The first public poll of 2015 ... 3News/Reid Research Poll, 20–28 January 2015.

The year closed with ... Roy Morgan New Zealand Poll, 9 December 2015.

Announcing in 2015 that he would not seek ... 'David Cameron "won't serve third term" if re-elected', *BBC News*, 24 March 2015.

Much has been made about Bronagh's influence ... Matt Young, 'New Zealand prime minister's wife, Bronagh, asked John Key to resign after eight years in office', News. com.au, 6 December 2015.

'That's for raping our sovereignty' Marika Hill, 'Steven Joyce hit by sex toy thrown by protester at Waitangi', Stuff, 6 February 2016.

He would later say ... 'PM's regret: That flag referendum', Radio NZ, 6 December 2016.

Auditor-General Lyn Provost found ... Inquiry into the Saudi Arabia Food Security Partnership, Controller and Auditor-General, 26 October 2016.

Buildings in Wellington ... Chloe Winter, 'Insurance claims total $1.84 billion for Kaikoura earthquake', Stuff, 21 June 2017.

Cullen, in a memorable ... Audrey Young, 'Cullen not apologising for "scumbag" taunt', *The New Zealand Herald*, 6 December 2007.

At that point National was ... 1 News/Colmar Brunton poll, 22–25 May 2006.

Second-term MP and Brash loyalist Judith Collins ... Judith Collins, *Pull No Punches*, Allen and Unwin, 2020.

Joyce had flirted ... 'Candidates' Bios, Alphabetically By Constituency', New Zealand National Party media release, 14 June 2002.

2: THE STAYER AND THE SPRINTER

Photographer Phil Reid captured ... Phil Reid, 'Long, lonely walk', *The Dominion Post*, 29 October 2003.

The Key–English management ... Ansuya Harjani, 'This will be the "rock star" economy of 2014', CNBC, 5 January 2014.

'I'm a stayer, he's a sprinter ...' *North and South*, August 2008.

Stranded in Gore ... Rt Hon. S. W. English, 'Valedictory Statement', *Hansard*, 1 March 2018.

Did they have an arrangement ... Tom Happold and Kevin Maguire, 'Revealed: Brown and Blair's pact', *The Guardian*, 6 June 2003.

Key was curiously absent ... Jenna Lynch, 'John Key expecting National candidate Parmjeet Parmar to lose Mt Roskill by-election', Newshub, 1 December 2016.

His post-2014 election ministry ... 'New National-led Administration announced', New Zealand Government media release, 6 October 2014.

In 2013 Key promoted Kaye ... 'PM announces changes to Cabinet line-up', New Zealand Government media release, 23 January 2013.

He was appointed ... 'Simon Bridges to be appointed a minister', New Zealand Government media release, 3 April 2012.

He was promoted ... 'New National-led Administration announced', New Zealand Government media release, 13 December 2011.

'I absolutely believe ...' John Key, 'Prime Minister John Key announces resignation', speech, 6 December 2016.

Key's nickname, 'the smiling assassin' ... 'Golden Boy', *Metro*, 26 April 2005.

3: THE PATIENT ENGLISH

With his gift of perfect timing ... Half Year Economic and Fiscal Update 2016, The Treasury, 8 December 2016.

Further, his insistence that ... Sam Sachdeva, 'John Key's eight-year reign comes to an end as Bill English gets head-start in leadership race', Stuff, 5 December 2016.

Her initial reaction was one of horror ... Tracy Watkins, 'Bill and Mary English on life after becoming PM', Stuff, 13 December 2016.

(English was the clear favourite ... Vernon Small, 'Bill English is the overwhelming favourite to replace John Key in our new poll', Stuff, 6 December 2016.

'I'll be focusing on building ...' Jo Moir, 'Judith Collins, Bill English and Jonathan Coleman are in the race to be Prime Minister', Stuff, 6 December 2016.

She revealed in her *Pull No Punches* memoir ... Judith Collins, *Pull No Punches: Memoir of a Political Survivor*, Allen and Unwin, 2020.

Collins would later admit ... Andrea Vance, 'The brutal business of politics: Judith Collins discusses memoir, John Key, David Bain, and being a survivor', Stuff, 28 June 2020.

Later, in a 2004 letter to Brash ... Nicky Hager, *The Hollow Men*, Craig Potton Publishing, 2006.

She contended that ... Vernon Small, 'Two way race emerging for Nat leadership with Coleman English's biggest threat', Stuff, 6 December 2016.

Journalists assumed they were a powerful alliance ... Lloyd Burr, 'Backbenchers "Four Amigos" key to future National leader's success', Newshub, 7 December 2016.

By the close of the week ... Isaac Davison, 'Bill English will be next Prime Minister, Judith Collins, Jonathan Coleman stand aside', *The New Zealand Herald*, 8 December 2016.

'There's a real sense ...' Brent Edwards, 'Battle of Bennett vs Bridges', *The Press*, 8 December 2016.

'He's got a big role to play ...' Jo Moir, 'Paula Bennett has won the battle for deputy Prime Minister and will team up with Bill English', Stuff, 10 December 2016.

With Bennett in place ... 'Joyce to be Finance Minister if English PM', Radio NZ, 8 December 2016.

Bridges and Adams won promotion ... 'PM announces Cabinet line-up', New Zealand Government media release, 19 December 2016.

Although he promised ... Claire Trevett, 'What Bill English promises to deliver to New Zealand, *The New Zealand Herald*, 12 December 2016.

Landing in a Defence Force helicopter ... Andrea Vance, 'PM Bill English: Frustrated Kaikoura locals say town is "the absolute pits"', Stuff, 15 December 2016.

'Trust your gut' ... 'Live: Bill English is NZ's new Prime Minister', Stuff, 12 December 2016.

4: JACINDAMANIA

His resignation triggered ... 'Mt Albert by-election date confirmed', New Zealand Government media release, 20 December 2016.

She had the dubious honour ... 'New poll ranks the nation's hotties', *The New Zealand Herald*, 13 February 2013.

On Waitangi Day 2017 ... 'Waitangi Day: Speech to Ngāti Whātua, Ōrākei Marae', 7 February 2017.

As the incumbent, National ... 'General Election to be held on 23rd Sept, 2017', New Zealand Government media release, 2 February 2017.

Speaking at the five-star ... 'Speech to Rotary Club of Auckland, 3 February 2017'.

But this in itself ... Hamish Rutherford, 'Net migration hits 71,000 as Kiwis turn their back on living overseas', Stuff, 27 February 2017.

Environment Minister Nick Smith responded ... '90% of rivers and lakes swimmable by 2040', New Zealand Government media release, 27 February 2017.

Winston Peters was on ... 1 News/Colmar Brunton poll, 11–15 February 2017.

The opening two Roy Morgan Research polls ... Roy Morgan Research, Finding 7127, 20 January 2017; Finding 7129, 27 February 2017.

Overturning Key's promise ... 'NZ Superannuation age to lift to 67 in 2040', New Zealand Government media release, 7 March 2017.

A Newshub-Reid Research poll ... Newshub-Reid Research poll, 10–19 March 2017.

A 1 News/Colmar Brunton poll ... 1 News/Colmar Brunton poll, 18–22 March 2017.

Joyce thumbed his nose ... Kevin Taylor, 'National accuses Government of "communism by stealth"', *The New Zealand Herald*, 11 June 2004.

Labour remained stubbornly ... 1 News/Colmar Brunton, 21–31 May 2017.

A few weeks later ... Newshub-Reid Research poll, 12 June 2017.

The Greens' fortunes were tied ... 'Green Labour agreement makes change of Govt possible', Green Party media release, 4 June 2016.

Bored reporters were shaken ... 'Mending the safety net', Metiria Turei speech to Green Party AGM, 16 July 2017.

The revelation worked ... 1 News/Colmar Brunton poll, 22–27 July 2017.

She then admitted ... Jenna Lynch, 'More questions raised about Metiria Turei's living situation', Newshub, 3 August 2017.

The backlash was too great ... 1 News/Colmar Brunton poll, 2–16 August 2017.

When Labour's internal polling saw ... UMR Research, July 2017.

When the 1 News poll dropped ... 1 News/Colmar Brunton poll, 22–27 July 2017.

'I'd be lying to you ...' Interview with Corin Dann, *Q+A*, TVNZ, 30 July 2017.

The following morning, Little told ... 'You don't get to form a govt at 24 percent — Little', Radio NZ, 31 July 2017.

Her new deputy, Kelvin Davis ... Dan Satherley, 'Jacinda Ardern reveals Labour's new campaign slogan: "Let's do this",' Newshub, 4 August 2017.

The next Newshub-Reid Research poll ... Newshub-Reid Research poll, 2–8 August 2017.

Treasury's Pre-election Economic and Fiscal Update ... 'The Pre-election Economic and Fiscal Update (PREFU) 2017', The Treasury, 23 August 2017.

National fell three ... 1 News/Colmar Brunton poll, 26–30 August 2017.

In the first clash ... *TVNZ Leaders Debate*, TVNZ, 31 August 2017.

A week later ... 'English, Ardern face off in *Stuff* Leaders Debate', Stuff, 7 September 2017.

Ardern went into the debate ... 1 News/Colmar Brunton poll, 2–6 September 2017.

It was a play National had used ... 'Key, Goff square off in Christchurch', Stuff, 2 November 2011.

The next poll ... Newshub-Reid Research poll, 6–11 September 2017.

There would be no new taxes ... Vernon Small, 'Read my lips, no new taxes says Labour', Stuff, 14 September 2017.

5: QUEENMAKER

Peters bristled at criticism ... 'Speech to a public meeting at the Rotorua Convention Centre', Winston Peters, 7 September 2005.

'I want to acknowledge ...' 'Election night remarks to the National Party', Bill English, SkyCity Convention Centre, 23 September 2017.

In 2008, a year dominated by a scandal … Claire Trevett, 'Key shuts the door on Peters and NZ First', *The New Zealand Herald*, 30 August 2008.

In the days following the election … Tracy Watkins, 'Peters launches legal action on leak', *The Press*, 8 November 2017.

His legal action … Catrin Owen, 'Winston Peters loses another legal battle over superannuation privacy breach', Stuff, 3 December 2021.

'I just felt it …' John Harvey and Brent Edwards, *Annette King: The Authorised Biography*, Upstart Press, 2019.

Barry Soper, of radio station Newstalk ZB … Barry Soper, 'NZ First has prided itself on transparency, so why are their board members a secret?', *The New Zealand Herald*, 12 October 2017.

'We've had to make a choice …' 'Post-Election Announcement Speech', Winston Peters, 19 October 2017.

6: KNIVES OUT

Fifteen years on … Tom Hunt, 'Flashback: Raging Bill English steps into the ring with the Psyclone', *The Dominion Post*, 3 June 2017.

Peters's own support base … Jack Vowles, Kate McMillan, Fiona Barker, Jennifer Curtin, Janine Hayward, Lara Greaves and Charles Crothers, *The New Zealand Election Study*, October 2017.

English told reporters … Henry Cooke, 'Bill English staying on through 2020', Stuff, 24 October 2017.

'Where's Winston …' Jo Moir, 'Government forced to do a deal with National after failing to have the numbers in the House', Stuff, 7 November 2017.

National was triumphant … Jo Moir, 'Ardern: we had the numbers', *The Dominion Post*, 8 November 2017.

The final 1 News/Colmar Bunton poll … 1 News/Colmar Brunton poll, 29 November – 5 December 2017.

They also dominated … Roy Morgan Research polls; Finding No. 7379, 29 October 2017; Finding No. 7419, 22 November 2017; Finding No. 7421, 18 December 2017.

'I found myself …' 'Adjournment — Sittings of the House', *Hansard*, 20 December 2017.

Former trade minister Todd McClay … Audrey Malone, 'National's blues', *Sunday Star-Times*, 10 December 2017.

'I just don't think we are looking …' Tracy Watkins, 'National knives are out over election loss', Stuff, 31 January 2017.

'Opposition is naturally a robust …' 'Rt Hon Bill English — State of the Nation 2018', New Zealand National Party, 31 January 2018.

National was still riding high … Newshub-Reid Research poll, 18–28 January 2018.

'I think we're energised …' Stacey Kirk, 'National Party looks inward as it prepares for battle from Opposition benches', Stuff, 8 February 2018.

'Now is the right time …' 'Bill English announces retirement from Parliament', New Zealand National Party media release, 13 February 2018.

'I'm announcing my candidacy …' @judithcollinsMP, Twitter, 14 February 2018.

'I'm one of the few people …' 'I'm that person — Judith Collins vies for National's leadership', Radio NZ, 14 February 2018.

'I'm 41 …' Derek Cheng, 'Simon Bridges: I have strong support for the leadership', *The New Zealand Herald*, 14 February 2018.

The canny publicist … 'Steven Joyce joins National leadership race', Newstalk ZB, 20 February 2018.

***New Zealand Herald* columnist Steve Braunias …** Steve Braunias, 'Loose goose Simon Bridges obvious pick as satirist-in-chief', *The New Zealand Herald*, 14 February 2018.

'The Tauranga MP …' John Armstrong, 'Opinion: Biggest challenge facing National Party's eventual new leader will be the Jacinda Ardern political juggernaut', 1 News, 13 February 2018.

A *Dominion Post* editorial asserted … 'Editorial: There is no promising National leader to replace Bill English', *The Dominion Post*, 13 February 2018.

Left-leaning website The Spinoff … Toby Manhire, 'Who will replace Bill English? The contenders for next National leader, power ranked', The Spinoff, 13 February 2018.

'We can't go into the election …' Stacey Kirk, 'Bridges leads Nats, Bennett deputy', *The Timaru Herald*, 28 February 2018.

The party tweeted the picture … @NZNationalParty, Twitter, 27 February 2018.

7: THE YOUNG AND THE RESTLESS

Born to Lisa Helmling … 'Maiden Statement: Jami-Lee Ross, 6 April 2011', *Hansard*, Vol. 671, p. 17791.

The Tongan capital had … James Ihaka, 'Divisions over city help for Tonga', *The New Zealand Herald*, 24 January 2007.

He challenged the Manukau mayor … Bernard Orsman, 'Brown puts ham on card', *The New Zealand Herald*, 11 June 2010.

He was accused of … Karen Mangnall, 'Len Brown faces up', *Manukau Courier*, 18 June 2010.

His stance of moral superiority … Ewan McDonald, 'Out-of-pocket money', *The Aucklander*, 1 July 2010.

Others accused him of racism … Yvonne Tahana and Viamoana Tapaleao, 'Māori flags to fly at Manukau Council', *The New Zealand Herald*, 28 March 2008.

'Start 'em early' … @jamileeross, Twitter, 26 February 2014.

In December, the neighbouring Botany seat … 'Pansy Wong returns from Parliament', New Zealand National Party media release, 14 December 2010.

'No one ever said democracy was cheap …' 'Musical chairs could be costly', *Sunday Star-Times*, 6 February 2011.

In a profile interview … Matt Bowen, 'Go out and vote', *Eastern Courier*, 18 February 2011.

'Besides advising him …' Nicky Hager, '*Dirty Politics*, 2018: Nicky Hager assesses the Jami-Lee Ross saga', The Spinoff, 25 October 2018.

A distraught Williamson had resigned … Jared Savage, 'Maurice Williamson resigns as a minister', *The New Zealand Herald*, 1 May 2014.

Liu's donations came to light … 'Party donations and loans by year', Electoral Commission, 24 February 2015.

The gift to National … Jared Savage, 'The Prime Minister, the dinner and the $25,000 donation', *The New Zealand Herald*, 21 February 2015.

'Loved the utu …' Nicky Hager, '*Dirty Politics*, 2018: Nicky Hager assesses the Jami-Lee Ross saga', The Spinoff, 25 October 2018.

'I had phone calls …' David Fisher, 'National candidate speaks out over harassment by rogue MP Jami-Lee Ross', *The New Zealand Herald*, 18 October 2018.

He alleged Ross used … Dan Satherley and Simon Shepherd, 'Jami-Lee Ross "makes Todd Barclay look like an angel"', *Newshub Nation*, 20 October 2018.

Schwaner, elected to the board … PJ Taylor, 'Local board member is sworn in, resigns, walks out', Stuff, 4 November 2016.

He played ping-pong … Steve Braunias, 'The great political ping-pong tournament: National leader Simon Bridges returns home for a beating', *The New Zealand Herald*, 31 March 2018.

Principal Gary Moore remembered … Torika Tokalau, 'Simon Bridges extends leadership challenge to Rutherford College head boy', Stuff, 12 April 2008.

By April it had a slim lead … 1 News/Colmar Brunton poll, 7–11 April 2018.

In August 2019, Newshub carried … Tova O'Brien, 'Simon Bridges' roadshow cash splash: $113k in taxpayer money on limos and hotels', Newshub, 13 August 2018.

He said he 'doubted' … Stacey Kirk, 'National demands independent probe into Simon Bridges' travel expenses leak', Stuff, 14 August 2018.

'Mr Bridges needs to reveal ...' Rt Hon Winston Peters, 'General Debate', *In the House NZ*, YouTube, 19 September 2018.

'It's a very separate matter ...' 'National MP Jami-Lee Ross stands down for health reasons', *Radio New Zealand*, 2 October 2018.

She claimed he had ... Melanie Reid, 'Jami-Lee Ross: Four women speak out', Newsroom, 18 October 2018.

Bennett told him ... Stacey Kirk, 'Tape exposes negotiations', *The Southland Times*, 6 November 2018.

Ross also taped that call ... 'Exclusive: Watch — Jami-Lee Ross admits to affairs with two women', Newstalk ZB, 19 October 2018.

'Later today Simon Bridges is ...' @jamileeross, Twitter, 15 October 2018.

The report pointed to Ross ... 'Simon Bridges: Statement on National Party Leak Inquiry', New Zealand National Party media statement, 15 October 2018.

The case relates to two ... Tim Murphy, 'Not one, but two $100k donations to National in court', Newsroom, 17 February 2020.

University of Canterbury professor ... 'Magic Weapons: China's political influence activities under Xi Jinping', Kissinger Institute on China and the United States, 18 September 2017.

'But it's very clear that the money comes ...' 'Academic warns against interference after National revelations', Radio NZ, 19 October 2018.

8: A TRAIN WRECK

'Two Chinese MPs ...' 'Jami-Lee Ross and Simon Bridges' phone call transcript', Stuff, 17 October 2018.

Nipping at his heels ... 1 News/Colmar Brunton poll, 5–19 October 2018.

'We've heard, listened, and acted ...' @winstonpeters, Twitter, 17 April 2019.

'We are already home' ... Michael Nielson, '"We are already home": Ihumātao group responds to Simon Bridges' comments', *The New Zealand Herald*, 12 August 2019.

The Treasury Secretary ... 'Further statement from Gabriel Makhlouf', The Treasury media release, 28 May 2019.

Come February, as MPs ... Newshub-Reid Research poll, 24 January – 2 February 2019.

UMR chief executive ... Hamish Rutherford, 'What the public is saying about Simon Bridges, according to Labour's pollsters', Stuff, 10 December 2018.

'We don't want to have years ...' 'No leadership "chopping and changing like Labour" for National: Judith Collins', Radio NZ, 12 February 2019.

Confident she was the public's favourite ... Toby Manhire, 'Poll gives Judith Collins slim lead as preferred National leader', The Spinoff, 22 February 2018.

Dalziel had to resign ... Kevin Taylor, 'Dalziel admits error over letter', *The New Zealand Herald*, 19 February 2004.

'You can't make an omelette ...' Andrea Vance, '"Crusher" Collins up close', *The Dominion Post*, 10 March 2012.

She loved the British prime minister's uncompromising ... 'Baroness Thatcher mourned', New Zealand Government media release, 10 April 2013.

In April, Newshub reported ... Jenna Lynch and Tova O'Brien, 'National MPs speaking out against leader Simon Bridges', Newshub, 16 April 2019.

His leadership, he felt, 'was damned ...' Simon Bridges, *National Identity: Confessions of an Outsider*, HarperCollins, 2020.

After Bridges proposed ... Reed Fleming, 'A short list of people who'd be fined under National's school leaver policy', The Spinoff, 4 October 2019.

A bizarre witch hunt ... Collette Devlin, 'Corrections' $1m slushy fund', *Sunday Star-Times*, 28 April 2019.

There was a strange episode ... Andrea Vance, 'Religious party idea "alluring"', *The Press*, 20 May 2019.

Her government acted swiftly … 'PM Statement on Christchurch mosques terror attack', New Zealand Government media release, 21 March 2019.

She climbed seven points … 1 News/Colmar Brunton poll, 6–10 April 2019.

Her response saw … 'White Island eruption: "How good is Ardern?" — World praises PM for disaster response', *The New Zealand Herald*, 10 December 2019.

Remarkably, National stayed ahead … 1 News/Colmar Brunton poll, 5–9 October 2019.

'We were down on our luck …' Bridges, *National Identity*.

'The decision for New Zealand …' @simonjbridges, Facebook, 20 April 2020.

It 'might be viewed …' Bridges, *National Identity*.

It was worse than … Newshub-Reid Research poll, 8–16 May 2020.

A couple of my colleagues … 'Simon Bridges to face National leadership challenge', Radio NZ, 20 May 2020.

Bridges was 'doing …' 'Todd Muller denies leadership ambitions despite endorsement by ex-PM', Newstalk ZB, 19 May 2020.

It was 'destructive' … Wynsley Wrigley, 'Bid to oust leader "nutty stuff": Tolley', *The Gisborne Herald*, 21 May 2020.

'As quick as that …' Bridges, *National Identity*.

9: INTO THE UNKNOWN

That morning the *Herald* … Matthew Hooten, 'Simon Bridges v Todd Muller — why National had to choose Muller', *The New Zealand Herald*, 22 May 2020.

The UK prime minister … 'Boris Johnson's funny *Love Actually* parody: Our final election broadcast', *The Conservatives*, YouTube, 10 December 2019.

'There is no Team Todd …' 'Todd Muller elected leader of the New Zealand National Party', New Zealand National Party media statement, 22 May 2020.

'More time for the most important …' @simonjbridges, Twitter, 22 May 2020.

By 2006, he was chief executive … Todd Muller CV, LinkedIn.

'This is my generation's …' 'Speech: Ardern — Labour's election campaign launch', New Zealand Labour Party media release, 20 August 2017.

'I've just had a gutsful …' 'Te Papa water display a "kick in the guts" for Kiwi farmers — Todd Muller', *The Country*, 16 December 2019.

'We will save jobs …' 'Todd Muller's Maiden Speech as National Party Leader', New Zealand National Party media release, 22 May 2020.

'He said to me …' 'Paula Bennett', *Matangireia* podcast (Series 2, Episode 1), Radio NZ, 26 May 2020.

A photograph from a 2019 profile … Alex Braae, 'The increasingly uncompromising Todd Muller', The Spinoff, 15 September 2019.

'I got one of those …' Dan Satherley, 'Todd Muller defends owning "MAGA" hat, says no one cares about his Hillary Clinton badge', *Newshub Nation*, 23 May 2020.

'MAGA caps are used …' @PouTepou, Twitter, 23 May 2020.

'That hat represents …' Amelia Wade, 'Muslim community to Muller: Keep your Make America Great Again cap at home', *The New Zealand Herald*, 24 May 2020.

'No, I'm not …' Henry Cooke, 'Nikki Kaye wrongly describes Paul Goldsmith as Māori as pressure over National's diversity grows', Stuff, 26 May 2020.

He was rattled … Todd Muller MP, Facebook, 24 September 2021.

'Even then, in an unformed …' 'Todd Muller Outlines National's First Term Priorities', New Zealand National Party press release, 14 June 2020.

'Today, he posed in front of …' Scott Palmer and Lisette Reymer, 'National leader Todd Muller lays out vision for New Zealand in key speech', Newshub, 14 June 2020.

The *Herald* published a flurry … 'Criticising National Party leader for upside-down Māori flag "cheap shot"', *The New Zealand Herald*, 15 June 2020.

Three days after … Hayden Donnell, 'Solved: The mystery of Todd Muller's upside down tino rangatiratanga flag photo', The Spinoff, 17 June 2020.

'The problem with doing poorly ...' @nealejones, Twitter, 14 June 2020.
National was up nine points ... 1 News/Colmar Brunton poll, 20–24 June 2020,

10: THE COUP THAT SHOULD NEVER HAVE HAPPENED
'Heaven knows how RNZ chose ...' Patrick Smellie, 'Team Muller sets out, with the emphasis on team', *BusinessDesk*, 22 May 2020.
'Our legacy isn't one of ruined buildings ...' 'Muller Speech: Our Plan to Get New Zealand Working', New Zealand National Party, 9 July 2020.
He tried to keep them ... Todd Muller MP, Facebook, 24 September 2021.
Labour's Megan Woods attacked ... Thomas Coughlan, 'National MP Hamish Walker defends remarks dubbed "racist" by Labour', Stuff, 2 July 2020.
The *Weekend Herald* revealed ... Amelia Wade, 'Covid 19 coronavirus patients' details leaked: Investigation launched as agencies scramble', *The New Zealand Herald*, 4 July 2020.
'Is it a deliberate leak ...' 'Criminal charges possible if leak source identified in Covid-19 privacy breach investigation', Radio NZ, 4 July 2020.
The party's health spokesman ... 'This Government can't be trusted with anything', New Zealand National Party media release, 4 July 2020.
The barrister concluded ... Mike Heron QC, *Investigation into COVID-19 active cases privacy breach*, Britomart Chambers, 29 July 2020.
'Clutha-Southland is a safe enough ...' 'Leak exposes National's indiscipline', *The Dominion Post*, 9 July 2020.
On the same day, the *Herald* ... 'Editorial: National MP Hamish Walker's resignation symptomatic of a party on the run', *The New Zealand Herald*, 9 July 2020.
Muller could no longer ... @ToddMullerMP, Facebook, 24 September 2020.
'It has become clear ...' 'Todd Muller resigns as Leader of the Opposition', New Zealand National Party media statement, 14 July 2020.
Collins had had a sleepless night ... Andrea Vance, 'Better the devil you know: the inside story of how Judith Collins became National's leader, Stuff, 19 July 2020.

11: THE HOSPITAL PASS
'I love it when people say ...' Andrea Vance, '"Crusher" Collins up close', *The Dominion Post*, 10 March 2012.
'I went and saw him, very grumpy ...' Andrea Vance, '"Crusher" Collins up close'.
'You cannot achieve ...' Andrea Vance, '"Crusher" Collins up close'.
'That vague ambition ...' 'Maiden statement of Judith Collins', *Hansard*, 29 August 2002.
'Nice bloke, shame he's ...' Andrea Vance, 'The brutal business of politics: Judith Collins discusses memoir, John Key, David Bain, and being a survivor', Stuff, 28 June 2020.
She passed on her best wishes ... 'Statement on resignation of Todd Muller', Office of the Prime Minister, 14 July 2020.
'I just admire him for ...' Zane Small, 'Political party leaders Jacinda Ardern, Winston Peters, David Seymour and James Shaw farewell Todd Muller', Newshub, 14 July 2020.
'Leading a divided ...' 'New Zealand First Statement on Muller Resignation', New Zealand First, 14 July 2020.
Kaye would later say ... Thomas Manch, 'Nikki Kaye: I'll most likely be growing veges on Great Barrier', *The Dominion Post*, 18 July 2020.
With her signature bellicosity ... 'Judith Collins is the new leader of the National Party, Gerry Brownlee is deputy — live updates', The Spinoff, 14 July 2020.
With Falloon at home ... Zane Small, 'Judith Collins confident Jacinda Ardern's office acted appropriately with Andrew Falloon information', Newshub, 21 July 2020.
'Today I spoke to ...' 'Statement from Rangitata MP Andrew Falloon', New Zealand National Party media statement, 20 July 2020.

The following morning Stuff reported … Henry Cooke, 'Andrew Falloon sent sexually explicit photos to another young woman', Stuff, 21 July 2020.

He has 'resigned …' 'Judith Collins "no longer trusts" disgraced MP Andrew Falloon's story', Newstalk ZB, 21 July 2020.

Police re-opened their investigation … 'No charges against former National MP Andrew Falloon over unsolicited images', Radio NZ, 18 December 2020.

'I am not going to be …' Jamie Ensor, 'Judith Collins claims to have received "tip-off" about Labour minister, passed to Prime Minister', Newshub, 22 July 2020.

But just to make sure … 'Judith Collins says she was contacted with allegations about Labour minister', Radio NZ, 22 July 2020.

'Over the course of …' 'PM statement on Iain Lees-Galloway', New Zealand Government media statement, 22 July 2020.

'I accept the Prime Minister's decision …' 'Minister steps down', New Zealand Government media statement, 22 July 2020.

'They made it very clear …' 'Paula Bennett', *Matangireia* podcast.

The first opinion poll … Newshub-Reid Research poll, 16–24 July 2020.

(Labour was on an unrealistic … 'Gerry Brownlee questions methodology used in latest Newshub-Reid Research poll', Radio NZ, 27 July 2020.

'Once things start getting …' Claire Trevett, 'Judith Collins sets her own sacking point: 35 per cent in the polls', *The New Zealand Herald*, 14 February 2018.

'If you had told me …' 'Speech: Labour Campaign Launch 2020', New Zealand Labour Party media release, 8 August 2020.

The change-up was 'squarely …' Duncan Greive, '"Paranoid storms": Judith Collins' former press secretary on National, leadership and oblivion', The Spinoff, 15 September 2020.

'Responsible economic management …' 'National releases its plan to restore NZ's prosperity', New Zealand National Party media release, 18 September 2020.

Three hours before … 'National has $4 billion mistake in its economic plan', New Zealand Labour Party media release, 20 September 2020.

'The mistake that was made …' Andrea Vance, 'Election 2020: "Labour Connect" the data analysis tool that boosted Jacinda Ardern's campaign', Stuff, 25 October 2020.

The leadership team had given … Thomas Coughlan, 'Judith Collins says no tax cuts from National this election', Stuff, 5 August 2020.

The tone was set by … 1 News/Colmar Brunton poll, 17–21 September 2020.

The symbolism of … Jason Walls, 'Election 2020: Judith Collins accused of "politicising" her faith to win over Christian voters', *The New Zealand Herald*, 4 October 2020.

Winston Peters mocked her … @winstonpeters, Twitter, 4 October 2020.

'I have a particular beef …' 'Collins talks housing, economy, faith and "wokeness" in first *Leaders Breakfast*', Newstalk ZB, 5 October 2020.

Lee panned the idea … Jenna Lynch, 'Leaked email: National MP criticises Judith Collins' "highly problematic idea" of reviewing Auckland Council', Newshub, 5 October 2020.

'National are still …' 'Leaked email reveals chaos in National', Labour Party media statement, 6 October 2020.

Collins was also facing allegations … Thomas Manch and Henry Cooke, 'Election 2020: Judith Collins denies fractures in caucus after scathing internal email leaked', Stuff, 6 October 2020.

Later, Collins would write … Judith Collins, in Stephen Levine (ed.), *Politics in a pandemic: Jacinda Ardern and New Zealand's 2020 election*, Victoria University Press, 2021.

Muller's former right-hand man … @MatthewHootonNZ, Twitter, 6 October 2020.

Paula Bennett, the former campaign chair … @paulalbennett, Twitter, 6 October 2020.

Grant Robertson couldn't help ... @grantrobertson1, Twitter, 6 October 2020.

She was heard to exclaim ... Stewart Sowman-Lund, 'Judith Collins walks into a nightmare on Ponsonby Road', The Spinoff, 7 October 2020.

Wilson, who shared duties ... Duncan Greive, '"Paranoid storms"'.

'What does a wealth tax mean? ...' Henry Cooke, 'Judith Collins tries to make wealth tax an issue, asking voters to trust her more than Jacinda Ardern', Stuff, 11 October 2020.

'National out to stop ...' 'National out to stop the Wealth Tax', New Zealand National Party media release, 11 October 2020.

'I don't believe ...' Thomas Manch, 'Collins on wealth tax warpath, Ardern claims "misinformation"', Manawatū Standard, 13 October 2020.

She dismissed ... 'Complaint number 20/531', Advertising Standards Authority Complaints Board, 28 October 2020.

David Clark, Mid Canterbury president ... 'Farmers want Labour to govern alone — Fed Farmers', Radio NZ, 19 October 2020.

However, the New Zealand Election Survey ... Josh van Veen et al, 'Anniversary of a landslide: new research reveals what really swung New Zealand's 2020 "COVID election"', The Conversation, 15 October 2021.

In a radio interview she'd said ... 'Gerry Brownlee on Judith Collins' obesity comments', Newstalk ZB, 14 October 2020.

In the last 1 News/Colmar Brunton poll ... 1 News/Colmar Brunton poll, 10–14 October 2020.

'I have to call you out on this ...' The Leaders' Debate, TVNZ, 15 October 2020.

12: CRUSHED

'The genesis of the many issues ...' 'Summary of New Zealand National Party 2020 Campaign Review', New Zealand National Party, February 2020.

'Boy, did we know this was going to be ...' 'Election night speech', Judith Collins, 17 October 2020.

In the live election coverage ... '"It's grim" — Simon Bridges gives blunt appraisal of failed National campaign', 1 News, 17 October 2020.

Brownlee was proud to have stepped up ... 'Statement on deputy leadership of the National Party', New Zealand National Party media release, 6 November 2020.

'We do not give our opponents ...' Vita Molyneux, 'Judith Collins reveals "confronting" election review wasn't compulsory reading for caucus', Newshub Nation, 20 March 2021.

Speaking to the Rotary Club ... 'Judith Collins — State of the Nation Speech 2021', New Zealand National Party media release, 26 January 2021.

Bridges launched several attacks ... @simonjbridges, Twitter, 19 February 2021.

'I've always made it very clear ...' 'Judith Collins distances herself from Simon Bridges' "wokester" comment about Police Commissioner Andrew Coster', Radio NZ, 24 February 2021.

'I respect Judith ...' Dan Satherley, 'Simon Bridges defies Judith Collins' order to stop criticising Police Commissioner because she's not his wife', Newshub, 26 February 2021.

The _Herald_'s political editor ... Claire Trevett, 'Is a Simon Bridges / Christopher Luxon leadership ticket on the cards?', The New Zealand Herald, 8 April 2021.

'Actually everyone is on-side ...' Henry Cooke, 'Still too early for Nats to peak — Collins', The Dominion Post, 15 April 2021.

He dismissed the 'rumour' ... '"Crazy silly talk": Bridges dismisses rumour of new leadership bid', Newstalk ZB, 8 April 2021.

'Politics is something ...' 'Air New Zealand chief executive Christopher Luxon resigns, hints at political move', The New Zealand Herald, 20 June 2019.

Key immediately began championing ... Henry Cooke, 'John Key endorses Christopher Luxon as "world class" National candidate', Stuff, 10 October 2019.

'My focus is to …' Chris Tobin, 'Luxon says "I'm just learning my job"', *The Timaru Herald*, 24 April 2021.

In a speech to the Ōrewa Rotary club … 'NATIONHOOD — Don Brash Speech Ōrewa Rotary Club', New Zealand National Party, 27 January 2004.

'There is nothing in being Māori …' 'Collins says her party won't stand for "racist separatism" New Zealand', Radio NZ, 28 April 2021.

Humiliatingly, in early August … Newshub-Reid Research poll, 22–29 July 2021.

'This Bill lacks common sense …' 'Conversion Practices Prohibition Legislation Bill — First Reading', *Hansard*, 5 August 2020.

She reportedly received … 'Young Nats turn on party over gay conversion stance', *The Otago Daily Times*, 7 August 2021.

In a statement Ross said … Bridie Witton, '"Deeply disappointed": Young Nats call for National Party to support conversion therapy Bill', Stuff, 5 August 2020.

In an emailed statement, … 'Judith Collins — New National portfolio allocations confirmed', New Zealand National Party media release, 28 August 2020.

He claimed Smith repeatedly said … Steve Kilgallon, '"Just a f…… secretary": Former MP Nick Smith bullied, harassed and swore at staff, according to a draft report', Stuff, 13 December 2020.

More than 35 staff had left … Andrea Vance, 'Parliamentary staff allege rampant bullying at the Beehive', Stuff, 21 April 2019.

An investigation by consultant … Debbie Francis, *Independent External Review into Bullying and Harassment in the New Zealand Parliamentary Workplace — Final Report, 21 May 2019.*

'I have decided to retire …' 'Nick Smith to retire from Parliament', New Zealand National Party media release, 31 May 2021.

Collins followed with a press release … 'Judith Collins thanks Dr Nick Smith for his service', New Zealand National Party media release, 31 May 2021.

It caused a minor public outcry, … Zane Small, 'Jacinda Ardern asks for "views based on fact" after National MP Harete Hipango accuses her of backing full-term abortions', Newshub, 28 July 2020.

She argued it was not a false quote … Ethan Griffiths, 'Whanganui MP Harete Hipango defends posting false Jacinda Ardern quote', *Whanganui Chronicle*, 25 September 2020.

Later, former MP Jo Luxton would reveal … David Fisher, 'Profile: Harete Hipango and how she upset her National colleagues', *The New Zealand Herald*, 17 January 2022.

Worried about her return … Jo Moir, 'National Party all out of love for returning MP', Newsroom, 16 June 2021.

'Social media has destroyed me …' Bridges, *National Identity*.

'My cute answer is …' Andrea Vance, 'Simon Bridges: Confessions of a political outsider', *The Dominion Post Your Weekend*, 14 August 2021

'Why is this all about me today?' 'Judith Collins defends move to Wellington during level 4: "I'll ask the questions"', 1 News, 1 September 2021.

Later she accused … Claire Trevett, 'Judith Collins accuses TVNZ *Breakfast* host Indira Stewart of having "a political agenda"', *The New Zealand Herald*, 2 September 2021.

'I think she's a big, fat hypocrite …' '"A big, fat hypocrite": Judith Collins lashes out at Dr Siouxsie Wiles over lockdown outing', Newstalk ZB, 10 September 2021.

'Judith's a friend …' Thomas Coughlan, 'Controversial blogger Cameron Slater still in regular contact with Collins — "Judith's a good friend"', *The New Zealand Herald*, 11 September 2021.

Wilson, in a podcast interview … Duncan Greive, '"Paranoid storms"'.

Collins accused Wilson … Luke Malpass, 'Judith Collins hits back at former staffer Janet Wilson over claims of a culture of fear and "paranoid storms"', Stuff, 15 September 2021.

Wilson's attack came on the back of … Matthew Hooton, 'The National Party death spiral', *Metro*, 7 September 2021.

A leaked UMR poll … Rachel Sadler, 'National Party slumps to 21.3 pct, ACT just 6 points behind in new NZ Taxpayers' Union poll', Newshub, 15 September 2021.

'We discussed our wives …' Zane Small, 'Simon Bridges regrets "inappropriate" remarks that upset Jacqui Dean, but will "consider" run for National leadership', Newshub, 25 November 2022.

'That's very flattering …' Tova O'Brien, 'Newshub-Reid Research poll: Simon Bridges isn't ruling out another tilt at National leadership — and he's got public's support, Newshub, 22 November 2021.

'This evening, with unanimous support …' 'Simon Bridges demoted following complaint', New Zealand National Party press release, 24 November 2020.

'What we saw yesterday …' 'Simon Bridges on being demoted: "What we saw yesterday was truly desperate stuff from Judith Collins"', Radio NZ, 25 November 2021.

'You cannot have a party …' 'National Party MP Simon O'Connor says Judith Collins cannot stay as leader', Radio NZ, 25 November 2021.

13: THE TEA PARTY

She was later jailed … 'Donna Awatere Huata jailed', *The New Zealand Herald*, 30 September 2005.

'Brash's leadership made ACT …' Rodney Hide, *My Year of Living Dangerously*, Random House, 2007.

In a newsletter … Bernard Orsman, 'Worth: ACT desperate in Epsom', *The New Zealand Herald*, 3 September 2005.

'They've cost Don Brash …' Claire Harvey, 'Brash texts congrats to Hide — and gets some advice back', *The New Zealand Herald*, 19 September 2005.

'We are going to support …' Dan Eaton, 'ACT will back a Nat government', *The Press*, 17 October 2008.

Reports emerged that Douglas … 'Bid to roll Hide defused', New Zealand Press Association, 21 December 2009.

Hide saw off the challenge … Martin Kay, 'Politics in the death zone a juggling act', *The Dominion Post*, 30 January 2010.

Roy gave an extraordinary speech … 'Self-Evident Truths and Black Swans', Heather Roy speech to the ACT New Zealand National Conference 2010, 27 February 2010.

Brash refused … Tracy Watkins, 'Brash launches bid to lead ACT party', *The Dominion Post*, 23 April 2011.

The duo were quickly nicknamed … Tracy Watkins, 'Triumph of the codgerati', *The Dominion Post*, 29 April 2011.

National's campaign manager … 'Key: tape dirty tricks', *Marlborough Express*, 14 November 2011.

Key later apologised … 'PM apologises to older NZers for any offence in "teapot tape"', Radio NZ, 27 January 2012.

At the same meeting … 'ACT choices huge risk for party', *3News*, 2 February 2014.

The party's support immediately slumped … *3 News*/Reid Research poll, 2 February 2014.

After dropping a clanger … Tim Batt, 'Mr Ryght: An interview with ACT leader: Jamie Whyte', *The Ruminator* [blog], 26 February 2014.

Seymour worked hard … Stacey Kirk, 'Small seat with the X-Factor', *The Dominion Post*, 13 September 2014.

A campaign video in which … Andrea Vance, 'ACT candidate's awkward video mocked', Stuff, 1 May 2014.

'The French, for instance …' 'ACT leader David Seymour: "French love the coq"', Stuff, 15 September 2015.

The week coincided with … 1 News/Colmar Brunton poll, 25–29 July 2020.

By October, 100 protestors … 'Gun owners force Winston Peters out of NZ First conference', Radio NZ, 19 October 2019.

Farmers were also attracted … Henry Cooke, 'ACT misses climate vote, allowing bill through unanimously', Stuff, 7 November 2019.

Nine months on … 'Seymour preferred as PM over Collins', *The Press*, 9 July 2021.

Ahead of the 2020 election … 'Māori Party launches extraordinary attack on National's new leader, calling him racist', 1 News, 11 June 2020.

Waititi — once a Labour Party candidate … Dale Husband, 'Rawiri Waititi: Unapologetically Māori', *E-Tangata*, 27 September 2020.

Labour no longer suits … Dale Husband, 'Rawiri Waititi: Unapologetically Māori'.

14: THIS IS YOUR CAPTAIN SPEAKING

'Proud as you may be …' 'National Party conference kicks off with nod for Simon Bridges from former Australian PM John Howard', *The New Zealand Herald*, 28 July 2018.

Bridges kept his powder dry … Zane Small, 'Simon Bridges regrets "inappropriate" remarks that upset Jacqui Dean, but will "consider" run for National leadership', Newshub, 25 November 2021.

'We are the reset …' 'Christopher Luxon's first speech as National Leader', New Zealand National Party media release, 30 November 2021.

The church's American-born pastor … Claire Trevett, 'National Party's Chris Luxon on God, John Key, ambition and sniffing capsicums', *The New Zealand Herald*, 8 February 2020.

'My faith is a very personal thing …' George Block, 'National chooses former Air NZ boss Christopher Luxon as Botany MP candidate', Stuff, 4 November 2019.

On his first day as … 'Christopher Luxon suggests extension of "no jab, no pay" policy', Radio NZ, 5 November 2019.

He believed the risk … Tim Murphy, 'A peek into the future', Newsroom, 15 September 2020.

Jacinda Ardern was raised a Mormon … 'New Zealand's new Prime Minister Jacinda Ardern quit Mormon Church to support gay rights', *Pink News*, 17 October 2020.

Luxon confronted the issue … 'Christopher Luxon Maiden Speech', New Zealand National Party media release, 24 March 2021.

Willis was a ballast … Henry Cooke, 'Christopher Luxon says he will vote for safe zones outside abortion clinics at second reading', Stuff, 1 December 2021.

The 52-year-old … Michael Neilson, 'National Party leader Christopher Luxon on why he stopped going to church', *The New Zealand Herald*, 5 December 2021.

Holland's successor … 'Keith Holyoake', *New Zealand Parliamentary Debates*, vol. 319, 14 July 1959.

It was an ideological shock … 'Our History', New Zealand National Party website.

Luxon's first job … 'Christopher Luxon — A Divided Society', New Zealand National Party media release, 21 February 2022.

He moved to the London … 'Air New Zealand Announces New Chief Executive Officer', Air New Zealand press release, 19 June 2012.

'I believe in a New Zealand …' 'Christopher Luxon Maiden Speech'.

In late January 2022 … 1 News/Kantar poll, 22–26 January 2022.